Walter Benjamin and the Architecture of Modernity

Anamnesis

Anamnesis means remembrance or reminiscence, the collection and re-collection of what has been lost, forgotten, or effaced. It is therefore a matter of the very old, of what has made us who we are. But *anamnesis* is also a work that transforms its subject, always producing something new. To recollect the old, to produce the new: that is the task of *Anamnesis*.

a re.press series

Walter Benjamin and the Architecture of Modernity

Edited by Andrew Benjamin and Charles Rice

re.press Melbourne 2009

re.press

PO Box 40, Prahran, 3181, Melbourne, Australia
http://www.re-press.org

© re.press 2009

British Library Cataloguing-in-Publication Data
A catalogue record for this book is available from the British Library

Library of Congress Cataloguing-in-Publication Data
A catalogue record for this book is available from the Library of Congress

National Library of Australia Cataloguing-in-Publication Data
Walter Benjamin and the architecture of modernity
/ editors Andrew Benjamin, Charles Rice.

ISBN: 9780980544022 (pbk.)
ISBN: 9780980544091 (ebook)

Series: Anamnesis.

Notes: Bibliography.

Subjects: Benjamin, Walter, 1892-1940—Influence.
Architecture—Philosophy. Architecture, Modern.
Interior architecture.

Other Authors/Contributors:
Benjamin, Andrew E.
Rice, Charles.

Dewey Number: 720.1

Designed and Typeset by *A&R*

This book is produced sustainably using plantation timber, and printed in
the destination market reducing wastage and excess transport.

Contents

Abbreviations

AP   Benjamin, Walter. *The Arcades Project.* Trans. Howard S. Eiland
         and Kevin McLaughlin. Cambridge, Mass.: Harvard UP, 1999.

GS   Benjamin, Walter. *Gesammelte Schriften.* Ed. Rolf Tiede-
         mann, Hermann Schweppenhäuser, Hella Tiedemann-
         Bartels and Tillman Rexroth. Frankfurt: Suhrkamp Ver-
         lag, 1972–89. 7 vols.

SW   Benjamin, Walter. *Selected Writings.* Ed. Marcus Bullock, Michael
         W. Jennings, Howard Eiland and Gary Smith. Cambridge:
         Harvard UP, 1996–2003. 4 vols.

introduction

Introduction

Walter Benjamin and the Architecture of Modernity

Andrew Benjamin and Charles Rice

Walter Benjamin's writings continue to play a fundamental role in the attempt to understand, evaluate and critique the complex interrelation of elements from which the architecture of modernity is constructed. To suggest that modernity has an architecture is to make the claim that its elements have points of connection and coherence. Amassing those points and thus allowing modernity to emerge as a genuine object of study necessitates that philosophical considerations work in and with studies of art, film, literature, and urbanism. Modernity demands a necessary interdisciplinarity. Responding to that demand does not mean the effacing of disciplines. Such a move would mute serious study by failing to grasp the multi-faceted nature of modernity. Interdisciplinarity is the construction of an affinity between disciplines in which it is in holding to their differences that there then can be points of accord. There is therefore an important relation between the nature of modernity and what is demanded in order that its architecture emerge as a genuine object of study.

The project of this collection is to continue to approach modernity through the interplay of its specific elements. Within that project Benjamin's work is provided with important moments of contextualization. At the same time that work is used to analyse specific moments within the modern. In this context emphasis has been given to aesthetics, the urban and the construction of images. These terms have real significance. Not only do they endure as central to Benjamin's own writings, they both name and capture an essential element of modernity. This is not to suggest that art has a privileged status within attempts to understand the modern. It is rather a materialist aesthetics, a position which, while not developed by Benjamin, is none-

3

theless compatible both with his writings and their legacy. This necessitates the interconnection between a historically orientated conception of experience and the material presence of aesthetic objects. To assert the importance of material presence is to insist on techniques and practices that are operative within and also essential to the he way art works, and thus also to the way art it is experienced.

The centrality of experience is twofold. In the first instance it allows for the introduction of a conception of history that is compatible with modernity. Modernity necessitates forms of interruption. Benjamin will refer to these interruptions in a number of ways. One of the most emphatic occurs in the use of the term 'caesura'.[1] The other aspect that accounts for experience's centrality has to do with the implicit critique, within Benjamin's writings, of Kant's account of experience. While Kant is correct to argue that experiences must have their conditions of possibility, the account that is given in the *Critique of Pure Reason* is such that it cannot take up the possibility that comes to define the modern, namely that space and time are already sites of historical conflict. As such the subject of experience within Kant's model is importantly different from the conception of the subject that is already at work within Benjamin's writings on the aesthetic. In addition, space and time within modernity, while accounting for the possibility of experience, are already the locus of the differing possibilities that give history a political determination. (The politics of history is more accurately a politics of historical time. The latter emerges in the nature of the contrast between historicism on the one hand and the insistence on the 'caesura' on the other.)

The aesthetic therefore is a point at which experience and art work continue to intersect. The aesthetic, moreover, in its insistence on experience, can be given a privileged position within analyses of modernity precisely because the affirmation of modernity on the one hand, and the counter move of historicism and myth on the other, are positions that are as much discursive as experiential. Benjamin's argument, for example, that perception is both historical and inextricably bound up with the development of the techniques of perception, is a claim that draws together experience, history and the material presence of objects. As such it is a clear instance of the approach that is central to his work and one that underscores the differing contributions made to this book.

The overall aim of this volume is to continue to develop through explication and critical engagement that which endures as implicit within Benjamin's project. In enduring as implicit it comes to define both the work's legacy and its future. As such Benjamin's work is able to acquire the force of the present.

---

1. See the discussion of this term in relation to Benjamin's conception of history in Andrew Benjamin. *Style and Time. Essays on the Politics of Experience*. Northwestern University Press: Chicago. 2006.

aesthetics and philosophy

I

Booking Benjamin: The Fate of a Medium

Henry Sussman

It's time, as we say in English, to throw the book at that polymorphous miscreant of reading and writing, Walter Benjamin, to book him, in the patois of American film noir. We can see already that in English there are some hang-ups between the book, whether a material object or a volume or space of writing, and the notion and conventions of legality. But in German, a bookseller, the manager of a market or trading place in which the historical Walter Benjamin spent a good number of his happier hours, is a *Buchhandler*, someone who handles and touches books, it might not be excessive to say, who fondles them, whereas in French, the culture of books is caught up both in their physical weight, *gravitas*, burden, but also in the promises in their de*liv*ery, of what they, in the expanse of their open-ended and engendering space, *convey*, the democracy to come in language that they affirm and promise.

I wander in today, a stranger in your midst, to ponder the vertiginous convergence of designs in books and the text that they encompass. Each text consequent and invasive enough to be memorable as a book is as much the result of a design, above all of a visual nature, as it is the residue of the traces of thinking. When we enter the domain of stylistics, when we take into account the conditions of verbal density, the span and fluidity of inscription, the familiarity or surprise of semantics, diction, and syntax also adding meaning and significance either to a singular text or a body of works, even when we enlarge the scope to encompass the expectations surrounding the aesthetic genres at play, we are characterising the discourse-design in effect for that text.

Contributing to schooled discourse, today as in Benjamin's time, entails a crisis of discursive models or subgenres. As I detail in a recent book, *The*

Task of the Critic, the contemporary cultural critic unavoidably trucks simultaneously in several discursive designs, at the very least what is recognisable as poetics, philosophy, close reading, and critique (Sussman, *Task* 1–36). It is no exaggeration to assert, as I do in that volume, that German Romanticism inscribed the enabling legislation for what we continue to recognise as cosmopolitan criticism, distinguishable by its abrupt turns and linkages, its fragmentary constitution, and its irony or multiple simultaneous levels of signification, in large measure by underscoring the discursive elements of such a critique appropriated from the existing genres and media of culture, among them poetry, drama, fiction and other narrative art, and even the fine arts. In such collations as the *Athenaeum* and *Philosophical Fragments*, German Romanticism launches modern cultural commentary, in other words, with a multifarious inquest into text or discourse design. As Benjamin devised specific and distinctive styles for his interventions, he was taking the Schlegels, Novalis, Tieck, and compeers both a step beyond and at their word. To decode and elucidate such diverse texts as 'Goethe's *Elective Affinities*' ('Goethes *Wahlverwandschaften*') (*SW* 1: 297–360; *GS* I·1: 123–201), 'The Critique of Violence' ('Zur Kritik der Gewalt') (*SW* 1: 236–52; *GS* II·1: 179–203), 'Food Fair' ('Jahrmarkt des Essens') (*SW* 2: 135–40; *GS* IV·1,2: 527–32), 'Franz Kafka' (*SW* 2: 794–818; *GS* II·2: 409–38), 'One-Way Street' ('Einbahnstraße') (*SW* 1: 444–88; *GS* IV·1: 83–148), and *The Arcades Project* (*Das Passagen-Werk*) (*AP*; *GS* IV·1, 2) is to a significant degree an exercise, with a full visual component, in the discernment and teasing out of textual design. The plurality of styles mobilized by the invariably occasional writing projects we score, whether concertedly designed or not, constitutes our fullest exercise of the freedom available to us.

Benjamin was a creature of the book at once voracious and overwhelmed by devotion. We all know this. This commonplace of cultural history can only make Benjamin endearing to us, just as we are endearing to ourselves by clinging to this eccentric medium, whose decisiveness in the storage and delivery or transmission of culture is already in question. A book encompasses a certain volume of text, itself, as we have already seen, the product of a certain process of design. The text's material or content is embodied in a book medium with certain design features of its own: typography, scale and layout of pages, binding, contents and design of the cover, and so forth. Yet in the sense that a book is a free-standing structure, we can also say that it has been modelled after an architectural blueprint. We can speak more compellingly of the architecture of books than of the architecture of discourse or text. Yet books, architecture, and even discourse itself are all inflected and imbued with significance by the elements and choices of design.

Just a word, if I may, on certain features of comparative discourse-design drawing Hannah Arendt close to Benjamin and then apart: assuming that all the works we keep coming back to again and again derive something from Derrida's notion—in *Specters of Marx*—of deconstruction as the experience of the impossible: the amalgam of textual functions that Arendt assembles and coordinates in *The Origins of Totalitarianism* as emblematic of her later works is nothing less than remarkable. Although a technically and very well-trained philosopher, she largely forgoes her discourse by formation and preference in favour of a most distinctive blend of the social history of the Jews in European modernity, the social psychology of mobs and their manipulators, and the sociology of class allegiances and rivalries (Arendt 54–88, 267–40). Like Marx in *Das Kapital*, she moves between the diverse registers of her discursive amalgam almost seamlessly. To the extent that at least in its day the Frankfurter Schule was an *Institut für Soziale Forschung*, an Institute for Social Research, Arendt presses a more compelling claim for membership than Benjamin, whose writing wanders into autobiographical memoir and seemingly inchoate collages of citations.

Arendt's brilliant analyses of such phenomena as totalitarian alliances between elites and mobs, the liquidation of entire classes, and the very easy expendability of human rights, would lose much of their power in the absence of her extensive historical backdrop to the experience of the Jews and other expendable minorities in modernity. In a highly unexpected fashion, Arendt fills in the occulted stages of modern European and Jewish histories in a fashion not unlike Deleuze and Guattari's demonstration of the persistence of antiquated stages of social formation—such as barbaric nomadism and feudalism—just at the periphery of contemporary liberal experience. By reconstructing the Jewish involvement in the scandals surrounding the construction of the Suez Canal or the mascotting of exotic Jews in certain Parisian salons on the eve of the Dreyfus case, she in effect performs the work of cultural psychoanalysis by reconstituting—at the level of philosophically-driven cultural studies—the stages that could have rendered the Jews so expendable at one fateful juncture of social forces in the twentieth century.

From the unavoidable perspective of discourse design, we can say that Arendt simply designs a discourse markedly different from Benjamin's. Benjamin is simply too taken up with the project of a critical redemption of contemporary culture; his allegiance is too invested in the transformations of the book and the vicissitudes of the book-medium, to accede to her historicism and work of psychosocial reconstruction.

Benjamin was before all else a citizen, habitué, cognoscente and transgressor of the history and tradition of the book. It will emerge as we pursue this impassioned lifelong liaison that the tradition and medium of the book is not the fading lily or lame-duck politician that it is often taken for in view of such phenomena as the overwhelming burgeoning of visual and cybernetic messaging and media, often blamed for a precipitous decline in the concentration and other cognitive faculties requisite for the decoding and comprehension of books. In the wider and virtual sense in which Benjamin and such contemporaries and *semblables* including Marcel Proust and James Joyce also took the book, the book is a volume of cultural process and understanding binding on a community of neighbours and readers. In a tangible sense, for these writers and the sociologists who theorised the wider implications of their contributions, the community itself, such as it exists, is tantamount to the readership of certain texts and discourses. Even as we shift over to digital data bases and as discourse is disseminated as much over the World Wide Web as between the covers of books, it will not be so easy to dispense with the communities and binding understandings and conventions ensuing from the medium of books as we may think. We can either place the book in the wider history of tele-technics, as Jacques Derrida[1] and Tom Cohen[2] do, or we can begin to imagine a history of the book that has already embarked on its digital future, where it is as much a game as an authoritative canon.

Given their architectural program, it may be said that books are the buildings in a virtual ecology or climate experienced as an urban landscape. Surely the work of Benjamin traces a confluence between the labyrinths according to which both textual constellations and modern cities are configured. The excitement in that sub-genre of Benjamin's work that might be characterized as urban memoir (I refer here to such works as 'One-Way Street' and 'Berlin Childhood around 1900') (*SW* 3: 344–413; *GS* IV·1: 235–304; *Berlin Childhood*) surely in large measure inheres in the close parallel tracks, traces almost indistinguishable, between the experience of discovering a city and the homecoming, on the part of those already tainted by the instincts of the omnivorous reader, to the world of books, to that *côté du chez Swann* so aptly demarcated as a zone, landscape, or climate characterised by the global meandering and interconnection of the sign and by the distinctive Proustian dissolve of the surface of appearance, Law, and convention into a subtext of smooth, fluid semiological resonance. For Benjamin, the discoveries, experiences, and shocks encountered in reading and in the modernised city, the city realised in the Paris of the Second Empire and afterwards, are inseparable.[3] Yet for the purposes of the present discussion, the history

---

1. An obvious place to take up this significant strand of Derrida's thought would be 'Freud and the Scene of Writing', in *Writing and Difference* (196–231). Among the other ports of call along this trajectory would be 'Ulysses' Gramophone' in *Acts of Literature* (253–309) and *Paper Machine*.

2. With the appearance of his two-volume *Hitchcock's Cryptonymies*, Tom Cohen goes to the head of that class of critical theorists thinking through the tangible impacts of the cinematic image, artificial memory, and the technocratic control, monitoring, and doctoring of information in the political and cultural spheres. Much of the foundational work that *Hitchcock's Cryptonymies* assumes was accomplished in the last six chapters of Cohen's *Ideology and Inscription*. Significant additional contributions to this vital current discourse include Friedrich A. Kittler's *Gramophone, Film, Typewriter* and Avital Ronell's *The Telephone Book*.

3. Indeed, in Benjamin's signal 'Unpacking My Library' ('*Ich packe meine Bibliothek aus*'),

and tradition of the book as a medium leaves a slightly different imprint and
thrust than the bold adventure into the city orchestrated by Walter the hip-
ster Benjamin, the city as the nexus of modern circulation, perception, cognition, experience and shock. The history and covenant of the book are too
binding, in several senses. I want to initiate the present exploration in keeping with the broader notion of the book, the one, I believe, studied and advanced by Benjamin, not merely as one medium for the dissemination and
storage of script among others, but as the very volume, space, forum, foyer,
scene and abyss for cultural articulation and public discussion and for critical apprehension. This longer trajectory of the book will continue to haunt
us in the sense of Hamlet's ghost, to rouse us to critical discrimination and
in some cases resistance, to prod us with the relentless stirrings of Being and
thinking, regardless of the techno-political regime under which information
happens to be registered, stored, disseminated, withheld or obliterated.

Benjamin was nevertheless savvy enough a dialectician of media to
know that the book-medium to which he was so devoted, at least in its time-
honoured forms, was not forever. The book medium is surely susceptible to
the progression that Benjamin sets out in 'The Work of Art in the Age of
its Technological Reproducibility' ('*Das Kunstwerk im Zeitalter seiner technischen
Reprozierbarkeit*') (*SW* 4: 252–6; *GS* I·2: 474–7, 487–92), one in which even the
most experimental and transgressive art forms and technologies of representation claim a foundation in prior media. The thrust of this meditation allows Benjamin to assiduously imagine the end of the very book tradition he
has served even with an ascetic devotion. In several senses, *The Arcades Project*
is his Book of the Future, his draft for the future of the book, a time-capsule
addressed to the future from a moment of unheralded achievement in sociopolitical, logistical, hegemonic, administrative, and informational control,
and by this I mean the cosmopolitan, urban nineteenth-century city, with
its backdrop in global commerce and trade. This extended work, which oc-
cupied him, at the diffuse extreme of his textual synthesis, from 1927 until
his death in 1940, may be accurately described as a text-medium website of
Paris in the nineteenth century: Paris both as the forerunner of certain re-
pressive political conditions that would dog and outlive him and as the world
of quintessential modern aesthetic innovation, the imaginary universe of his
personal and creative escape.

It may be no accident that in their different ways, Marcel Proust and

---

the panorama of the cities in which he made his memorable acquisitions is inseparable
from the autobiographical account of himself as a collector and the conceptual distinctions between the collector, the borrower, and the writer. See this text in *Selected Writings*:
'Memories of the cities in which I found so many things: Riga, Naples, Munich, Danzig,
Moscow, Florence, Basel, Paris; memories of Rosenthal's sumptuous rooms in Munich, of
the Danzig Stockturm, where the late Hans Rhaue was domiciled, of Süssengut's musty
book cellar in North Berlin; memories of the rooms where these books had been housed
… ' (2: 492; *GS* IV·1: 396).

James Joyce joined Benjamin in the emission of complex messages sent out ahead to the future of the book, no doubt conceived and transmitted under a shroud of crisis. As Benjamin was prescient in noting, Proust dissolved the conventional novel in the reconfiguration of a genre sensitive and welcoming to the catastrophes in authority, certainty, objectivity, the stability of the physical world, the integrity of media and art forms, and the exclusiveness and duration of selfhood and identity that had pervaded the fields of knowledge, perception, and cognition. Hovering above the hybrid narrative form, the polyglot linguistic medium, the nearly illegible semantic, syntactic and grammatical discourse that Joyce devised for *Finnegans Wake*, his ultimate novel, as its bibliographical talisman, is a singular and unforgettable book, *The Book of Kells*, surely, in Benjamin's words on Proust, as much of a genre and tradition-maker as a breaker. As Joyce tarries at the very end, on the literal limit of the bibliographic forms, traditions, and conventions that he has unleashed and unravelled in the modernist experimentation of *Ulysses*, he too experiences a state of crisis, appealing to one of the notable fundaments and exceptions in the book's long and storied run.

The direction in which we are inexorably headed is toward an inventory and census of the Benjaminian library. We ask not so much which books Benjamin encountered and read, for his own works are quite explicit about disclosing their raw materials, and the remarkable scholarship that has risen to the occasion of Benjamin has been persistent in filling in necessary additions to our knowledge. We ask ourselves instead on which books, not only the notable exceptions comprising *The Origin of German Tragic Drama* (*Ursprung des deutschen Trauerspiels*) (also *GS* I·1: 203–430) and *The Arcades Project*, did Benjamin's practices of reading and writing predicate? What are the scale, design, architecture, and other salient features of these books, that are just as much hypothetical as actual, that have been shelved both in Borges's Library of Babylon and in the Parisian Bibliothèque Nationale? It was in the latter archive of course, that Benjamin, when Paris no longer provided any cover whatsoever, deposited the manuscript of *The Arcades Project* with George Bataille, who fulfilled his custodial charge, the obligation of the Talmudic *shomair hinam* (remunerated watchperson). In what senses are the books comprising Benjamin's virtual library both the highest syntheses in the history of their medium and the departure points for as yet unrealised and unmastered programs of inscription and information? The assayer of the Benjaminian library would surely have to base his or her inventory on at least the following major categories of volumes: the illustrated or illuminated book, the Talmudic book or hypertext, the mystical book, the compendium or encyclopaedia, and the dissolving or interstitial book, the volume inscribed with the traits of its own future. Each of these collections arises at a particular conjunction of discourse-design with book-design; we need to constantly remind ourselves that these two items are not exactly the same matter. Because of my earlier encounters with *The Arcades Project* as a radical book-experiment complying with parameters of the Talmudic work, the hypertext, and the encyclopaedia in Benjamin's collection (Sussman, *Task* 100–28; Sussman, *boundary 2*) I will be unpacking, in my not-so-brief overview of books of the Benjaminian library, only the illuminated book, its mystical counterpart, and the dissolving variety that opens up the entire tradition.

THE ILLUMINATED BOOK

Even as Benjamin initiates his life-long nomadic quest for a discourse in which he is definitively at home, a search perhaps futile in the end but on the way unearthing the bewildering profusion of dialects in which he became proficient, among them philosophy-based literary critique, travel literature, food criticism, personal memoir, and radio-talk, he is aware of the profound synergy initiated by the incursion of images into text, particularly in the sphere of children's literature. The picture-book is an indispensable element of the Benjaminian library from the moment that he openly assumes the guise of a book-collector, a real one, a role delineated from that of a seller or even the writer.[4]

The encounter with Benjamin transpiring in a truly inventive library or collection may well be as instructive as the illuminations gained from acts of reading his prose. Anyone fortunate enough to have wandered into Richard Macksey's library in the Guilford section of Baltimore, a collection in the letters, arts, and sciences never at rest, has gained an even more tangible access to the real collector's devotion and discipline than the reader of 'Unpacking my Library'. The line from the obsessions, dissimulations, and triumphs encountered in book-collecting and chronicled in that essay, one of Benjamin's most elegant and compelling, to Macksey's book-filled house, is direct. The rare privilege of witnessing, over the years, the development of this collection, the rhizomatic growth and movement of its sub-sections toward one another, and into more and more sections of the house, has been the purest possible Benjaminian experience.

The window that the illustration introduces into the printed medium bears a privileged a special relation to childhood, which for Benjamin is less a zero-point of human development than the initiation of perception and sensibility into the wonders of language and reading. Childhood sensibility, in other words, is the initial emergence of and encounter with the vari-

---

4. See one of Benjamin's signature essays, 'Unpacking my Library' (*SW* 2: 492): 'O bliss of the collector, bliss of the man of leisure … For inside him there are spirits, or at least little genii, which have seen to it that for a collector—and I mean a real collector, a collector as he ought to be—ownership is the most intimate relationship that one can have to things'.

ants of colour, touch, sound and play persisting under siege during the later
phases of life, but in childhood comprising the very basis and structure of
aesthetico-cultural experience. The illuminated book is not merely the ves-
tige of a childhood whose magical evanescence is first invoked and com-
modified by the Romantics; it is, in its many guises—from the *Shah-nameh*
and the *Book of Kells* to *Der Wunderschirm: Eine Erzählung* ⁵—a window on the
particular propensities to linguistic play and dissonance hard-wired into the
individual. It is in this sense that Proust's *Recherche*, setting out with a scene
of bedtime reading between a little boy and his mother, a scene emblematic
of the profound intimacy, wonder, distraction, separation and suffering ac-
cruing from the encounter with signs, is, as its multiple volumes appear during the 1910s and 1920s already primed with one of its most astute readers,
Walter Benjamin.

Benjamin may draw our attention, in 'Unpacking my Library', to the
'childlike element which, in a collector, mingles with the element of old age'
(*SW* 2: 487). But the world of '*Old Forgotten Children's Books*' ('*Alte vergessene Kinderbücher*') (*SW* 1: 406–13; *GS* III: 14–22), the title of a book by collector and
exhibitor Karl Hobrecker that Benjamin reviewed in the *Illustrierte Zeitung*
in 1924, is not the domain of antiquated and outmoded relics; it is, rather, a
riot-house of colours, games, and mixtures:

> Since the Enlightenment, this has been one of the mustiest speculations
> of the pedagogues. Their infatuation with psychology keeps them from
> perceiving that the world is full of the most unrivalled objects for chil-
> dren's attention and use. For children are particularly fond of haunting
> any site where things are being visibly worked on [*geneigt, jedwede Arbe-
> itsstätte aufzusuchen, wo sichtbare Betätigung an den Dingen vor sich geht*]. They
> are irresistibly drawn by the detritus generated by building, gardening,
> housework, tailoring, or carpentry. In waste products they recognize the
> face that the world of things turns directly and solely to them [*In diesen
> Abfallprodukten erkennen sie das Gesicht, das die Dingwelt gerade ihnen, ihnen al-
> lein zukehrt*]. In using these things, they do not so much imitate the works
> of adults as bring together, in the artifacts produced in play, materials of
> widely differing kinds in a new, intuitive relationship [*Mit diesen bilden sie
> die Werke von Erwachsenen nicht sowohl nach als daß diese Rest- und Abfallstoffe in
> eine sprunghafte neue Beziehung zueinander setzen*]. (*SW* 1: 408; *GS* III: 16)

Children serve Benjamin, in this brief extract, as vehicles for two of his
prized hobby-horses: they defy the pedagogical heritage of Rousseau and
the Enlightenment, which would treat them as miniature men and women,
prematurely overburdened with the baggage of reason and by implication,
the moral imperative; and, in the open-ended and combinatorial thrust of

---

5. For an illustration of the cover of this volume, see Walter Benjamin, 'The World of
Children's Books', (*SW* 1: 441).

their play, from which they emerge as proto-modernists of the first order.[6] In preparing his culture to receive and welcome the innovations of modernism, to which he is particularly attuned, Benjamin enlists a *Kinderbrigade* of his fellow urban explorers and innovators. In their intuitive relation to matter and materials and their inborn gift in improvisation, the children of Benjamin are already, in their sensibilities, structural anthropologists of mythology, visual cubists, editors of film-montage, and jazz musicians, even if, in 1924, Benjamin does not yet venture all these connections. The children of Benjamin are not so much imprinted with intuitive senses of purpose and rectitude as they are with the marks of modernist sensibility and improvisation, including a susceptibility to what Benjamin will later call shock. Benjamin already circles about this link between childhood and shock in his review of *Old Forgotten Children's Books* by tracing the heritage of illustrated books back to the Baroque period, when it was, in its representational program, infused by an allegorical shorthand and violence. The value of any future education for these children would be to prolong and interrelate these predilections for radical juxtaposition and experiment, not to eventuate at the well-tempered man and woman.

In keeping with his work in the Youth Movement and his emerging political philosophy, Benjamin deduces the artefacts of child-culture, including the illustrated book, from the habits and relations of childhood, not the reverse.

> Children thus produce their own small world of things within the greater one. The fairy tale is such a waste product—perhaps the most powerful one to be found in the spiritual life of humanity; a waste product that emerges from the growth and decay of the saga. Children are able to manipulate fairy tales with the same ease and lack of inhibition that they display in playing with pieces of cloth, ... and combining its various elements [*Kinder bilden sich damit ihre Dingwelt, eine kleine in der großen, selbst. Ein solches Abfallprodukt ist das Märchen, das gewaltigste vielleicht, das im geistigen Leben der Menschheit sich findet: Abfall im Entstehungs- und Verfallsprozeß der Sage*]. The same is true of songs. And the fable ... We may alsoquestion whether young readers admire the fable for the moral tagged on at the end, or whether they use it to school their understanding, as was the traditional wisdom ... Children enjoy the spectacle of animals that talk and act like people far more than they enjoy any text burdened with good thoughts ...

One thing redeems even the most old-fashioned and self-conscious prod-

6. For my overall apprehension of the centrality and indispensability of childhood to Benjamin's notions of criticism, I am most indebted to Martin Blumenthal-Barby, an advanced graduate student of Germanic Languages and Literatures at Yale University, whose study-in-progress devoted to this topic will surely comprise an important contribution to the Benjamin literature.

ucts of their era: their illustrations ... The collections of fables show that
related formulas recur in the remotest places with larger or smaller variations. In like fashion, picture-books go back even further, as we can see
from the way in which, for example, illustrations of the Seven Wonders
of the World can be traced back to the copper engravings of the seventeenth century, and perhaps to earlier times. We may perhaps venture to
surmise that the illustrations of these works have some connection with
the emblem books of the Baroque period. (*SW* 1: 408–9; *GS* III: 16–7)

In his apprehension that children in effect carry over material relations
and tactile habits to intellectual (or mythical, or narrative) property, Benjamin radically pre-empts Lévi-Strauss's approach to science, experimentation, and classification as conducted by so-called primitive peoples. Moral
fables spin or tease out the permutational play of formulae and fragments
of narrative sequences in which children are particularly adept. Children's
books, forgotten or not, illustrate—literally—this playful repetition with *dif-
férance*. The Baroque, among many things, is a site where the putative child,
the unabashed learner from repetition and trial-and-error, the by no means
naive exploiter of the materials at hand, interfaces with the studied tedium
of adulthood, the latter perspective one that any cultural critique approach-
ing the thresholds of its own spontaneity and its own impossibility wishes to
avoid.

Benjamin's encounter with Karl Hobrecker as a purveyor and historian of children's literature serves him well in his engagement with the perception and sensibility of the child. The Benjaminian child, for example,
enjoys a privileged rapport with and experience of colour, which for Benjamin infuses the world, cutting through its spatial, authoritarian and logical compartments. It is a form of interconnectedness that Deleuze and Guattari associate both with the schizophrenic mentality and the experience of
the body without organs. Benjamin distinguishes the colouring in paintings
from that in children's books:

> When in paintings the colors, the transparent or glowing motley of tones,
> interfere with the design, they come perilously close to effects for their
> own sake. But in the pictures in children's books, the objects depicted
> and the independence of the graphic design usually exclude any syn-
> thesis of color and drawing. In this play of colors, the imagination runs
> riot [*Bei den Bildern der Kinderbücher bewirkt es jedoch meist der Gegenstand und
> die Selbständigkeit der graphischen Unterlage, daß an eine Synthese von Farbe und
> Fläche nicht gedacht werden kann. In diesen Farbenspielen ergeht sich aller Verant-
> wortung entbunden die bloße Phantasie*]. After all, the role of children's books
> is not to induct their readers directly into the world of objects, animals,
> and peoples—in other words, into so-called life. Very gradually their
> meaning is discovered in the outside world, but only in proportion as
> they are found to correspond to what children already possess within

themselves. (*SW* 1: 410; *GS* III: 18–9)

The meaning of colour, as children encounter it in illustrated books, is precisely *unbound*: its fidelity to the known features of objects in the empirical world is limited. The worldly place and context of the objects represented in the illustrated book will dawn upon the youthful reader only as his or her experience evolves. As Benjamin characterises the impact of colour on the childhood imagination, his description is akin to that of a developmentally specific Derridean archi-trace, the irreducible mark of articulation that conditions all further thinking and expression. Indeed, the play of colour in the illustrated book stages an early symbolic encounter between the imagination and the law. The colour 'not confined to illustrating objects ... must be full of light and shade, full of movement, arbitrary and always beautiful,' writes Benjamin in 'A Child's View of Color'. The completely absorbing, fully entrancing childhood experience of colour plays around and against the symbolic order, the division of labour between form and function. Whereas colour occupies a specific place in the 'world order' that it is incumbent on the adult to furnish, '[i]n a child's life, color is the pure expression of the child's pure receptivity ... The concern of color with objects is not based on their form ... It cancels out the intellectual cross-references of the soul and creates a pure mood' ('*Sie hebt die intellektuallen Verbindungen der Seele auf und schafft die reine Stimmung ohne darum die Welt aufzugeben.*') (*SW* 1: 51; *GS* VI: 111).

Colour is a primary medium for the child's playful and ultimately short-lived resistance to the adult law. There is a magical, if not mystical quality to the child's encounter with colour: 'The order of art is paradisiacal because there is no thought of the dissolution of boundaries—from excitement—in the object of experience. Instead the world is full of colour in a state of identity, innocence, and harmony. Children are not ashamed, since they do not reflect but only see' (*SW* 1: 51). It is precisely a quasi-mystical phenomenon, 'the struggle between light and darkness', that Benjamin discloses in Goethe's Romantic account of colour in *The Theory of Colours*.

> The *Theory of Colors* takes up a position diametrically opposed to Newton's optics. The basic disagreement underlying Goethe's often bitter polemic, prolonged over many years, is this: whereas Newton explained white light as the composite of the different colours, Goethe declared it to be the simplest, most indivisible and homogenous phenomenon known to us [*Newton erklärt das weiße Licht als eine Zusammensetzung aus farbigen Lichtern, Goethe dagegen als das einfachste, unzerlegbarste, homogenste Wesen, das wir kennen*] ... The *Theory of Colors* regards the colors as metamorphoses of light, as phenomena which are formed in the course of the struggle between light and darkness. Together with the idea of metamorphosis, the concept of polarity, which runs like a thread through Goethe's entire scientific enterprise, is of decisive importance here. Darkness is not merely the absence of light [*Die 'Farbenlehre' nimmt die Farben für Metamorphosen des*

Lichtes, für Erscheinungen, die im Kampf des Lichtes mit dem Dunkel sich bilden. Neben dem Gedanken der Metamorphose ist hier für Goethe bestimmend der der Polarität, der sein ganzes Forschen durchzieht. Dunkel ist nicht bloße Abwesenheit des Lichtes]... (*SW* 2: 173–4; *GS* II·2: 720–1)

Goethe's treatment of colour is infused by a cosmic struggle between darkness and light. In its transformation from the completely absorbing and entrancing medium of childhood apprehension into an interstice at which Goethe's incipient Romanticism arrives at a mystical world-view, colour gathers momentum as a force of socio-cultural reform and redemption. Toward the end of his full-fledged early work of philosophically inspired literary criticism, 'Goethe's *Elective Affinities*', Benjamin becomes obsessed by the hope that ' "shot across the sky above their [the novelistic characters'] heads like a falling star" ... That most paradoxical, most fleeting hope finally emerges from the semblance of reconciliation, just as, at twilight, as the sun is extinguished, rises the evening star which outlasts the night' (*SW* 1: 354–55). Benjamin discerns, in other words, the workings of the possibilities for a messianic redemption of the world at the stratospheric limits of Goethe's chemical and alchemical novel of erotic affiliations, set amid the trappings of neo-classical architecture. In degraded form, the falling star that Benjamin tracks in Goethe's novel of the displacements and limits of erotic possibility continues its trajectory across the sky of Benjamin's Second Empire capital, where it is ironically transformed from the vehicle of the wish in folktale into the white roulette wheel ball of the gambling casino.[7] More importantly, Goethe emerges from a figural network in which childhood is both a mystical fascination with play and colour and a prefiguration of radical modernistic experimentation as the legitimizing vehicle of mystical apprehension in German letters.

Throughout his treatment of Goethe's novel, Benjamin is attentive to the play of *Schein*—semblance, appearance, but also glimmer—within it. *Schein* is a term with impeccable credentials in German idealist philosophy. In the Hegelian *Phenomenology of Mind*, for instance, *Schein* is the semblance at the heart of the *Erscheinung* or manifestation, by which *Geist*, spirit or mind, in heavily onto-theological fashion, makes its presence known and felt in the world. In Benjamin's approach to Goethe's novel, *Schein* is a swing-term, what Derrida would call a hinge (*Of Grammatology* 66–73, 265), linking literature to philosophy, enabling 'all genuine works' to find 'their siblings in the realm of philosophy' (*Und alle echten Werke haben ihre Geschwister im Bereiche der Philosophie*) (*SW* 1: 333; *GS* I·1: 172). In a fashion that we will pursue later in this inventory, Benjamin somehow manages to add a mystical resonance to the glittering play of Christian, idealist semblance, one emerging from far afield. Against the backdrop of the childhood apprehension of colour in il-

---

7. This in 'On Some Motifs in Baudelaire' (*SW* 4: 330–1).

luminated books, Benjamin enlists Goethe, whose invention and exemplarity encompass both Enlightenment and Romantic ages, in the service of a redemption of the world both mystical and messianic, one grounded among other sources in the literature of Jewish mysticism. The yearning for a graft or trunk or direct line between the Judaic messianic imagination and the mainstream of German letters is acted out in a dream recorded in 'One-Way Street', in which Goethe's hospitality to Benjamin's relatives brings him to tears. 'Goethe rose to his feet and accompanied me to an adjoining chamber, where a table was set for my relatives … Doubtless there were places for my ancestors, too … When the meal was over, he rose with difficulty, and by gesturing I sought leave to support him. Touching his elbow, I began to weep with emotion' (*SW* 1: 446; *GS* IV·1: 87). It is precisely at this juncture that the shelving of the illuminated Benjaminian book merges into the holdings in mystical literature, a register we have yet to explore.

Although residing at the very gateway to reading and informed cultural discourse, the illustrated books in the Benjaminian library are far from a simple matter. If they serve as primers, they already sustain a colloquy of different voices and mixed messages, the aesthetic, the modern, the Germanic, the Judaic, and the messianic, to which I add the programme of radical change, exemplified best of all by the Marxian analysis of and proposal for capital. Not only an adept practicing modernist, the Benjaminian child is, willy-nilly, a proto-Marxist. Children's book illustrator Johan Peter Lyser figures in '*Old Forgotten Children's Books*' as 'a bohemian figure from those days' who effects a 'merging of all intellectual classes and modes of action' ('*Das Ineinandersinken aller geistigen Schichten und Aktionsweisen*') (*SW* 1: 410; *GS* III: 19). Under the stewardship of artists such as Lyser, children's literature becomes a site for challenging the given division of labour between classes and the effects of the Derridean 'Law of Genre'.[8]

As Karl Marx set about decrying the debilitating socio-cultural changes wrought by the factory system, no impact inspired him to purer outrage than child-labour as a developmentally specific squandering of human potential. Like the Benjaminian child, Marx, in his own dance between the discourses of algebraic calculation, detached sociological observation, evolutionary history, outraged polemic and theoretical speculation, violates the laws of order and good sense. When he addresses the impact of child-labour under the factory system, Marx metamorphoses himself from the revolutionary social thinker with whom we are most familiar and comfortable into a developmental psychologist:

> It appears, for example, in the frightful fact that a great part of the chil
> dren employed in modern factories and manufactures are from their

---

8. Derrida's construct of the Law of Genre and his fullest elaboration of it emerges in his reading of Blanchot's 'Folie du jour'. See Jacques Derrida, 'The Law of Genre' (*Acts of Literature* 223–35).

earliest years riveted to the most simple manipulations, and exploited for years, without being taught a single kind of skill that would afterwards make them of use, even in the same factory. In the English letterpress printing trade, there formerly existed a system … of advancing the apprentices from easy to more and more difficult work. They went through a course of teaching until they were finished printers. To read and write was for every one of them a requirement of their trade. All this was changed by the printing machine. It employs two sorts of worker. On the one hand, there are adults, tenters, and on the other hand there are boys … whose sole occupation is either to spread the sheets under the machine, or to take from it the printed sheets. They perform this task, in London especially, for 14, 15 and 16 hours at a stretch … A great proportion of them cannot read, and they are, as a rule, utter savages and very extraordinary creatures … As soon as they get too old for such children's work, that is at about 17 years old, at the latest, they are discharged from the printing establishments. They become recruits for crime. (Marx 615)

We must not overlook the Marxian impulse behind Benjamin's reverence for the child, to whatever degree it is also inflected by a Romantic aura and by the child's pivotal placement in the process of messianic repair and correction. The child is not only a playful resistor of norms and an endlessly inventive player. The child is potential for human realisation and progress, ravaged and subjected to irreversible degradation once reconfigured as the ward of voracious capitalism. The design of the illustrated children's book that Benjamin collects with the purpose of introducing it to his readership's sensibility is as much to spare the unborn victims of capital and its attendant circumlocutions and calculations as it is to fetishise the auratic freshness of early experience. Romanticism, Marx, Jewish mysticism, and modernistic improvisation converge here. However playful its provenance, under Benjamin's stewardship the illustrated book attains a certain gravity in advance of its age. He assigns it a daunting and strategic role in the extension of culture.

THE MYSTICAL BOOK

We discover the placement of the mystical book in Benjamin's library as we address key anomalies in some of his most liminal and haunting works. Why would he in the Kafka essay commemorating the tenth anniversary of the Czech author's death—an author who did so much to translate into the modes and formats of twentieth-century configurations of power and signification—devote so much material to Kafka's totemism, his relation to prehistory, and his human and animal ancestors? Why, in 'The Critique of Violence', in which Benjamin seriously investigates the rationale for violent proletarian insurrection, would he elaborate the position of divine violence, which although arbitrary and always at the extreme limit of credulity, furnishes an alternative to mythic violence? We are familiar with this latter form of unrest, the mythic, expressing itself externally as warfare and internally as state repression, from its basis in an ideological constriction and fetishisation imposed upon the free play of signs. This process, for Benjamin, is as old as recorded history itself; it is what Roland Barthes, in the 1950s, taking either a blind or explicit cue from his predecessor, referred to as mythology.

It is when such questions arise that the gates (or covers) of the mystical book in the Benjaminian library swing open. In the background to this literature is mysticism in general and Jewish mysticism in particular, among whose signal accomplishments included, in the Zohar, the opening of a sublime Judaic afterlife whose spectral landscape found its most receptive European home in German letters, particularly during the Romantic moment; also Benjamin's lifelong collaboration and commiseration with Gershom Scholem, who, while Benjamin confined his critico-cultural interventions to the secular sphere, blazed a backward trail from twentieth-century Zionism to the literatures of the Kabbalah and Zohar. The supplemental tension in which Benjamin places the Judaic, on the one hand, and the Greco-Christian on the other, is not unlike a parallel pulsation that Derrida pursues, particularly in such early works as *Of Grammatology*, 'Plato's Pharmacy', and 'The Double Session', the latter his study of the poetics of Stéphane Mallarmé, between the discourse of philosophy and its literary sibling. In general, we can say that for Benjamin, the Judaic, particularly in its mystical aspect, implicates a vaster time-scheme than the history of dialectical movements, developments, and structures emerging from the doubled sources of Greek mythology and idealist philosophy and Christian theology.

The Judaic, furthermore, in the hope that it holds out for the redemption of a morally polarised and intrinsically flawed world—not entirely unlike certain aspects of Indian and Chinese civilizations—also encompasses the possibility of circumventing certain rationalist dynamics and eventualities. This is not to suggest that the Judaic, in its exceptions to the dialectical, as Benjamin can discern it in the writings of Buber and Rosenzweig as well as of Scholem, is entirely devoid of the arbitrary. On the contrary, the Judaic gains a good measure of its sublimity, one also achieving a particular intensity in writers ranging from Kleist and Büchner to Celan, precisely in furnishing a lieu for an arbitrariness that will not submit to reason.

It is in this context that Benjamin, at the outset of dire conditions of political repression, in 'Critique of Violence', his inquiry into legitimate grounds for the general proletarian strike, one that might extend from figural to actual violence, goes to the extreme lengths of articulating and invoking 'divine violence'. Benjamin takes Georges Sorel at his word—to the effect that 'the proletarian general strike sets itself the sole task of destroying state power. It "nullifies all the ideological consequences of every possible social policy … The revolution appears as a clear, simple revolt, and no place is reserved either for the sociologists or the elegant amateurs of social reform or for the intellectuals'" (*SW* 1: 246). But against the grain of Sorel's 'reject[ion of]every kind of program, of utopia … for the revolutionary movement', Benjamin disallows any 'objection … that seeks, on grounds of its possibly catastrophic consequences, to brand such a general strike as violent' (*SW* 1: 246).

'Critique of Violence' not only spells out through meticulous argumentation the conditions under which the particular violence of the general proletarian strike would be warranted, it also furnishes a methodological template for the 'critique of all legal violence' (*SW* 1: 241). Benjamin indeed examines in the course of a brief essay the variations linking and separating such social controls as militarism, universal conscription and the death penalty. Benjamin's reasonings take up precisely the gauntlet that Sorel has thrown down to 'intellectuals who have made it their profession to think for the proletariat' (*SW* 1: 246). The general proletarian strike becomes viable only through a concerted labour of distinction-making: between the 'natural law, which regards violence as a natural datum' and furnishes a critique of ends, as opposed to positive law, which lays the blame for violence at the feet of history, and delivers the critique of means; between the law-making and law-preserving functions of violence (the one the inaugural event in the formulation of laws; the latter an incipient violence always in potentia from the state). The ignominy of police brutality consists in its suspension of the distinction between law-making and law-preserving violence:

> It is lawmaking, because its characteristic function is not the promulgation of laws but the assertion of legal claims for any decree, and law-preserving, because it is at the disposal of these ends [*Sie ist rechtsetzende— denn deren charakteristische Funktion ist ja nicht die Promulgation von Gesetzen, sondern jedweder Erlaß, den sie mit Rechtsanspruch ergehen läßt—und sie ist rechtserhaltende, weil sie sich jenen Zwecken zur Verfügung stellt*]. The assertion that the ends of police violence are always identical or even connected to those of general law is equally untrue. Rather, the 'law' of the police really marks the point at which the state, whether from impotence or because of the immanent connections within any legal system, can no longer guarantee through the legal system the empirical ends that it desires at any price to attain. Therefore the police intervene 'for security reasons' in countless cases where no legal situation exists [*Daher greift 'der Sicherheit wegen' der Polizei in zahllosen Fällen ein, wo keine klare Reschtslage vorliegt*]. (*SW* 1: 243; *GS* II·1: 189)

Benjamin has initiated his own chess game with systems of law and justice that allow escalating abuses by the state; this as much by dint of being opposed to the law's own logico-rational underpinnings. Even in the logical construction and disposition of his own essay, Benjamin demonstrates that there is an ample scaffolding of logical operations and moral principles for the negotiation of violence by civil society. Police rule, as he indicates in the above citation, sets in not through the bypassing of the abundant legal literature of natural law versus positive law, the relative validities of ends versus means and so forth, but through a short-circuiting of this substantial defensive apparatus. In moments of authoritarian repression, the system of the law does not so much void itself or cancel itself out as implode under the inertia and equilibrium wrought by its distinctions. In this sense, the legal crisis resulting in police violence, which includes the suppression of workers' resistance, is a practical instance of the proliferation of insubstantial 'differences that are not differences' marking the limit of the Hegelian understanding or *Verstand* (Hegel 94–6, 99–102).

The proletarian general strike emerges in Benjamin's parlance not merely as a recourse to justice unavailable through any other means but also as the expansion of a system as repressively closed off and involuted as it is corrupt. The proletarian general strike, in other words, opens up the conceptual-structural configuration in which the class interests of workers are systematically devalued and underrepresented. By the time of 'Critique of Violence' Benjamin is already beginning to discern the historical coherence and perdurance of this gridlocked system, lending it something of the cohesion that Derrida can extrapolate in his notion of 'Western metaphysics'. The grounding of the proletarian general strike will demand an expansion—historical, conceptual and literary—of the logical grid arising in myth and prevailing through the only too-familiar cycles of absolutist tyranny, revolution, civil adjudications of violence and abuses of civil law by the very state agencies of moderation. In this piece of writing, Benjamin has anticipated the ploy of the rigorous deconstructionist; he is riding logic to its very ends to demonstrate how arbitrary and illogical these eventualities are. It is precisely here in Benjamin's argument where he appeals to the divine violence that in its sublime arbitrariness circumvents the mythic violence lending itself only too well to the various outcomes of the play of force and law; it is at this point as well that he opens up the temporal framework of Greco-Christian metaphysics and law to the somewhat wider (and indeed on some level timeless) horizon of Judaic creation.

Both subsequent history and Jacques Derrida, in 'Force of Law', will demonstrate that the appeal to a divine violence, 'without warning, without threat' and not stopping 'short of annihilation' can be a double-edged sword (*SW* 1: 250). It can indeed be directed against those whose interests it might otherwise protect. At a moment in history when the ordeal of reading a newspaper is exacerbated in no small measure by system-wide, near-global attenuation of religious fundamentalisms and ethnic strife, we need to underscore the irresponsibility and risk, by any and all parties, of invoking 'divine violence'.

Much as mythic violence may initiate cycles of casuistry and bad faith
in government and the civil sphere, in Benjamin's account divine violence is
not exactly unproblematic either: it is abrupt, bloody, disproportionate, and
hyper-arbitrary. It shows no mercy and may exact inexplicable vast tolls in
sacrifice. Benjamin situates the educational system under the aegis of divine
violence: his very first political activity was dedicated to the Youth Movement's program of educational reform. With respect to such phenomena as
the recalibration of laws in the wake of military treaties, Benjamin dem-
onstrated striking acuity toward his particular historical moment. But like
the rest of us, he was blind addressing the future. Within the framework of
the specific text, 'Critique of Violence', such moves as the bracketing of the
Niobe myth by the biblical account of Korah give an early indication of
where the mystical book, particularly the book conditioned by the Jewish
mysticism of which Scholem was such a powerful avatar, places within the
body of Benjamin's writing.

> [T]he mythic manifestation of immediate violence shows itself funda-
> mentally identical with all legal violence [*zeigt die mythische Manifestation
> der unmittelbaren Gewalt sich im tiefsten mit aller Rechtsgewalt identisch*] … Just
> as in all spheres God opposes myth, mythic violence is confronted by the
> divine. And the latter constitutes its antithesis in all respects. If mythic
> violence is lawmaking, divine violence is law-destroying; if the former
> sets boundaries, the latter boundlessly destroys them; if mythic violence
> brings at once guilt and retribution, divine power only expiates; if the
> former threatens, the latter strikes; if the former is bloody, the latter is le-
> thal without spilling blood. The legend of Niobe may be contrasted with
> God's judgment on the company of Korah … Mythic violence is bloody
> power over mere life for its own sake; divine violence is pure power over
> all life for the sake of the living. The first demands sacrifice; the second
> accepts it [*Die mythische Gewalt ist Blutgewalt über das bloße Leben um ihrer
> selbst, die göttliche reine Gewalt über alles Leben um des Lebendigen willen. Die erste
> fordert Opfer, die zweite nimmt sie an*]. (*SW* 1: 249–50; *GS* II·1: 199–200)

In seeking a framework and pretext for the general proletarian strike,
even at the cost of his own logical inconsistency (for the configuration in
which he places mythical and divine violence here is nothing if not strin-
gently dialectical), Benjamin is willing, to borrow a phrasing from his major
Kafka essay, to 'move divine time'. The general proletarian strike comprises
a severe challenge to the Western tradition of conceptualising, making and
adjudicating laws and punishment for their violation. Yet it is backed, in the
logic of Benjamin's argument, by an alternate tradition, one characterised,
if by nothing else, by a sublime arbitrariness, one capable of suspending the
rule of logic, and by cosmic time.

This alternate tradition subtends the manifest wish, in the dream recounted in 'One-Way Street', for an intimacy between Judaic and German letters (parallel to the graft that Faust makes to the very bedrock of Greek culture when, in *Faust II*, he marries Helen of Troy), and it makes its influence felt, often surprisingly and with seeming irrelevance, in a wide range of Benjamin's addresses to cultural artefacts.

In view of the preceding discussion and its distinction between mythical and divine violence, and the timeframes from whence they proceed, it is perhaps not difficult to understand why Benjamin, in his 1934 Kafka essay discerns Chinese, Greek, Judaic, and even Indian forerunners, his term is 'ancestors', to Kafka's fiction-making. In this line of inquiry, Benjamin is of course taking his cues from Kafka, whose Poseidon sits 'at his desk, going over the accounts' (Kafka 434), a twentieth-century bureaucrat, and whose Abraham appears 'with the promptness of a waiter' (*SW* 2: 808). In one respect, Kafka continues the ploy, along the lines of Baudelaire's angel in 'Perte d'auriole', of inserting cultural figures of venerable pedigree in a contemporary setting, depicted in all its realistic wrinkles. But Benjamin figures the complementary side to this vast temporal reversal or metalepsis as a case of premature cosmic old-age:

> To speak of any order or hierarchy here is impossible. Even the world of myth, which comes to mind in this context, is incomparably younger than Kafka's world, which has been promised redemption by myth. But if we can be sure of one thing, it is this: Kafka did not succumb to its temptation … Among Kafka's ancestors in the ancient world, the Jews and the Chinese (whom we shall encounter later), this Greek one should not be forgotten. Ulysses, after all, stands at the dividing line between myth and fairy tale. Reason and cunning have inserted tricks into myths; … and fairy tales for dialecticians are what Kafka wrote when he went to work on legends. He inserted little tricks into them [*Und Märchen für Dialektiker schrieb Kafka, wenn er sich Sagen vornahm. Er setzte kleine Tricks in sie hinein*]; then he used them as proof 'that inadequate, even childish measures may also serve as a means of rescue'. With these words, he begins his story 'Das Schweigen der Sirenen' (*The Silence of the Sirens*). For Kafka's Sirens are silent [*Die Sirenen schweigen nämlich bei ihm*]. (*SW* 2: 799; *GS* II·2: 415)

Although the expression is as stunningly trenchant as Benjamin can often be, we can well understand how Kafka could have devised 'fairy tales for dialecticians'. Kafka's fictive ploys of logic, spatiality and temporality are indeed legendary and unavoidable. But Kafka's cosmic timeframe, the fact that 'Kafka did not consider the age in which he lived as an advance over the beginnings of time. His novels are set in a swamp world' (*SW* 2: 808), remains a puzzle unless Kafka's fiction occupies a cosmic sweep of time, the eons of mystical apprehension.

We remember in Benjamin's 'Critique of Violence' how the dialectical operations of mythical violence and justice were both meticulous in their distinctions and constrictive in their compulsion. In the citation immediately above, Ulysses is an interstitial figure, hovering 'at the dividing line between myth and fairy tale'. He thus claims a dual citizenship in the progression of myth into civil law instrumented by dialectical logic and resulting in mythical violence but also in the incomparably broader scope, international and intercultural as well as historical, claimed by fairy-tale and legend. This latter literature, of course, like the particular aura of colourful illustrations, enjoys a particular intimacy with children, their play and their culture. I would suggest that those aspects of Ulysses making him an emissary to the world of *Old Forgotten Children's Books* also make him figure in the cosmic universe of Benjamin's mystical book-holdings, a world proceeding, among other sources, from the literature of Jewish mysticism as penetrated and purveyed by Scholem. Where Ulysses belongs both to myth and fairy tale, the dialectical does commerce with the mystical, and the Greek joins the Judaic, as in Joyce's trenchant phrase from *Ulysses*, 'Jewgreek Greekjew' (32, 165, 378, 411).

In an act of authentic critical impossibility and creation, Benjamin links Kafka's dealings with the prehistorical pretext to world literature to the sordid bureaucratic spaces that fill his novels. 'We do not know the makeup' of the suffocating, phantasmatic family from Kafka's very early life. Benjamin writes that he 'composed of human beings and animals. But this much is clear: it is this family that forces Kafka to move cosmic ages in his writings. Doing this family's bidding, he moves the mass of historical happenings the way Sisyphus moved the stone' (*SW* 2: 808). It is with bemused admiration that Benjamin characterizes Kafka's Archimedean feat of moving, with his imagination, the building blocks of a broader, more anthropologically resonant tradition than the Western canon alone. The women in the world literature mobilised by Kafka's imaginary, like the vague and innocent sister of 'Der Schlag ans Hoftor' ('The Knock on the Manor Gate'), do not stand out clearly, like Penelope, heroically devising to restore the unity of her world. They are, also like Leni of *The Castle*, 'swamp creatures', who arise from 'swampy soil' (*SW* 2: 809).

The communication with the prehistoric and animal worlds distinguishing Kafka's modernist innovation embarks him, in Benjamin's scenario, on an exploration of oblivion itself, of the collective and cosmic unconscious. Kafka becomes the psychoanalytical explorer of prehistory in its anthropological as well as cultural dimensions. It is no accident that Benjamin cites Franz Rosenzweig on the Chinese ancestor cult in illuminating Kafka's uncanny gravitation toward oblivion. In the passage that inspired Benjamin to this particular thrust of his reading, Rosenzweig, in *Stern der Erlösung* (*Star of Redemption*), an overview of the tradition of redemptive history in Judaism, accounts for the transformation of spirit, or *Geist* in its Hegelian sense, into spirits. In Rosenzeweig's terms: 'All spirit must be concrete, particularized, in order to have its place and *raison d'être*. The spiritual, if it plays a role at all, turns into spirits. These spirits become definite individuals, with names and a very special connection with the name of the worshiper ... Unhesitatingly, the fullness of the world is filled to overflowing with their fullness' (*SW* 2: 810). Kafka's special relation to the amorphous creatures who teem out of this inchoate history, in Benjamin's scenario, marks him a partner in a cosmic process of the redemption of the world, *tikkun olam*, in a framework whose application and potential surpass its grounding in Judaic texts.

> What has been forgotten—and with this insight we stand before another threshold of Kafka's work—is never something purely individual. Everything forgotten mingles with what has been forgotten of the prehistoric world, forms countless uncertain and unchanging compounds, yielding a constant flow of new, strange products. Oblivion is the container from which the inexhaustible intermediate world in Kafka's world presses toward the light ... To Kafka, the world of his ancestors was as unfathomable as the world of realities was important, and we may be sure of that, like the totem poles of primitive peoples, the world of ancestors took him down to the animals. (*SW* 2: 809–10; *GS* II·2: 430)

Under Benjamin's scrutiny, Kafka looks backward to a past of sublime number, scale and non-definition. The oblivion with which Kafka trucks is reminiscent of the uncanny afterlife through which the rabbis wander in pairs throughout the Zohar, often under cover of night, looking backward upon a world they have departed as they deliver elucidations of the Torah whose thrust is far more poetic than legalistic (this even when the same rabbis have figured earlier in the Talmud as legalists). It can be well argued, I believe, as I do elsewhere (Sussman, 'Afterlife of Judaism' 95–116; *Actualities* 196–220), that the legends of the Zohar not only mark a new relation between Judaic theology and the afterlife but also a pre-modern Judaic receptivity to literature itself, to literature as literature. Sholem even went so far as to collect some of the most compelling of the anecdotal and allegorical rabbinic commentaries of the Zohar into a slim volume, *Zohar: The Book of Splendor*. Kafka's decisive 'Parable of the Doorkeeper' is written very much under the aura of the afterlife of the Zohar, and Benjamin's own poetic compression and condensation shift into high gear as he undertakes formulating the particularly Kafkan oblivion.

But the dimension of cosmic time that Benjamin also associates with divine violence not only extends backwards. The dimension of Jewish mysticism in Kafka's work becomes most explicit when it figures, even ironically, the possible redemption of the swamp world from which so many of the characters press forward. At the moment that it allows for the repair or redemption of the world, the cosmic time of children's literature, of fairy tale and legend, becomes messianic time. In the world of Kafka, we would of

course expect the agents of the messiah, the Judeo-Christian counterparts to
bodhisattvas, to be screwball in some quintessential way. From the students
common to *Amerika* and *The Trial* to the bumbling assistants of *The Castle*, the
agents of redemption are not who we expect them to be. As Benjamin characterizes them in two related passages:

> In Indian mythology there are the *gandharvas*, mist-bound creatures, be-
> ings in an unfinished state. Kafka's assistants are of that kind: neither
> members of, nor strangers to, any of the other groups of figures, but,
> rather, messengers busy moving between them. Kafka tells us that they
> resemble Barnabas, who is a messenger. They have not been completely
> released from the womb of nature ... (*SW* 3: 798)

> The gate to justice is study. Yet Kafka doesn't dare attach to this study
> the promises which tradition has attached to the study of the Torah. His
> assistants are sextons who have lost their house of prayer; his students are
> pupils who have lost the Holy Writ (*Schrift*). Now there is nothing to sup-
> port them on their 'untrammelled, happy journey'. (*SW* 2: 815)

Whether the agents of redemption elicit our laughter or our homesick-
ness, they are messengers from the domain of mystical thinking and figu-
ration without which, according to Benjamin, the full sweep of Kafka's imagination and writing cannot be taken into account. In militating for this
dimension of Kafka criticism, Benjamin continues in his role as an *agent
provocateur* for the instatement of the Judaic to its full role in German letters
and for the contrary movement, recognition on the part of Jewish authors of
the hospitableness to key elements of the Judaic imaginary shown by German literature. This is a major file in his ongoing self-delegated portfolio.
The role demands that he plumb to the innermost depths of Goethe, Schiller, Hölderlin, Kleist, Schlegel, Hebbel, Keller, George, Hofmannsthal, Brecht and others so that he can read them both as concretions of the ongoing
Western and European curricula and in a second light. Exegeses underwrit-
ten by such a split identity are inevitably scored with the hidden dimensions
of a secret or a shibboleth, one into which Scholem deeply delves in his sur-
veys of the messianic literature. Paul Celan, at certain pivotal moments in
his poetic composition, acknowledges the cryptic side of his linguistico-exis-
tential predicament and the messages with which he responds to it, a point
not lost on Jacques Derrida in his Celan elucidations (*Sovereignties* 22–6, 29-
33, 45, 48, 50).

It is indeed a mystical *Schein* or light—in the sense in which I have been
developing this term—that Benjamin casts upon Goethe's *Elective Affinities*,
even while he rigorously sets about the task of a philosophically trained critic in the sphere of German letters. He reminds us that Goethe himself has
launched '[h]ope ... across the sky above their [the characters'] heads like
a falling star', hope even in the face of the constitutional indirections and

failures of love, intimacy, and commiseration. The hope toward which Benjamin gazes as much for his own edification as that of his readers is one only comprehensible in terms of the messianic dream of the end of *Galut* or exile: '[T]hat most paradoxical, most fleeting hope finally emerges from the semblance of reconciliation, just as, at twilight, as the sun is extinguished, rises the evening star which outlasts the night. Its glimmer, of course, is imparted by Venus. And upon the slightest such glimmer all hope rests' (*SW* 1: 355). Benjamin's wish for a synthesis between the major strands of his study and his most compelling interests is embedded in the fragmentary phrase 'semblance of reconciliation' (*Schein der Versöhnung*). This briefest of genitive constructions merges the *Schein* of semblance and appearance, the facilitating link in the transition between sensible and supersensible worlds in systems as far-reaching as Kant's and Hegel's, to the mystical yearning for a connectedness in the universe made possible by the undoing of exile. In the 'system' of Lurianic kabbalism, according to Scholem, the second major phase in the Jewish mystical adventure,

> redemption is synonymous with emendation or restoration. After we have fulfilled our duty and the emendation is completed, all things occupy their appropriate places in the universal scheme, then redemption will come *of itself*. Redemption merely signifies the perfect state, a flawless and harmonious world in which everything occupies its proper place. Hence the Messianic ideal, the ideal of redemption, receives a wholly new aspect. We all work, or are at least expected to work, for the amendment of the world and the 'selection' of good and evil. (Scholem, *Messianic Idea* 47)

In Benjamin's account, such a world of mystical harmony and reconciliation flashes above the horizon of Goethe's *Elective Affinities*. His appeal to the semblance of reconciliation furnishes the exception to Plato's dictum 'that it is absurd to desire the semblance of the good'. Once again, the experiment of Western idealism finds a certain culmination and fulfilment among the reaches and reconciliations of cosmic space.

Between the twelfth century and the expulsion of the Jews from Spain in 1492, Scholem argues, Kabbalists could hope 'for a particular and mystical redemption for each individual, to be achieved by escaping from the turbulence, perplexity, chaos, and storms of the actual course of history. The early Kabbalists were at liberty to ponder such questions as "What is the nature of Creation?" and "Whence have we come?" For they believed that ... to know the secret of our beginnings, whence the imperfections of this distorted and dark world in which we are stranded, with all the storms and perturbations and afflictions within it—to know all this would teach us the way back to "our inward home"' (*Messianic Idea* 41). 'The *Zohar*', the primary corpus of Jewish mysticism of this pre-exilic period, 'follows Talmudic Aggadah in seeing redemption not as the product of inward progress in the historical world, but as a supernatural miracle involving the gradual illumination of the world by the light of the Messiah'. The Zohar itself takes the bold step of imagining a messianic redemption taking place amid the relative objectivity of the external world. The messiah's work is redemption by means of illumination, a Judaic spin on the spiritual centrality of acts of exegesis and criticism, one that could not have been lost on Benjamin or Scholem.

The post-exilic universe-picture, as we might imagine, was not nearly as rosy for the Kabbalists. Once again they contended with exile or *Galut*, the loss of a discursive as well as a geographical community. Those who stayed behind in Spain underwent the circumlocutions of feigned, doubled and secret identity. Under such conditions, the mission of the messiah himself took on untoward complexity. The redemption of the world might just as well be achieved through messianic apostasy as through impossible perfection and exemplarity. In the wake of 1492, the stage gradually became set, in Scholem's account, for the actual messianic adventures and catastrophes in the 17th and 18th centuries surrounding Sabbatai Zevi and Jacob Frank, among others. The transgressive undercurrent entering Jewish messianism in the aftermath of the great pre-modern exile from Spain, itself an imaginary replay of the parallel events in Biblical times, is also not without interpretative repercussions for a commentator such as Benjamin, invested for long stretches of his critical run in a Judeo-Germanic graft under the aura of modernism. The Jewish mystics 'began to seek explanations' for the 1492 expulsion. They posed such questions as 'What had happened? What brought on the affliction and suffering? What is the nature of the gloomy world of Galut? They sought an answer to such questions in terms of their basic mystical outlook … And by connecting the notions of Galut and redemption with the central question of the essence of the universe, they managed to elaborate a system which transformed the exile of the people of Israel into an exile of the whole world, and the redemption of their people into a universal, cosmic redemption' (*Messianic Idea* 42-3).

It fell to the Lurianic messianism of the decades following 1540 to meld the dream of messianic redemption with the destructive forces at play in a world of Galut. According to the Lurianic Kabbalah, this is 'a terrible and pitiless state permeating and embittering all of Jewish life … but … also the condition of the universe of the whole, even the deity' (*Messianic Idea* 43). Scholem pegs this as 'an extremely bold idea', demanding destructive action along with creativity, forming a context for the notorious Kabbalistic *shevira ha-kelim* or 'breaking of the vessels' in which the divine attributes have been disbursed (*Messianic Idea* 45). Lurianic Kabbalism thus adds a strain of violence to the mystical imperatives of reparation and redemption. It is one that may be recognisable to us in the more disruptive features of Benjaminian shock, not only a condition of an industrial landscape increasingly under the sway of the assembly line and its spasmodic gestures (*SW* 4: 316-21, 324, 327-31); also in the storm that has gotten caught in the Angel of History's wings, drawing him 'irresistibly into the future, to which his back is turned, while the pile of debris before him grows toward the sky. What we call progress is *this* storm' (*SW* 4: 392).

Under the aura of the mystical book in Benjamin's library, exegesis needs to keep its eye on the prize of cultural repair and correction. It needs at the same time to calibrate its interventions of system-scrambling disruption. Does this sound at all familiar? Lurianic Kabbalism, according to Scholem, ushered in a new twist to 'an old rabbinic concept ... "a commandment which is fulfilled by means of a transgression" ... We know that even before his apostasy, Sabbatai Zevi violated several of the commandments'. There is no more distinctive signature to Benjamin's imprint than the sustained coordination between redemptive exegetical striving and twentieth-century violence throughout his script. So much of his commentary emanates from the obscure writing-desk shared by the angel of interpretation and the avatar of shock. The mystical books in his library may well serve as a commanding context in which he incorporates one additional Talmudic legend into his celebratory essay on Kafka, one explaining 'why Jews prepare a festive meal on Fridays':

> The legend is about a princess languishing in exile, in a village whose language she does not understand, far from her compatriots. One day this princess receives a letter saying that her fiancé has not forgotten her and is on his way to her.—The fiancé, so says the rabbi, is the Messiah; the princess is the soul; the village in which she lives is in exile is the body. She prepares a meal for him because this is the only way in which she can express her joy in a village whose language she does not know.—This village of the Talmud is right in Kafka's world. For just as K. lives in the village on Castle Hill, modern man lives in his own body; the body slips away from him; is hostile toward him. It may happen that a man wakes up one day and finds himself transformed into vermin. Strangeness—his own strangeness—has gained control over him [*Denn so wie K. im Dorf am Schloßberg lebt der heutige Mensch in seinem Körper; er entgleitet ihm, ist ihm feindlich. Es kann geschehen, daß der Mensch eines Morgens erwacht, und er ist in ein Ungeziefer verwandelt. Die Fremde—seine Fremde—ist seiner Herr geworden*]. (*SW* 2: 805-6; *GS* II·2: 424)

THE DISSOLVING BOOK

> It has rightly been said that all great works of literature establish a genre or dissolve one—that they are, in other words, special cases. 'On the Image of Proust' (*SW* 2: 237)

No one with Benjamin's exquisite attunement particularly to the destructive as well as generative forces and flows released by modernization could be accused of a facile conviction in the permanence of books, whether as a medium or a culture. Some books are acquired only to be released again to the general flow of printed matter, even by the 'genuine' collector. The forces of commerce, capital, industrialisation, mass-production, and the regimentation of the masses making *Les Fleurs du mal* 'the last lyric work' with 'a broad European reception'(*SW* 4: 341), impact not only on communities of folktale and the ritual calendar, but community as such including the implicit community crystallising around each book. When the community of the book is dismembered, when each book abandons its potential to become a quasi-institution of discourse, then the prospects for the book as a medium of information and thinking has undergone a detrimental reversal. History is only too replete with instances and explanations of the crisis of the book during the last two decades of Benjamin's life. However, the ground and pretexts have shifted since that time, perhaps from politics to technology, those of us charged with disseminating the topography, sensibility, and skills of the broader literacy surely today face a constitutional crisis of reading and its potential communities.

To any thinker as sensitive as Benjamin to the vicissitudes of book-culture, assaults on the book are registered on the design, architecture and volume of actual books. *The Arcades Project*, Benjamin's encyclopaedic and hypertextual time-capsule of Paris in the Second Empire, obsessed him from 1927 or so until the time of his death in 1940. Itself a resource book (or, as we would now say, a text-medium website) consisting of citations that Benjamin collected from an astonishing range of first-hand, historical, and contemporary accounts and commentaries (social psychology, urban studies, art history and critical theory number among them), only occasionally interspersed with observations posited by Benjamin himself, *The Arcades Project* subtends some of his most pointed and memorable literary studies, written at the very opposite extreme of compression and shorthand. *The Arcades Project*, in its omnivorous openness to relevant materials and in the linear progression of its Convolutes, is positively cloudlike in consistency in comparison to such carefully orchestrated essays as 'The Storyteller', 'Paris, the Capital of the Nineteenth Century' (in both its versions), and 'On Some Motifs in Baudelaire'. *The Arcades Project* is Talmudic in its obsession with registers of signification and commentary, in its fascination with the spatial zones, vertical as well as lateral, of Paris, its commerce and its activities, legitimate or not; it is encyclopaedic in the sheer range of factors and materials surrounding Paris's (also known as modernity's) development, achievements, and political vicissitudes that it takes in; it is hypertextual to the degree to which the individual Convolutes supplement and enlarge upon one another. This hypertextual supplementation can transpire even within the compass of a single Convolute, as, within Convolute O, 'Prostitution and Gambling', the

segues between the materials related to both of these vices, themselves supple-
ments to the humdrum balance sheets of the legitimate economy, are more
telling and suggestive than the nitty gritty transactions endemic to these
spheres.

It is then fated, absolutely unavoidable, that *The Arcades Project*, with all
the innovation that it brings to the architecture and design of books, its consisting almost entirely of citations, its opening up a display-space for its materials as much *visual* as verbal, the hypertextual mutual referencing of its
various sections, its thematic omnivorousness—and the internal apparatus
of sub-directories that this necessitates—it is inevitable that this work also
foretells a devastating constitutional crisis in the medium, culture, community and consistency of the book. As in the epigraph to this section from 'On
the Image of Proust', *The Arcades Project* is both the founder, the progenitor
of the new electronic book (or whatever name we attach to it) in its rhizomatic configuration, a medium still in the moment of its becoming, and the
confirmation of the demise of the book-medium as Benjamin encountered
it at the outset of his intellectual life and throughout the preponderance of
his research.

Benjamin, in other words, is as much the avatar of the dissolving book,
the book that provides for its own marginality and dispersion, as he is the
champion of the Age of the Book in all its classicism and in all the vitality
of its remarkable run. With Benjamin as its ringleader, as the leader of its
pack (this latter term in its Deleuzian sense)[9], the entire historical production of the book circles around to face its radical reconfiguration, if not its
flat-out annihilation. We encounter the dissolving book, whose aftermath
remains entirely uncertain, not only in *The Arcades Project*, with its open-ended receptivity and citationality, its soft and amorphous contours, its endless circulation about its motifs and theoretical interests. We run into the
dissolving book in a large share of Benjamin's primary inspirations and in
generative experimental works that were configured by others under the
aura of Benjamin's age. A tragically incomplete list of these manifestations
would include: the soft structure, macro- and microcosmic, or the fractal
miniaturisation,[10] making Proust's *Recherche* possible, a gay romance scored
between the margins of a straight one, leaving room for an astonishingly
broad network of rhizomatically interconnected social relations; the Creole

---

9. Kafka's 'Josephine the Singer' is a precise literary instance of what Gilles Deleuze and
Félix Guattari mean by a pack leader, as opposed to the head of a standard sociopolitical
(and dialectically configured) organization (Deleuze and Guattari 51-57, 233-34, 239-50,
287-88, 305-09).

10. J. Hillis Miller has written surprisingly and compellingly about the persistence and
miniaturisation of telling tropes in Proust, which he relates to fractals. See his 'Fractal
Proust' (349-77, 395, 439-49). For a brief general introduction to fractals, their structure,
and their contribution, see Fritjof Capra (142-53).

that Joyce fashions for *Finnegans Wake*, a language drawing on national histories and ethnic traditions while paying none of them credence, the draft, rather, for an incipient global language;[11] fiction in Borges's counterworld of Tlön, that 'has but a single plot, with every imaginable permutation' (Borges 77); finally, but not last, the crumbling columns of type configured, in *Glas*, by a deconstructive encounter between Hegel and Genet, a Talmudic work whose demarcated sectors of text have been constructed precisely in order to fall apart and together (Sussman 'Hegel' 260-92). Ever so slightly afield from this body (or perhaps swamp) of intransigent works but thoroughly participating in it is the unique patois that Gertrude Stein devised for *The Making of Americans* and other of her productions, a discourse abundantly inventive of grammatical variants and new possibilities for expression at the same time that it suspends and frustrates its reader's addictions to making clear and easy sense.

Benjamin peered over into a future of the book that he would not, having transformed himself into the consummate citizen of its past, fully inhabit. It remains for us to render tribute to this inclination and this tradition by struggling to explore and comprehend it; to furnish it with a memory, however artificial; *and*, frontally and without a hitch, to embrace its mutants and mutations.

---

11. This tack, understanding the hybrid, interlinguistic, at times exasperating patois of Joyce's *Finnegans Wake* as the preliminary dialect of a global language in the most idealistic sense, has been explored most productively by my colleague at Buffalo State College and doyen of the rich cultural life around Joyce in Western New York, Laurence Shine.

2

On the 'Vital Significance' of Kitsch: Walter Benjamin's Politics of 'Bad Taste'

Winfried Menninghaus

In a programmatic statement Benjamin portrays *The Arcades Project* as a work on kitsch: 'We construct here an alarm clock that rouses the kitsch of the previous century to "assembly"' (*AP* H1a,2).[1] What predestines 'that strange … form of matter' which is 'kitsch' (*GS* V·1:500 K3a,1) to be at once the repository and explosive charge of an originary historiography (*Urgeschichte*) and politics of the 19th century? The very word 'kitsch' is, in fact, an invention of the 19th century. Kluge's *Etymologisches Wörterbuch der deutschen Sprache* has this to say:

> Originated c. 1870 in painting circles. Origin unclear. Perhaps linked to *kitschen* 'to scrape together/smooth down sludge on the street' (from *Kitsche*, the instrument with which this is done). Thus the original meaning would be 'daub'. Another possibility would be a connection with *verkitschen* = 'sell off cheaply'.[2]

Other monosyllabic German words that end in 'tsch'—*Quatsch* (nonsense, rubbish), *Klatsch* (splash; smack; gossip), *Matsch* (mush; slush; sludge), *pitsch*, *patsch* (pitter-patter), *ritsch*, *ratsch* (rip!), *futsch* (bust)—share with *Kitsch* two basic features:

1. They tend to describe 'lowly' objects or actions, aesthetically reinforcing this content by their decidedly non-exquisite phonetic appear-

---

1. Please note that I have corrected or altered the text of the existing English translations where I found this necessary or at least advantageous.

2. Avenarius reports another derivation based on personal recollection: 'Kitsch, trash, specifically of pictures, originating in Munich. If English or American buyers did not want to invest much for a picture there, they demanded a sketch. This gave rise to the term kitsch, originally in artistic circles in the 70s' (quoted in Ludwig 21).

ance which in many cases conjoins low discourse with a slight degree of funniness, and hence they are not part of elevated or formal discourse, representing rather a vulgar and/or childish mode of expression (see also *Kladderadatsch* (crash-bang-wallop)).

2. They are suggestive of blurred distinctions or the active suspension of distance and differentiation and tend to have an element of 'debasement' (*Kuddelmuddel* (hotchpotch)) about them. This also applies to quite a few adjectives and verbs that correspond phonetically to the forms *kitschig* (kitschy), *verkitscht* (reduced to kitsch) and *verkitschen* (to reduce to kitsch): *glitschig* (slippery), *pitschen* (to pitter-patter), *zerquetschen* (to squash), *verquatschen* (to waste time with idle chatter). Presumably it was this existing paradigm of tsch-words that prepared the way for the new coinage. The rapid international success of this relatively new but etymologically still obscure word is amazing: by the turn of the century it had been adopted unchanged by English (British and American), French, Spanish, and other languages. By the laws of (linguistic) evolution this is a strong indication that the emergence of the word met a widespread and urgent need. Benjamin's writings on Baudelaire, Proust, Surrealism ('dream kitsch'), and above all his *The Arcades Project*, provide a theoretical narrative as to why 'kitsch' emerged as a problem solving device in the context of the 19th century. From the very beginning, his work on kitsch is informed by avant-garde uses of kitsch and hence does not accept the key opposition most other theorists of kitsch rely on: namely, the opposition of kitsch and art proper, or high art, and more precisely of kitsch and avant-garde art.

The very first book dedicated to the topic of kitsch appeared in 1925; its title—*Der Kitsch: Eine Studie über die Entartung der Kunst*—makes use of the term *Entartung*, or 'degeneration', which was shortly after adopted by the Nazis for the purposes of both their racist agenda and their polemical stance vis-à-vis modernist art (Karpfen). Benjamin's work on kitsch begins in the late 1920s and extends until his death in 1940. Benjamin appears not to have known Fritz Karpfen's book nor Hans Reimann's *Das Buch vom Kitsch* of 1936. While the word kitsch rapidly became internationalised, research on the topic appears to have remained a German specialty until the 1970s. An article by Clement Greenberg dating back to the late 1930s is perhaps the most remarkable exception to this rule (3ff.); the article firmly subscribes to the irreconcilability of avant-garde and kitsch und furthermore offers some critical remarks on the use of kitsch in Nazi politics. Within the context of more recent kitsch scholarship, Benjamin's work has thus far gone totally unnoticed, even though his unique ways of addressing kitsch are unparalleled both in his time and in more recent research on kitsch. My article is confined to reconstructing the basic configuration Benjamin sets up for dealing with the 'vital importance' (*AP* N1,11) of aesthetic failures.

Although Benjamin does not offer an exhaustive definition of kitsch in any of his works, his use of language does provide clear semantic clues. Kitsch, according to Benjamin, undermines the distinction between art and utilitarian object. Art in the exalted sense 'begins at a distance of two meters from the body. But now, in kitsch, the world of things advances on the human being; it yields to his uncertain grasp' (*SW* 2: 4). Kitsch does not have the austere remoteness of classical works of art, and this absence of reverential distance also means that kitsch provokes another kind of intimacy. It has—as Benjamin says with no trace of irony—'something that is warming', is even conducive to ' "heart's ease" ... Kitsch ... is ... art with a 100 percent, absolute and instantaneous availability for consumption' (*AP* K3a,1). Kitsch offers instantaneous emotional gratification without intellectual effort, without the requirement of distance, without sublimation. It usually presents no difficulties in interpretation and has absolutely nothing to do with an aesthetics of negativity. It is unadulterated beauty, a simple invitation to wallow in sentiment—in short a true antidote to any Adorno-type aesthetics of negativity. Practically all studies on kitsch agree on this key feature. The question is, what specifically drew Benjamin's attention to the aesthetic and political aspects of this world of 'bad taste'?

Defining kitsch in terms of a saving of intellectual effort and the suspension of normative taboos is rich in implications. For Freud, these behavioural mechanisms are typical of both humour and, more broadly, of the libidinous regression to infantile gratifications which have normally fallen victim to the reality principle and cultural prohibitions. Benjamin's constant references to childish perception in *The Arcades Project* are largely based on the hypothesis—common to both Romanticism and psychoanalysis—that children enjoy an experiential advantage as a result of their incomplete submission to the taboos and laws of the symbolic order. Benjamin directly evokes the child's way of touching things at their 'not always seemliest' spot as a model of the adult's contact with 'dream kitsch': 'And which side does an object turn toward dreams? What point is its most decrepit? It is the side worn through by habit and patched with cheap maxims. The side which things turn toward the dream is kitsch' (*SW* 2: 3) Thus, intellectual, infantile and dream-related devices of saving effort and avoiding censure come together in the same hackneyed libidinous stuff called kitsch. Most other authors of Benjamin's time tended to identify the moment of regression to infantile wishful thinking as an attack on art proper from the part of industrialised mass production—an attack which needed to be rejected by remaining true to bourgeois high standards. In contrast, Benjamin from the very beginning, while never fully embracing kitsch, found something not just understandable and admit table in it, which would be the condescending approach, but identified it as a phenomenon of utmost political significance.

What bearing does the elementary semantics of 'kitsch' have on the key issues of *The Arcades Project*? First of all, the disappearance of the difference between work of art and utilitarian object is the very essence of architecture. We do not look at a building or an interior in the same concentrated manner in which we view a painting or a statue, but simply walk past or through them. We use them, we have a tactile relation to them: 'Architecture is not primarily "seen", but … sensed by those who approach or even enter it as a surrounding space [*Umraum*] *sui generis*—that is, without the distancing effect of the edge of the image space [*Bildraum*]' (*SW* 2: 670). The absence of a distancing picture frame on the one hand and distracted, largely unconscious, partially tactile apperception without focused intellectual effort on the other—these are only the first, most general features which enable Benjamin to let his analyses of architecture and kitsch overlap. In addition, there are other, more specific affinities. What is Benjamin actually investigating in the arcades and other forms of 19th century architecture that interested him, the railroad stations, exhibition halls, winter gardens and department stores? He mentions more than once that the arcades belong to the avant-garde of iron and steel architecture. But he has hardly discovered anything new in this regard. The great majority of the entries in *The Arcades Project*, which in a classical sense bear on architectural history are direct quotations from Siegfried Giedion's standard work *Bauen in Frankreich* [*Construction in France*]. Benjamin makes not the slightest attempt to compete with Giedion in the latter's own field. Instead he opens up a new field that Giedion has quite deliberately neglected. One might call this field *para-architecture*: it encompasses objects, actions and all kinds of ornamental accretions in and around buildings. Giedion dismissed these 'artistic drapings' as 'musty' remnants left behind in the successful modernisation of architecture as it proceeded to create structures of pure iron, concrete and glass. Benjamin, on the other hand, in typical Surrealist fashion, focuses firmly on this dated 'dream kitsch':

> 'Apart from a certain *haut-goût* charm,' says Giedion, 'the artistic draperies and wall-hangings of the previous century have come to seem musty' … We, however, believe that the charm they exercise on us is proof that these things, too, contain material of vital importance for us … In any case, material of vital importance politically; this is demonstrated by the attachment of the Surrealists to these things, as much as by their exploitation in contemporary fashion. In other words: just as Giedion teaches us to read off the basic features of today's architecture in the buildings erected around 1850, we, in turn, would recognize today's life, today's forms, in the life and in the apparently secondary, lost forms of that epoch. (*AP* N1,11)

Benjamin thus seeks the channel for the unconscious 'dream energies' linked to architecture—and for their potential effect on posterity—precisely in those 'musty' para-phenomena that Giedion dismisses as nothing more than the slag left behind by technical evolution. This change of perspective from the technical and structural aspects of buildings to their arabesque drapings (*AP* K1a,6) results in a very different perception: 'It is remarkable that constructions in which the expert recognizes anticipations of contemporary building fashions impress the alert but architecturally unschooled sense not at all as anticipatory but as distinctly old-fashioned and dreamlike. (Old railroad stations, gasworks, bridges.)' (*AP* K1a,4). No other theoretician of kitsch from 1900 through today has made such a provocative claim: namely, that in the now kitschy ornaments of the epoch around 1850–70 we need to search for decisive clues to understanding the situation of the 1930s.

It is Benjamin's non-expert para-architecture that 'rouses the kitsch of the previous century to "assembly"'. To it we owe the rich parade of past specialities which Benjamin presents to the reader with all the pride of a collector. It is not the construction of the entrances to pubs, railroad stations or arcades (*AP* 871–2) that interests Benjamin, but the para-objects in the space of this 'threshold magic' (*Schwellenzauber*): 'The hen that lays the golden praline-eggs, the machine that stamps our names on nameplates, slot machines, fortune-telling devices, and above all weighing devices' (*AP* I1a,4). Not the walls of the arcades, but the 'false' and cheap 'colorful language of the posters' that 'flourished' there is evoked (*GS* V·1:235 G1a,1). Two early drafts entitled 'Arcades' contain almost nothing but lists of curiosities, of which some have an affinity to kitsch while nearly all fall under the more comprehensive category of 'bad taste':

> In the arcades, one comes upon types of collar studs for which we no longer know the corresponding collars and shirts. If a shoemaker's shop should be neighbor to a confectioner's, then his festoons of bootlaces will resemble rolls of licorice. Over stamps and letterboxes roll balls of string and of silk. Naked puppet bodies with bald heads wait for hairpieces and attire. Combs swim about, frog-green and coral-red, as in an aquarium; trumpets turn to conches, ocarinas to umbrella handles; and lying in the fixative pans from a photographer's darkroom is birdseed. The concierge of the gallery has, in his loge, three plush-covered chairs with crocheted antimacassars ... (*AP* 872)
>
> ...
>
> They are the true fairies of these arcades (more salable and more worn than the life-sized ones): the formerly world-famous Parisian dolls, which revolved on their musical socle and bore in their arms a doll-sized basket out of which, at the salutation of the minor chord, a lambkin poked its curious muzzle. (*AP* a°,1)

Interiors, the second main element of Benjamin's para-architecture after arcades, enable him to indulge in analogous descriptions: 'To render the
image of those salons where the gaze was enveloped in billowing curtains
and swollen cushions, where, before the eyes of the guests, full-length mirrors disclosed church doors and settees were gondolas upon which gaslight
from a vitreous globe shone down like the moon' (*AP* I1,8). Benjamin grate-
fully borrows Franz Hessel's formula of a '"dreamy epoch of bad taste"'
(*AP* I1,6) ('träumerischen Zeit des schlechten Geschmacks', *GS* V·1:282 I1,6).
Even the Eiffel Tower fits neatly into this panorama. From Egon Friedell's
Kulturgeschichte der Neuzeit Benjamin quotes the following apt comment: 'It is
characteristic of this most famous construction of the epoch that, for all its
gigantic stature, ... it nevertheless feels like a knickknack' (*AP* F5a,7) ('doch
nippeshaft wirkt', *GS* V·1: 226 F5a,7). The great literary models for *The Arcades Project* likewise offer abundant material for a protohistory of bad taste.
Polemics against 'good taste' are part of the agenda of Baudelaire, Rimbaud
and the Surrealists. Proust praises Baudelaire's work for its violations of any
'purity of style' (*AP* J44a,1), and Anatole France provides Benjamin with the
following remark on Baudelaire: '"His legend, created by his friends and ad-
mirers, abounds in marks of bad taste"' (*AP* J17a,1). On Proust's interior Benjamin notes: 'Maurice Barrès has characterized Proust as "a Persian poet in
a concierge's box". Could the first person to grapple with the enigma of the
nineteenth century interior be anything else?' (*AP* I2,4).

What does Benjamin hope to gain from hunting down all these dated
and aesthetically dubious items for his project of a new historiography? The
answer I would like to offer combines Benjamin's theory of 'experience' with
the elementary findings of his historical analysis. What Benjamin calls *Erfahrung* (experience), as distinct from *Erlebnisse* (conscious experiences), has
little to do with the modern scientific concept of empiricism. Experience in
Benjamin's sense includes unconscious desires, manual skills, and religious
rituals. The concept combines a profound relationship between 'experience'
and self with a radical openness to, indeed dependence on, tradition: 'Experience is a matter of tradition, in collective existence as well as private life.
It is less the product of facts firmly anchored in memory than of a convergence in memory of accumulated and frequently unconscious data' (*Illuminations* 157). Both experience and tradition, according to Benjamin's diagnosis,
are put in question by the modern world we live in. By isolating the mass of
news items from one another the modern method of disseminating information prevents their integration in 'deeper' layers of experience (*GS* I: 611; *Illuminations* 159); a similar function is performed by the reflective mechanisms
habitually used to overcome shock in modern city life (*GS* I: 614; *Illuminations* 161ff.). Although the modern traumas caused by technical accidents and
warfare of unprecedented destructive power break through the neutralising
effects of consciousness, they create no narratable tradition and hence also

contribute to the *Erfahrungsarmut* (*SW* 2: 214) (poverty of experience; *SW* 2: 732). At the same time traditional symbolic and social orders (religion and family) lose their power to provide an authoritative interpretation of power-ful desires:

> A generation's experience of youth has much in common with the expe-rience of dreams. Its historical configuration is a dream configuration. Every epoch has such a side turned toward dreams, the child's side ... But whereas the education of earlier generations explained these dreams for them in terms of tradition, of religious doctrine, present-day educa-tion simply amounts to the distraction of children. (*AP* K1,1)

When traditional authorities no longer offer widely believed interpre-tations of it, the dreamy and childlike side of existence 'sinks' (*AP* K1,4) into speechlessness and loses its symbolic representation; it ceases to be part of a collective consciousness in the form of narratives and instructions. In the 19th century, Benjamin holds—continuing Giedion's train of thought (*AP* K1a,5)—'the individual consciousness more and more secures itself in reflecting, while the collective consciousness sinks into ever deeper sleep' (*AP* K1,4, see also *Illuminations* 159 and *AP* M21a,2). Only in this distinc-tive sense of powerful collective desires, which are no longer 'interpreted' in terms of traditional symbolisms and thus no longer have any (semi)conscious representation, does Benjamin speak of the 'dream-filled sleep' (*AP* K1a,8) (*Traumschlaf* (*GS* V·1: 494 K1a,8)) of the 19th century. And just because of this desymbolising shift to the unconscious, this removal of linguistic represen-tation, Benjamin assumes that 'the forms of appearance taken by the dream collective ... characterize [... the 19th century] much more decisively than any other' (*AP* K1a,6). Benjamin's project of leading the dream side of the 19th century to the edge of 'awakening' thus bears a very specific historical signature. It is aimed at a new kind of 'dream and child side', and it has to perform an archaeological feat for which traditional rites and symbolisms no longer provide any preparation.[3]

How is it possible under these conditions to achieve an integral experi-ence of one's own past? Bergson's, Dilthey's, Klages', and Jung's attempts 'to lay hold of the "true" experience as opposed to the kind that manifests itself in the standardized, denatured life of the civilized masses' (*Illuminations* 156) are treated by Benjamin as mere symptoms of the crisis, not as adequate so-lutions to the problem: they are said to lack any real, historically specified memory, and their tendency toward bourgeois restoration is blamed to end with Klages and Jung in an affinity to 'fascism' (*GS* I·2: 608–9, *Illuminations*

---

3. Proust's great project of a radically individualised remembrance is a response to the same situation of lost tracks: 'Proust could emerge as an unprecedented phenomenon only in a generation that had lost all bodily and natural aids to remembrance and that, poorer than before, was left to itself to take possession of the worlds of childhood in merely an iso-lated, scattered, and pathological way' (*AP* K1,1).

156–7). Bergson, Dilthey, Klages, and Jung would clearly dismiss kitsch as precisely what prevents genuine experience. Only Proust's work is accepted by Benjamin as a successful 'attempt to produce experience synthetically, as Bergson imagines it, under today's conditions' (*Illuminations* 157).[4] Proust is thus one of the great models for *The Arcades Project*; with the qualification, however, that the latter might extend beyond the 'hopelessly private character' (*Illuminations* 158) of Proust's undertaking.

Benjamin's own attempt at synthetically mining the 'raw material' (*AP* K1a,5) of emphatic experience from a century hostile to experience rests on a radical assumption, namely that the modern vehicle of the deposed 'tradition' is fashion. However much Benjamin's diagnosis of the crisis of 'experience' as being a crisis of 'tradition' appears to converge with conservative doctrines of cultural decadence, this impression is utterly dispelled when we see Benjamin's surprising proposal for a way out of the crisis. Not conservative 'values', but the most fleeting and ephemeral of all cultural phenomena—fashion—is to be the medium for reconstructing a functional equivalent of emphatic experience in modern life:

> Energies of repose (of tradition) which carry over from the nineteenth century. Transposed historical forces of tradition. What would the nineteenth century be to us if we were bound to it by tradition? How would it look as religion or mythology? (*AP* C°,5)

Why and how should fashion of all things provide such opportunities for genuine experience and even open up 'forces of tradition'? Benjamin's strategic decision to entrust the matter of 'experience' to a focus on fashion, rests on three elementary historical assumptions. The first is: 'It is … in this century, the most parched and imagination-starved, that the collective dream energy of a society has taken refuge with redoubled vehemence in the mute impenetrable nebula of fashion, where the understanding cannot follow' (*AP* B1a,2). Fashion thus inherits the fading 'dream energies' of other symbolic media (religion, family, traditional mythology) and thereby gains a 'redoubled vehemence', even tending to become the sole representative for social strategies of imaginary self-interpretation. For Benjamin, the aesthetisation of the *Lebenswelt* and the loss of significance that traditional forms of negotiating social 'affects' undergo are concomitant. Secondly, by interpreting fashion in terms of fetishistic objects of desire and veneration, Benjamin not only refers to the concept of fetishism in Marx and Freud, but likewise to its use in the ethnology of 'primitive peoples', thus establishing a direct functional analogy of fashion and archaic religious practices. Fashion provides quotidian cult objects; it is therefore not by coincidence that we speak of 'cult movies', 'cult novels', cult jeans'. Thirdly, the 19th century is the first centu-

---

4. This attempt is founded on a crucial modification of Bergson's concept of memory, namely the confrontation between voluntary and involuntary memory.

ry of fashion in another important sense: more and more objects are manufactured for purposes of fashion only (*AP* B7,7),[5] and the rapidly accelerating rate of obsolescence of technical and practical everyday objects emphasizes their transitory nature much more than in earlier times:

> In the nineteenth century, the number of 'hollowed-out' things increases at a rate and on a scale that was previously unknown … (*AP* N5,2).

> The old prehistoric dread already envelops the world of our parents because we ourselves are no longer bound to this world by tradition. The perceptual worlds (*Merkwelten*) break up more rapidly; … [their mythical aspect] comes more quickly and more brutally to the fore, and a wholly different perceptual world must be speedily set up to oppose it. (*AP* N2a,2)

> A definitive perspective on fashion follows solely from the consideration that 'to each generation the … [last fashion to go out of style] seems the most radical anti-aphrodisiac imaginable … Thus, the confrontation with the fashions of previous generations is a matter of far greater importance than we ordinarily suppose. (*AP* 64)

It is observations of this kind that Benjamin compresses into one of the most striking gnomes of *The Arcades Project*: 'Being past, being no more, is passionately at work in things' (*AP* D°,4) ('Vergangen, nicht mehr zu sein arbeitet leidenschaftlich in den Dingen' *GS* V·2: 1001 D°,4). This applies particularly to the confrontation with outdated fashions which still haunt the history or prehistory of a generation. For it is only the relative proximity to the démodé which enables the full extent of the difference to be realised.[6] This gives rise to a hypothesis as to why the preoccupation with bygone fashions of all things can act as a substitute for the extinct 'forces of tradition' and remembrance. As the mutual repulsion of fashions also contains a system of mutual references, they forge—at least for short periods—a link between the generations: a 'tradition' not of unchanged 'values', but of continued feedback loops aimed at emphasising differences. For the sake of being perceptible at all, fashion's emphasis on the 'newest' requires 'the medium of what has been', an at least subcutaneous awareness of past fashions: this, according to Benjamin, constitutes 'the true dialectical theater of fash-

---

5. Fashionable brand names and personalised 'designer labels' have only been able to establish themselves in such a big way thanks to industrial mass production and modern sales channels; the old way of having clothing or interior furnishings made by hand to individual specifications was much slower to undergo changes in style and execution.

6. Hence Benjamin's conviction that there are only short time windows—a historical 'moment of recognition'—for the discovery of past dream energies, and that the special task of his *The Arcades Project* can only be fulfilled 'now': 'I have found that aspect of 19th century art that is only discoverable "now", which it never was before and never will be again'. (*'Ich habe denjenigen Aspekt der Kunst des neunzehnten. Jahrhunderts gefunden, der nur "jetzt" erkennbar ist, der es nie vorher war und der es nie später sein wird.'* *GS* V·2: 1148)

ion' (*AP* B1a,2). What we 'passionately' experience in the confrontation with
the fashions of previous generations is, in Benjamin's view, the bewildering
fact that these past fashions subcutaneously have a powerful bearing on our
own 'dream energies'. (That is why they are a key to our 'awakening'.) That
is why fashions can lead the same worlds of things (*Dingwelten*) that they con-
sign to oblivion to a 'passionate' afterlife at the level of historical observation
and thus promote the working-through of our own past: 'Fashions are a drug
designed to compensate, on a collective scale, for the fateful effects of oblivion' (my translation) ('*Moden sind ein Medikament, das die verhängnisvollen Wirkun-
gen des Vergessens, im kollektiven Maßstab, kompensieren soll*' *GS* V·1: 131 B9a,1).

From this survey of Benjamin's understanding of experience and fashion I would now like to return to the phenomena of kitsch and bad taste. The
Surrealist polemic against the well-educated (*bien élevé*) 'good taste' is directed not least at the 'stupid' way in which it takes certain taboos and prefer-
ences for granted (Aragon 21ff.). The aesthetic imperfection of the dusty and
outdated has the advantage of entailing less sublimation and self-sufficiency,
and hence of allowing greater scope for everyday 'dream energies'. Benjamin always had a great interest in nascent and dying forms that did not appear bearing the seal of perfection. In this regard, his habilitation thesis on
German tragedy in the Baroque period anticipates—and not just in its theory of allegory—the main lines of his work on the para-architecture of the
19th century. Benjamin repeatedly stressed that German Baroque drama
'never achieved that suppleness of form which bends to every virtuoso touch,
such as Calderón gave the Spanish drama' (*Origin* 49). It is this aesthetic 'insufficiency' (*GS* I·1: 409), this failure to achieve a 'well-wrought' (*Origin* 55)
form which Benjamin takes as the point of departure for a dynamic insight
revealing the 'artistic will' (*Kunstwollen*, *GS* I·1: 235) and the afterlife of an art
form rather than appraising the perfection of individual 'works of art'. This
approach, based on Alois Riegl's concept of *Kunstwollen*, finds its continuation in *The Arcades Project*. There is no longer any talk of 'artistic will' (*Origin*
55), but of 'dream energies' and 'powerful desires' as well as of the 'will to
happiness' (*SW* 2: 239) (*Glückswillen*, *GS* II·1: 313). In both cases, the imperfection, the stale and démodé nature of the observed phenomena is used as
a tracking device revealing both the failures and the unfulfilled potential—
or, metaphysically speaking, the 'weak messianic power'—of past energies
of daydreaming.

The history of aesthetics knows of numerous observations to the effect
that perfection of form can check the flow of emotion. A remark of Edmund
Burke may represent many: 'We shall have a strong desire for a woman of
no remarkable beauty, whilst the greatest beauty … excites nothing at all of
desire' (91). What is aesthetically imperfect or entirely incompatible with *bon
goût* may turn out to have the advantage of not having to pay the price of
sublimation works of high art require us to live up to. Put in positive terms,

the objects of 'bad taste' may offer a less restricted channel for desire, emotion and their recollection. Benjamin took this idea further than anyone before him. The following sentences are to be treated with all seriousness and taken literally:

> Can we say that all lives, works, and deeds that matter were never anything but the undisturbed unfolding of the most banal, most fleeting, most sentimental, weakest hour in the life of the one to whom they pertain? (*SW* 2: 238)

> [T]he sentimentality of our parents, so often distilled, is good for providing the most objective image of our feelings. The long-windedness of their speeches, bitter as gall, ... [condenses, in our perception, into an arabesque rebus]; the ornament of conversation was full of the most ... [intricate] entanglements. Within is heartfelt sympathy, is love, is kitsch. (*SW* 2: 4)

> What the child (and, through faint reminiscence, the man) discovers in the pleats of the old material to which it clings while trailing at its mother's skirts—that's what these pages should contain. Fashion (*AP* K2,2).

'Arabesque rebus' (*krauses Rätselbild*), 'picture puzzle' (*AP* I1,3) *Vexierbild* (*GS* II·2: 601, V·1: 281 I1,3), 'intricate arabesques' (*SW* 2: 238) (*verschlungene Arabesken GS* II·1: 311), dissolved 'ornaments of forgetting' (*SW* 2: 238) (aufgelöste'*Ornamente des Vergessens' GS* II: 311)—these terms not only allude, as has often been remarked, to Freud's definition of the dream as a 'picture puzzle' or 'rebus' (Freud 1: 280); their earliest historical model is the Romantic poetics of enigmatic scripture (*Rätselschrift*), of 'hieroglyphs' and exuberant 'arabesques'. And in the last quoted sentences Benjamin, as a specialist on Romanticism, uses another term which belongs both to the idea of the Romantic and to the analysis of kitsch: 'sentimental'. Friedrich Schlegel's famous definition—'The Romantic is that which presents a sentimental subject matter in a fantastic form' ('Gespräch über die Poesie' 333)—has a decidedly antithetical character. The 'fantastic form' which for Schlegel was largely synonymous with 'grotesque displacements' and 'arabesque' ornamentation[7] provides an (ironic) antidote under the protection of which 'a sentimental subject matter' remains amenable to artistic portrayal. Apart from this very specific licence, Schlegel, too, primarily referred to 'sentimentality' in its 'usual notorious meaning' of being 'shallowly emotional and lachrymose ... full of those familiar noble feelings, the consciousness of which makes people of no character feel so unutterably happy and grand'. In fact, classical and Romantic art are very much about checking and transfiguring the popular emotionalism of the sentimental novel. Precisely for this reason,

---

7. See Schlegel 'Athenäums-Fragment 305' (217) and the numerous comments on 'fantastic', 'arabesque', 'grotesque' and 'sentimental' (Polheim).

the sentimental proper is pushed outside ambitious art and became a reservoir for low key kitsch. However, although Romantic literature, and German Romantic literature in particular, *are responsible for the emergence of kitsch rather through criticising and transfixing than through merely embracing it*, the terms 'Romantic' and 'sentimental' have become closely associated in the coarsening consciousness of posterity. And this rather dubious association is a historical proto-model for kitsch. In the perception of a (supposedly) sober posterity both the Romantic and the sentimental are in constant danger of spilling over into *Gefühlskitsch* ('maudlin kitsch').

Thus it is no accident that Benjamin's text on 'dream kitsch' begins with the blue flower: 'No one really dreams any longer of the Blue Flower. Whoever awakes as Heinrich von Ofterdingen today must have overslept ... No longer does the dream reveal a blue horizon. The dream has grown gray. The gray coating of dust on things is its best part. Dreams are now a shortcut to banality' (*SW* 2: 3). Benjamin himself does not go so far as to dismiss the Romantic model as proto-kitsch. All the less so, since early German Romanticism already propagated aesthetic licenses not just of the evil, the ugly and the disgusting, but also of the banal. Transformed Romantic licences and surrealist devices thus join forces in the hypothesis quoted above:

> For the sentimentality of our parents, so often distilled, is good for providing the most objective image of our feelings. The long-windedness of their speeches, bitter as gall, ... [condenses, in our perception, into an arabesque rebus]; the ornament of conversation was full of the most ... [intricate] entanglements. Within is heartfelt sympathy, is love, is kitsch. (*SW* 2: 4)

The circle closes: sentimentality and kitsch, a pseudo-Romantic alloy, are propagated surrealistically as the primum movens of a revolution in our way of seeing. According to Schiller's classic analysis, the category of the sentimental inevitably implies a reference to childhood and the past. By this standard Benjamin is—next to Freud—probably the most sentimental of the great 20th century thinkers. Pushing the surrealist approach to kitschy outdated fashions even further, Benjamin arrives at the generalised claim that all 'living forms' of art must at least dialectically engage in negotiating kitsch:

> [Among] the consecrated forms of expression, kitsch and art stand irreconcilably opposed. But for developing, living forms, what matters is that they have within them something stirring, useful, ultimately heartening—that they take 'kitsch' dialectically up into themselves ... while yet surmounting [it]. Today, perhaps, film alone is equal to this task—or, at any rate, more ready for it than any other art form. And whoever has recognized this will be inclined to disallow the pretensions of abstract film, as important as its experiments may be. He will call for a closed season on—a natural preserve for—the sort of kitsch whose providential

site is the cinema. (*AP* K3a,1)

In defiance of the modernist insistence on 'pure' forms, on a stripping down of ornament and emotion, and on a radical 'negativity' of expression, Benjamin demands that works of art should 'have within them something stirring, useful, ultimately heartening' and explicitly advocates treating kitsch as a protected species. He even did not hesitate to speak repeatedly and emphatically in these contexts of 'happiness' (*Glück*) or the 'will to happiness'—regardless of whether he was talking about film or Proust. It is important to note that Benjamin by no means simply embraces kitsch, thus reversing its negative evaluation, but calls for strategies of dialectically acknowledging and overcoming it rather than merely condemning it as an instance of bad taste. A limited licence of kitsch is, in varying degrees, advocated by other authors, too. However, Benjamin is totally unique in the narrative he offers to account for the emergence of 19th century kitsch. While other authors diagnose a decline of taste or refer to the unfolding of a presumed anthropological disposition (Giesz' *Kitschmensch*, 68–75), only Benjamin offers a strictly historical explanation, one whose core is the changing relation of art and technology.

In the architecture of the 19th century Benjamin diagnoses a fundamental change whose effect was to promote kitsch, if it not making it possible in the first place: 'In the nineteenth century the forms of construction [have been emancipated] from art, just as in the sixteenth century the sciences freed themselves from philosophy. A start is made with architecture as engineered construction. Then comes the reproduction of nature as photography' (*AP* 13). Architecture is no longer one of the fine arts but has become the domain of engineers at the École Polytechnique. Its exclusion from the fine arts was mainly the result of technical innovations. The introduction of steel girders and concrete elements fundamentally revolutionised the relationship between 'construction material and construction design' (my translation) ('*Baustoff und Bauform*' (*GS* V·1: 220 F3a,5)) and brought about both new structural possibilities and technical necessities: '[In former times], technical necessities in architecture (but also in the other arts) [did not] determine … the forms, the style, as thoroughly as they do today, when such technological derivation seem actually to become the signature of everything now produced' (*AP* F3a,5). The enhanced role of the structural engineer as an expert in ever more complex techniques, which represent a radical break with the traditional method of placing one stone on top of another, reduces the scope of the architect's activity. This loosens the inner links between construction and aesthetic design and turns the latter into a merely decorative stylisation of a construction increasingly dictated by industrial techniques. The historicising masks and architectural kitsch of the 19th century thus have a precise historical 'signature': they are both the effect and symptom of a disintegration of building and fine art under the pressure of rapidly changing techniques. The widening gap between the new technical possibilities and the traditional aesthetic role of architecture is being filled by largely random decorations and masquerades (*GS* V·1: K1a,6, L1a,3; *AP* K1a,6, L1a,3). Even Haussmann's use of aesthetic perspectives to embellish his grand boulevards is seen by Benjamin as a kitschy application of aesthetic ornaments to a town-planning technique essentially dissociated from all traditional forms of the fine arts: 'Haussmann's predilection for perspectives, for long open vistas, represents an attempt to dictate art forms to the technology ... of city planning. This always results in kitsch' (*AP* E2a,7).

Whether in the arabesques of the new iron and glass structures, in the 'perspectives' of Haussmann's boulevards (*AP* E2a,7), or in the opulently appointed bourgeois interiors, Benjamin always sees kitsch as a product of the contemporary distortions in the relationship between art and technology. Art, Benjamin suspects, 'no longer finds the time' to keep up with the tempo dictated by technology and fashion:

> From a European perspective, things looked this way: In all areas of production, from the Middle Ages until the beginning of the nineteenth century, the development of technology proceeded at a much slower rate than the development of art. Art could take its time in ... [playfully referring to the technological standards and procedures in a variety of ways]. But the transformation of things that set in around 1800 dictated the tempo [of technological change upon] ... art, and the more breathtaking this tempo became, the more ... [fashion came to dominate and spread through] all fields. Finally, we arrive at the present state of things: the possibility now arises that art will no longer find time to adapt somehow to technological processes. [Advertising] ... is the ruse by which the dream forces itself on industry. (*AP* G1,1)

For Benjamin there can no longer be any question of art being 'autonomous'. Ever since it ceased to be faster and more advanced than the technical devices in everyday use, art finds itself in the increasingly precarious situation of having to react to technological developments. Instead of freely, 'playfully' and self-assuredly 'referring to the technological processes in a variety of ways', it lacks the time and pace 'to adapt somehow to technological processes'. The constrictions imposed by engineering on architecture and by photography on painting are but two examples among many. Benjamin tends to see all art which dissociates itself from technological evolution as being trapped in a social limbo. On the other hand a particularly technology-intensive art form, such as film, is for that very reason crucial to the development of art as such:

> Film: unfolding ... of all the forms of perception, the tempos and rhythms, which lie preformed in today's machines, such that all problems of contemporary art find their definitive formulation only in the

context of film. (*AP* K3,3)

> [F]ilm today articulates all problems of modern form-giving as questions
> of its own technical existence—and does so in the most stringent, most
> concrete, most critical fashion ... (*AP* Q1a,8)

At a higher level of abstraction this systematic linkage of all art-relat-
ed problems to technical hardware ('today's machines') and the programs
they are based on leads to a question which Benjamin describes as the basic
'problem concerning the form of the new art' (*Formproblem der neuen Kunst*):
'When and how will the worlds of form which, without ... [any contribution
on our part], have arisen, for example, in mechanics, in film, in machine
construction, in the new physics, and which have subjugated us ... reveal
themselves to us as natural forms?' (*AP* K3a,2). In other words, when and
how will the forms of modern science and technology acquire a secondary
sensual immediacy for our perception as a result of their assimilation by art?
In view of the revolutionary technical developments that 'have arisen and
subjugated us without any contribution on our part', the outmoded para-architecture and plush interiors of the 19th century are seen by Benjamin as
attempts to offer—in mask-like arabesques—a refuge for powerful desires
that have been deprived of their traditional symbolisms. Furthermore the
wealth of technical possibilities that accrue to art and handicrafts without
any contribution on their part (*ohne eigenes Zutun*) provokes all kinds of design
attempts that no longer have any expertise or tradition to build on, attempts
which tend to enrich all the more 'the dreamy epoch of bad taste' with additional phenomena:

> 'Every tradesman imitates the materials and methods of others, and
> thinks he has accomplished a miracle of taste when he brings out por-
> celain cups resembling the work of a cooper, glasses resembling porce-
> lains, gold jewelry like leather thongs, iron tables with the look of rattan,
> and so on. Into this arena rushes the confectioner as well—quite forget-
> ting his proper domain, and the touchstone of his taste—aspiring to be
> a sculptor and architect.' Jacob Falke, *Geschichte des modernen Geschmacks*
> [History of Modern Taste], p. 380. This perplexity derived in part from
> the superabundance of technical processes and new materials that had
> suddenly become available. The effort to assimilate them more thor-
> oughly led to mistakes and failures. On the other hand, these vain at-
> tempts are the most authentic ... [testimonies] that technological pro-
> duction, at the beginning, was in the grip of dreams. (*AP* F1a,2)

It is in the countless aesthetic 'mistakes and failures' of the 19th century that Benjamin discovers 'the most authentic testimonies' (my translation)
('*echteste Zeugnisse*' *GS* V·1: F1a,2) and 'signal[s] of true historical existence' (*AP*
K1a,6): testimonies of an historically new configuration of art and technology and at the same time testimonies of how, at the newly precarious inter-

faces of art and technology, 'dream energies' can bring into being a world of
new objects—including that 'stuff which the nineteenth century has accumulated in that strange and perhaps formerly unknown … [form of matter]
which is kitsch' (*AP* K3a,1). Benjamin recognises an irresolvable ambiguity.
On the one hand the 'mistakes and failures' are signs and testimonies of the
historically determined 'dream energies' and as such represent the 'will to
happiness' of a generation. This is why Benjamin does not simply embrace
a modernist position advocating a dismissal and overcoming of ornament.
On the other hand, the pertinent phenomena remain 'mistakes and failures', since they fail in their task of 'reveal[ing]' to us in aesthetic 'form' the
'worlds of form which … have arisen, for example, in mechanics, in film,
in machine construction, in the new physics, and which have subjugated us'
(*AP* K3a,2). Furthermore, Benjamin sees a large proportion of the phenomena he investigates in para-architecture and interior design not just as failed
responses to technology, but as attempts to avoid the challenges issuing from
technology by means of ornament, draping, and historicising 'masks' (*AP*
K1a,6).

In its politics and historical philosophy *The Arcades Project* is animated by
the assumption that the difficult task—which the kitsch of the 19th century
failed to achieve—of integrating the advanced state of technology into the
'expression' of social dream energies has two grave consequences:

1. Art no longer enjoys a position of superiority that enables it to 'play-
    fully refer to the technological standards and procedures in a variety
    of fashions'; this places it at a historical disadvantage and dooms it to
    an escapist limbo.

2. At the same time technology, having outrun the pace and reach of
    artistic development and control, likewise eludes social and political
    control and can thus wreak its destructive effects unhindered.

It was Benjamin's hope that film, and in some cases advertising as well
(*AP* G1,1), would draw the lessons from the 'mistakes and failures' of the 19th
century. Only this, Benjamin literally believed, could have prevented the
catastrophe of fascism and National Socialism. Much like Benjamin's historiography, Nazi politics heavily invested in kitsch. Where the Nazi propaganda is not openly aggressive, it frequently makes use of kitsch, a typical
example being the caring Führer with a child in his arms. While Benjamin
advocates a dialectical overcoming of kitsch, Nazi politics simply exploits
its potential for sentimental indulgence. Interestingly, by the time Benjamin
was still working on his Arcades-kitsch-project, there was a veritable debate
on kitsch within the Nazi party.[8] Some high-ranking members of the party
condemned kitschy elements of its self-presentation as an offence to genuine

---

8. See Friedrich 41–2. (Benjamin is not mentioned in this article.)

German folk culture and strongly recommended a change in Nazi aesthetics. The debate made its way up to the very top level of the Nazi hierarchy, with Goebbels finally decreeing that the party could and should not refrain from recourse to kitsch. Thus, Nazi politics could, in fact, serve as a prime example of what it means not to strive, as was Benjamin's intention, for an 'awakening' from kitsch. This is not the time to discuss how 'realistic' Benjamin's dialectical politics of kitsch was. I merely note in conclusion that Benjamin's project was far more radical than anything I have expounded here. He intended to displace his readers to the threshold of 'awakening' not by means of the arguments that I have advanced here, but above all by the (Surrealist) 'explosion' (*AP* K3a,1, *SW* 2:208) which was to be produced by the direct confrontation of his contemporary readers with the 19th century dream energies stored in things. These were to 'strike' (*zustoßen*) the reader like the taste of the 'madeleine' strikes Proust's narrator. The problem of presentation in *The Arcades Project* was to simulate this 'striking' (*Zustoßens*) by means of its own literary form: 'In order to understand the arcades from the ground up, we sink them into the deepest stratum of the dream; we speak of them as though they had struck us' (*AP* F°,34). Nothing less than this 'striking'—with the desired result of an 'explosion'—is behind Benjamin's consistent policy of refraining from any idealistic arguments or 'moral metaphor' in favour of a 'one hundred percent image space' (*SW* 2: 217). The 'dream kitsch' of the 19th century was for Benjamin a—if not *the*—main repository of the energy represented by this image space.

   To sum up, we can say that there are four fundamental hypotheses on which Benjamin's program to 'construct here an alarm clock that rouses the kitsch of the previous century to "assembly"' (*AP* H1a,2) is based:

1. Benjamin shares the assumption of Darwin, Freud and today's evolutionary psychology that social systems essentially function through religious, political and/or aesthetic media that elicit, bind and channel powerful *social* emotions. That is why he did not want to abandon the field of aesthetisised emotion to the fascist politics that used mass media coverage to stage grandiose spectacles designed to work as analogues of archaic communal rituals. Benjamin's project of a counter-politics likewise draws on what he literally calls our 'most primordial … [emotions], fears and images of yearning' (*AP* K2a,1) as well as on aesthetic perception and modes of collective participation, thus entailing a decisive break with any purely rational or moralistic leftist politics. However, Benjamin's politics of affect seeks to draw strength not from the myth-making, pseudo-religious posturing which exploits narcissistic megalomania and promotes xenophobic aggression, but from the more diffuse aesthetic 'dream energies' of everyday life, disseminated as they are over a wide variety of often banal things. Rec-

ollecting the affective charges of these outdated things was entrusted
with the task of disseminating the false pathos, the decidedly propa-
gandistic sublime of the fascist politics of affect. Put in a more contemporary idiom, one might say that Benjamin tries to 'renegotiate'
affective potentials which he hoped could fight the disastrous success
of Nazi propaganda in generating emotional support for its political
agenda.

2. In the 19th century, Benjamin saw a cultural evolution that weakens
   the traditional means of a social politics of affect (religion, family, social status, and class distinctions) in favour of fashion and an aesthetisised *Lebenswelt*. Technology plays a major role in this development.
   Our 'most primordial emotions, fears and images of yearning' are
   shifted into an imaginary space with radically new properties. They
   have, according to Benjamin, 'taken refuge ... in the mute impenetrable nebula of fashion, where the understanding cannot follow' (*AP*
   B1a,2).

3. The relations between art and technology have undergone a fundamental change in the modern era. Art has largely lost its role of playfully being ahead of technology and is in danger of losing its ability to
   aesthetically master the latter's potential, being reduced to providing
   mere drapery. At the same time it turns out that the technically most
   sophisticated forms of artistic creation and communication—such as
   film or today's Internet—fit in very well with the generation of collective desires and reach the largest public. Hence Benjamin's conclusion that only such an art which transforms the most advanced technological possibilities into quasi-natural modes of sensuous perception will live up to the challenges of cultural evolution. The possibility
   that art might be relieved of the need to compete with technology and
   open up new horizons for itself by detaching itself from the latter's dynamic development is not seriously considered by Benjamin.

4. Benjamin sees the kitsch produced in the 19th century as an 'authentic testimony' of an effort aimed at solving a problem that emerged
   only in this period. Even though this effort has failed to arrive at integrating technology and social energies of desire or wishful thinking in the first place, it still 'contains' retroactively—precisely in its
   objects becoming démodé and dying out—'material of vital importance for us ... In any case, material of vital importance politically' (*AP* N1,11). Or to put it in evolutionary terms: Benjamin's project
   amounts to retroactively turning a partly failed cultural adaptation
   of the recent past into a powerful resource for dealing with present
   and future challenges. As kitsch was a powerful tool in fascist politics,

Benjamin's strategy of aiming at a dialectical use of kitsch had clearly singled out a worthy target for political intervention. In fact, Benjamin was the only author to devise a politics which did not leave this historically novel and powerful phenomenon aside.

History did not give Benjamin's *The Arcades Project* the opportunity of 'striking' his contemporaries and—perhaps—'rousing' or 'awakening' them. This much is certain: *The Arcades Project* was not supposed to be an academic work, but a Surrealistically inspired political intervention. If Benjamin sought to dig out, salvage and reactivate the 'weak messianic power' of past desires precisely in the 'kitsch' of his parents' generation, he did not imply that this politics could be applied to other periods. In fact, he firmly held, that this would be a unique reply to an historically unique constellation. There is no way to tell whether or not his politics would have made any difference. Obviously, it is easier to dismiss his project as hopelessly out of proportion with the reality of National Socialism than to subscribe to its ambitious claims. However, I do believe that Benjamin's work on kitsch can serve as a powerful incentive to look into novel ways of writing history from below—from quotidian things and their affectice significance and to design a politics which pays sufficient attention to the fact that politics always relied on and played upon our emotions.

3

Modernity as an Unfinished Project: Benjamin and Political Romanticism

Michael Mack

POLITICAL ROMANTICISM VERSUS POLITICAL THEOLOGY

It is quite well known that Benjamin was fascinated by German romanticism throughout his intellectual career. Andrew Benjamin has recently distinguished between an understanding of Benjamin as a romantic and an
understanding of romanticism's legacy in Benjamin's notion of modernity.
This legacy of romanticism consists in a novel notion of temporality. It is this
new comprehension of time which romanticism bequeaths to modernity:

> In order to develop an understanding of modernity defined in terms of
> historical time, a distinction needs to be drawn between a conception of
> the modern conceived as the current state of progress and modernity as
> interruption. The first is the linear conception of development through
> continuity that is the implicit understanding of historical time in the
> Enlightenment, especially Kant. Working against this tradition involves
> deploying motifs from Romanticism, more specifically the conception of
> caesura in Hölderlin's theoretical writings. (A. Benjamin *Style* xv)

This novel romantic conception of temporality precisely informs Benjamin's understanding of modernity as interruption: it is a break not only
with the past but also with the present.

This article achieves the aim of delineating the relevance of a Spinozist
non-hierarchical vision for modern thought by tracing its social and political revision from Benjamin's study of early romanticism to his work on the
architecture of modernity as developed in *The Arcades Project*. Why was Benjamin's study of early romanticism the ground on which he built his theory
of modernity? Raising this question does not necessarily pave the way for a

portrayal of Benjamin as closet romantic. He was clearly at pains to differentiate his intellectual position from a nostalgic longing for the return of the past; a sentiment which one could ascribe to a commonplace understanding of romanticism. Rather than celebrating the past as 'romantic' escape from the present, Benjamin makes problematic our understanding of both the present and what it means to be present. Is our presence preconditioned by a peculiar absence? Benjamin questions the autonomy of the present and that which is often conflated with it: the modern. He was fascinated by the continual co-presence of an apparently absent past within the presence of modernity.

More important, the past in question here has undergone a substantial change: it survives in modernity in radically changed form but at the same time it becomes itself a force that makes transformation possible insofar as it upends the presumed understanding of the modern as a self-sufficient, autonomous project. In other words, past and present crisscross each other in a dialectical force field, where each actualises the potentialities of the other so that the past brings out the hidden core of the present and the present unveils the secret potentialities within the past. As Werner Hamacher recently expressed it:

> When past things survive, then it is not lived-out (*abgelebte*) facts that survive, facts that could be recorded as positive objects of knowledge; rather what survives are the unactualised possibilities of that which is past. There is historical time only in so far as there is an excess of the unactualised, the unfinished, failed thwarted, which leaps beyond this particular Now and demands from another Now its settlement, correction and fulfilment. (41)

Here history clearly is not a completed project. Neither is it one that is hierarchically structured along the line of time's projected 'progress' which supposedly finds its culmination and completion in the attainment of modernity.

Benjamin proposes an alternative image of modernity: one that is not hierarchical and one that does not incorporate a homogenous understanding of time. In the Arcade project he detects in the buildings of modernity what he calls 'images in the collective consciousness in which the old and the new interpenetrate' (*AP* 4). These wish images undermine the hierarchical prioritisation of the present over and above the past, because they evidence dissatisfaction with current modes of production and social organisation. Not being satisfied with the present they turn to the past. They commingle the present as rejection of presence with the past as an opening that could liberate the current state of affairs from past and future injustices.

History thus emerges as the renewing force of what is absent, insignificant and forgotten. Modernity describes the birth of what has been suppressed and repressed: it instantiates the promotion of the demoted historical past. This attempt to rescue those who have been marginalised and forgotten is affiliated with an idiosyncratic type of theology: one that avoids dogmas and a specific doctrine. As Irving Wohlfarth has recently pointed out, Benjamin's theology attempts to redeem the current state of nature which is based on the production of refuse (or in other words 'waste') and the refusal to include those who have been excluded from a hierarchical construction of society: 'The question of the rest—Nature's silent plea for a second hearing, the little hunchback's yearning to be included in our prayers—is finally, a theological undertaking' (Wohlfarth 30). There is a striking connection between Benjamin's non-dogmatic approach towards the theological and a romantic comprehension of the lyrical: Herder's and Goethe's romanticism mainly consists in the literary formulation of a theology that has been peeled of its exclusivist and dogmatic kernel.

In this context David E. Wellbery has called Goethe's lyric writings of the 1770s 'a poetic religion of *Liebe*', which 'as a supernatural guidance, as presence even in absence … is the sublimation of the originary donation and therewith the ontological form of poetic speech' (383). Poetry understood as a religion of love outdoes the cruelty of political theology that authorises authority figures to kill those who, in a hierarchical construction of society, are below them and might thus be perceived as a threat to their hold on power. Significantly, Carl Schmitt formulated his Politische Theologie as a response to the egalitarianism of the romantics, which, in his Politische Romantik, he explicitly branded as opponents of the ruler's right to declare the state of exception. Developing and radicalising Hobbes, Schmitt singles out fear as the prime force that authorises the power of the ruler and allows him to declare a state of emergency (which, according to Benjamin, is perpetual).

Strikingly, Schmitt singles out romanticism as a subversive force that threatens to unravel the social grid of political theology. What characterises the subversion that Schmitt detects in political romanticism? It is precisely absence of fear: it is Goethe's religion of love that undermines the anxiety-inducing hierarchy which structures the workings of political theology. Schmitt therefore advances a new politicised understanding of romanticism with the following question: 'Would it not be simple to say that romanticism is everything that can be psychologically or conceptually derived from the belief in the *bonté naturelle*—in other words, the thesis that man is good by nature?' (Schmitt 1) The thesis according to which humanity is intrinsically good pre-empts political theology because it is the focus on the forces of 'evil' which authorises the ruler to use absolute power in order to combat and defeat those forces in the quasi apocalyptic battle that characterises the state of exception.

Schmitt goes on to align political romanticism with Spinozism which he contrasts with the modern abstract rationalism of Descartes, Hobbes and

Kant: 'Spinoza's system, however, is the first philosophical reaction—and one analogous to this post-Kantian [i.e. romantic] reaction—to the modern abstract rationalism defended at that time by Descartes and Hobbes, to a mechanistic world view' (Schmitt 54). The romantic celebration of the *bonté naturelle* presupposes a Spinozist coincidence between ethics (thought) and ontology (being). Schmitt thus identifies political romanticism with Spinoza's one-substance philosophy: 'Thought and being become attribute of the same infinite substance' (54). Whereas Schmitt's political theology furthers hatred and violence, Spinoza's one-substance philosophy eventuates in a levelling of hierarchical distinctions and other forms of exclusionary devices that promote the use of brute force. According to Schmitt, Spinoza's *Ethics* gives rise to political romanticism which manifests itself in 'general disintegration' (75): 'If this general disintegration, this playful sorcery of the imagination, remained in its own sphere, it would be irrefutable within the confines of its orbit. But it intermixes with the world of commonplace reality in a capricious and arbitrary fashion' (75). Schmitt sees in romanticism not a self-enclosed aesthetic sphere. On the contrary he is startled by the political repercussions of the Romantics' aesthetic appropriation of Spinoza's non-hierarchical vision (i.e. Spinoza's one-substance philosophy). In this way Schmitt takes issue with Novalis' inclusive notion of religion (Bible), artistic creation (genius) and nationality (what it means to be German):

> He [i.e. Novalis] believes in the Bible; but every authentic book is a Bible. He believes in genius; but every person is a genius. He believes in the Germans; but there are Germans everywhere. In spite of the alleged historical sensitivity of romanticism, for him the German character is not limited to a state and a race. It is not even limited to Germany. (Schmitt 75)

Schmitt focuses on the levelling of racial, national ('not limited to a state and race') and geographic distinctions ('not even limited to Germany'). Why does he do so? A focus on race, nationality (and also religion) is closely connected to what Schmitt misses in the work of Novalis and that of other exponents of political romanticism, namely political hatred and outrage over the injustices of foreign domination' (129). Benjamin's interest in the interruptive potential of romanticism has much to do with this levelling approach to various hierarchical structures that give rise to hatred and violence.

Avant la lettre, Goethe questions Schmitt's notion of political theology by formulating a poetic religion of love. Wellbery focuses on the way in which Goethe transforms authoritarian and violent aspects of traditional religious language in poems like 'Harzreise im Winter':

> The religion of fear (and of destiny) projects a god in which death and sovereignty are condensed in the terrifying physiognomy of a punitive paternal authority. In the religion of thanks, however, this personifica-

tion dissolves, the Other relinquishes its characteristics as phantasmatic object and becomes the law of an invisible ethical bond. The religious celebration is conducted with symbolic tokens (the altar) and commemorates (gives thanks for) the institution of the communal religious law as a divine gift. Such is the poetic insight attained in and through the quest and proclaimed in the psalm this text [i.e. 'Harzreise im Winter'] purports to be. *It is an insight into the nonobjectival character of the Other, the vision (but, of course, a nonperceptual, sublime vision) of the Other as the ethical relation of gift and gratitude that is the foundation of communal solidarity.* (Wellbery 389)

Goethe's lyric poetry thus celebrates the transmutation of a politics and religion that is grounded in both fear and the perpetuation of violence to one that does away with hierarchical rankings within theology and society at large.

Romantic literature is the site where a meeting between self and other occurs that avoids the power relations implicit in what Carl Schmitt would later call the 'state of exception'.[1] Eric Santner has recently linked Schmitt's concept of the state of exception to a phenomenon that first Herder and then Goethe critiqued as 'natural history' (*Naturgeschichte*). The term 'natural history' refers 'not to the fact that nature also has a history but to the fact that the artefacts of human history tend to acquire an aspect of mute, natural being at the point where they begin to lose their place in a viable form of life (think of the process whereby architectural ruins are reclaimed by nature)' (Santner 16). The romantics respond to destruction and decay in a Spinozist mode insofar as they do away with the opposition between the natural and the societal: nature emerges as life-enhancing rather than destroying force, as Spinoza's *conatus*, which 'is simply a thing's special commitment to itself' (Goldstein 160). According to Spinoza, this natural desire to persist is however always already rational and ethical, 'because, having stood beside oneself and viewed the world as it *is*, unwarped by one's identity within it, one will understand that there is nothing of special significance about one's own endeavour to persist and that doesn't pertain to others' same endeavours' (Goldstein 185). This recognition of nature as foundational to ethics—rather than as opposed or inferior to it—preconditions Goethe's and Herder's nonhierarchical poetic vision of a new religion based not on dogma but on love of the neighbour.

BENJAMIN'S CRITIQUE OF TELEOLOGY

Like Hannah Arendt, Benjamin links the future to the significance of

---

1. For a discussion of Benjamin's critical reinterpretation of the state of emergency as continuity as the everyday occurrence of catastrophe see my 'Transzendentaler Messianismus und die Katastrophe der Entscheidung. Anmerkungen zu Carl Schmitts und Walter Benjamins Eschatologie'.

the 'insignificant' past. Following Herder's and the early romantics' Spinozist critique of the hierarchical demotion of 'primitive' history, Benjamin's
notion of the modern radically breaks with teleological conceptions of history and time. The presence of messianism in Benjamin's thought indicates
that he has not completely abandoned a concern for the construction of a
better future. This messianic element is, however, part of an unpredictable
realisation. It manifests itself in what Benjamin understands by the term
'awakening'. The awakening breaks with historical continuity: it is an interruption. Benjamin's conception of interruption is significant because it offers
an alternative to teleological thought.[2]

If one can speak of teleology in Benjamin's work then it is a teleology
that outdoes itself: it does not know what it is truly about; one simply cannot
force or even foresee the coming of the Messiah.[3] The distance Benjamin
establishes towards teleology marks his critical stance towards the enlightenment.[4] As Andrew Benjamin has pointed out, the romantic notion of in-

2. Recently Andrew Benjamin has distinguished between Walter Benjamin's notion of
interruption and utopianism. Utopianism is teleological: it is goal oriented and attempts to
predict the future. Benjamin's messianic interruption is unpredictable: 'Awakening is the
construction that is the allowing. The formalism provides for history and marks the force
of strategy. In contradistinction to this positioning, utopianism empties time by giving the
future an already determined, even if idealized, content. Utopianism cannot sustain potential. Within it structure and content have to be given in advance. Such a possibility is
predicated upon the effacing of potential. Only through the retention of potentiality and
a formalism that will always allow for content—a possibility actualized by the moment of
interruption—will a politics of time be possible. What is at stake is an interruption; its possibility depends upon potentiality; its occurrence allows. Rather than the cessation inau-
gurated by violence, here the interruption—what for Hölderlin would have been the coun-
termeasure of the caesura—is occasioned strategically' (A. Benjamin *Style* 38).

3. I owe this argument about the presence of a weak teleology in Benjamin's work to discussions with Gyorgy Markus.

4. Andrew Benjamin has acutely analysed the way in which Benjamin's romantic underpinnings depart from a Kantian Enlightenment conception of a teleological history.
Modernity understood as interruption claims romanticism rather than the Enlightenment
as the blueprint for the modern: 'Interruption as the defining motif in Benjamin's thought
dominates both his engagement with Romanticism and his move to the writing of another
construction of history. In both instances the interruption—analyzed in terms of the caesura—is unthinkable outside its relation to the Absolute. In regard to Romanticism, the
presence of the Absolute is explicable in terms of retention of key elements of Schlegel's
philosophical and critical project. In the case of the *Arcades Project* the Absolute returns as
time. Two important conclusions can be drawn from this setup. The first is that it must
force a reconsideration of the role of the Absolute within philosophical thinking; even that
thinking whose ostensible concern is a theory of modernity. The second is connected insofar as what must be taken up is the extent to which a theory of modernity will depend
upon a philosophy of time that has its point of departure in Early Romanticism, rather
than in the march of teleological time implicit, for example in Kant's construal of the relationship between history and the Enlightenment. In sum interruption will continue to
figure since the hold of continuity makes modernity an unfinished project.' (A. Benjamin,
'Benjamin's modernity' 113)

terruption contradicts Enlightenment descriptions of history's teleological continuity: 'Indeed, it can be further argued that thinking the particularity of modernity as an interruption depends upon the successful distancing of the conception of historical time within the Enlightenment tradition' (A. Benjamin 'Benjamin's modernity' 97–8). Benjamin's notion of the modern thus modernises a conception of diversity that was first developed in the literature of the age of Goethe in its reworking of Spinoza's *Ethics*. In his *Ethics* Spinoza interpreted perfection not in terms of teleological fulfilment of a single entity. Rather he argued that it encompasses the sustainability of life. He understood life not as homogeneous but as diverse. The literature of the age of Goethe made Spinoza's concept of the sustainability of the diverse applicable to a new understanding of history that departs from Kant's teleology. This article analyses Spinoza's hidden legacy (or in Benjamin's terms his *Nachleben*/'afterlife'[5]) within Benjamin's reading of romantic texts as the blueprint for the architecture of the modern.

This hidden Spinozist viz. romantic aspect of Benjamin's approach towards modernity may help explain the tension in his thought between destruction and preservation, between the eschatological and the utopian, between the progressive and the traditional, between the materialist and the theological.[6] Why does Benjamin advocate Divine violence while at the same time granting profane history its right to find fulfilment in its striving for happiness? As I have shown elsewhere, with a despairing gesture Benjamin saw in the reinforcement of a Kantian divide between freedom (the intellectual/spiritual) and nature (the profane) its messianic overcoming (Mack *German Idealism*). To reinforce this dualism between the rational and the natural means to accept a certain level of violence. The violence in question is perpetrated on the demoted body of the profane. This demotion of nature is a crucial theme in Benjamin's book about Baroque tragic drama and in his essays 'Capitalism as Religion' and 'Critique of Violence'. The disgust with nature, with the body, with the profane brings about the desire to read the world allegorically. Baroque allegory, in Benjamin's understanding, immanently transcends the immanent to the point of annihilating it.

---

5. For a discussion of Benjamin's term *Nachleben* see Andrew Benjamin's 'Benjamin's Modernity', p. 112.

6. Esther Leslie has recently attempted to play down this tension by arguing that Benjamin criticises rather than celebrates the destructive force of capitalism (87–112). Howard Caygill affirms this tension between the redemptive and the catastrophe while at the same time uncovering the presence of a third position that avoids any form of violence: 'The presence of a non-messianic political theology in "On the Concept of History" does not replace the messianic, but situates it in a more complex configuration. The middle and the final theses perhaps should be seen as posing an alternative within the alternative to catastrophe. Decision, in this case, would not be simply between the alternatives of a catastrophic or the messianic end of history, but between the end of history and its radical and immanent transformation' (Caygill 226).

This is exactly what he perceived to be operative in the nonsignifying eco-
nomical transactions that characterise the religion of capitalism.

Related to capitalist economics as it emerged within the Christianity
of the Reformation and fully develops into the commodification of life as
analysed in *The Arcades Project*, the reformationist aesthetics of the baroque
destroys profane bodies. This commandment of the destruction of the profane rules the workings of allegory, just as it seems to motivate the abrupt
coming of a redeemed society: '[t]he human body could be no exception to
the commandment which ordered the destruction of the organic so that the
true meaning, as it was written and ordained might be picked up from its
fragments' (*Origin* 216).[7] As a self-enclosed entity, the profane seems to be deprived of meaning. Such absence of signification engulfs the whole of nature
(human nature included) into a maelstrom of guilt. Benjamin foregrounds
this point in his essay on Goethe's *Elective Affinities* when he writes, 'With the
disappearance of supernatural life in man, his natural life turns into guilt,
even without his committing an act contrary to ethics. For now it is in league
with mere life, which manifests itself in man as guilt' (*SW* 1: 308).

In his 1921 essay 'Capitalism as Religion' Benjamin analyses capitalist
economics as a theology of guilt. Rather than working for a change of heart,
Christianity that has become capitalism tries to declare the whole of life
guilty so that redemption can only be attained in complete despair, which
heralds the utter destruction of profane life:

> Capitalism is entirely without precedent, in that it is a religion which of-
> fers not the reform of existence but its complete destruction. It is the ex-
> pansion of despair, until despair becomes a religious state of the world
> in the hope that this will lead to salvation. God's transcendence is at an
> end. But he is not dead; he has been incorporated into human existence.
> (SW 1: 289)[8]

There is a sense in which Benjamin is fascinated by the apocalyptical
aspects of the religion of capitalism. He seems to dwell on the *Zertrümmerung*
(complete destruction) unleashed by capitalist economics in a way similar to
which the allegorist dwells on the *Trümmer* (ruins) to which profane life has
been transformed in Baroque tragic drama.

Are these landscapes of destruction however to be read in a literal sense?
Or rather, does Benjamin celebrate destructive force as that which makes incomplete the presumed and presumptuous completion of any kind of work

---

7. 'Der menschliche Körper durfte keine Ausnahme von dem Gebot machen, das das
organische zerschlagen hieß, um in seinen Scherben die wahre, die fixierte und schriftge-
mäße Bedeutung aufzulesen.' *GS* IV: 145

8. 'Darin liegt das historisch Unerhörte des Kapitalismus, daß Religion nicht mehr Reform des Seins sondern dessen Zertrümmerung ist. Die Ausweitung der Verzweiflung zum
religiösen Weltzustand aus dem die Heilung zu erwarten sei. Gottes Transzendenz ist ge-
fallen. Aber er ist nicht tot, er ist ins Menschenschicksal einbezogen.' *GS* VI: 101.

whether it is that of the profane or that of the spirit/intellect (viz. that which the German term *geistig* denotes)? Modernity's destructive force would then be that which renders modernity incomplete: it would not necessarily destroy the past which precedes the presence of the modern but it would shatter modernity's pretended position—posing as the temporal endpoint where history's long progress finds its culmination. The profanity of destruction thus coincides with revelation: it is a heuristic device that sheds light on the fragmentary nature of immanent autonomy and historical fulfilment. In an important essay Phillipe Simay has recently distinguished Benjamin's understanding of destruction from that of Hannah Arendt: 'Destructivity is not just, as Arendt thought, a simple destruction. Its first nature is to reveal. Attacking the conservative mode, destructivity casts light on that dark part which tradition strives to mask behind normative continuity. It unveils its violence' (Simay 144). The destructive work of the profane would thus further the cause of redemption.

This article questions Benjamin's dualism between the profane and the redeemed. Benjamin puts this dualism into question. While there is a sense in which one can interpret his thought in terms of a somewhat despairing Kantianism, that is, of Kantianism that despairs of itself, there is also a sense in which he continues a romantic critique—a critique that manifests itself in what Hölderlin perceives as caesura and Benjamin describes as interruption—of Kant's hierarchical divide between freedom and nature. What I have called elsewhere Benjamin's 'transcendental messianism' outdoes itself if one locates this problematic notion on the ground of an idiosyncratic modernity, one that is not Kantian but Spinozist and romantic (Mack *German Idealism* 155–67). As we shall see the modernity of this romanticism resides in its refusal to assume self-contained forms of identity.[9] On this view, notions

---

9. In an intriguing discussion of Benjamin's image of Proust, Carol Jacobs has discussed non-identity and noncoincidence as key characteristics of the work of remembrance: 'Spontaneous remembrance at first seems very like that memory that satisfies an elegiac desire for coincidence with past happenings, but it brings us instead to a world of nonidentity. As the children play their game, the rolled-up stocking seems, like the *mémoire involuntaire*, to promise access to a plenitude behind it; but what seems to function as container and a sign for fullness is found to have always from the first been a mere stocking, an empty sign. The children's play with the stocking is like a particular gesture of Proust: just as the children cannot satiate their desire to transform the pouch and its contents into the stocking, "so Proust could not get his fill of emptying the dummy, the Self, with a grasp in order over and over to bring in that third thing—the image". The *Attrappe* (which may be translated as 'dummy,' 'imitation,' or 'trap') for which Proust reaches seems to signify the hidden presence of the self. But the grasp that should render this contents (sic!) present only leads to a voiding of the self. The dummy that seemed to promise the plenitude to self was always a mere image, just as the full pouch of the children was always a mere stocking. The gesture of Proust, like that of the children, is only a game. His insatiable desire is not the longing for the presence of the self, but rather simply to repeat the movement, to transform the dummy over and over into an empty image.' (44–5)

such as the profane and the theological lose their semantic stability.

In his 'Theological-Political Fragment' Benjamin seemingly separates the profane from the messianic only to establish their mutual dependence at the end. Politics as the realm of the profane desires a state of happiness but it can reach this state only by way of self-loss.[10] Losing itself, the profane gives way to the reign of the messianic. This is why neither the political nor the theological coincides with itself. Both entities are incomplete. Rather than being autonomous, their seemingly teleological strivings for either profane happiness or messianic redemption diverge from the straight lines of their respective initial constructions and turn into what is on the surfaces of their appearance their respective opposite. One path destroys itself at the point it enters the pathway of its other.

Is this what Benjamin understands by destruction? If so, his notion of violence is in fact non-violent. It denotes not the annihilation of a given work but its incompletion. The profane finds its fulfilment at the point where it interrupts itself and enters into the realm of theology. Mutatis mutandis, theologians betray theology when they depict it as autonomous completion. Theology does not coincide with itself. It requires the profane as its subject matter in a way similar to that in which philology needs a textual basis in order to do its work. Benjamin draws on this non-coincidence of the theological with itself in the N convolute of *The Arcades Project*: 'Bear in mind that commentary on a reality (for it is a question here of commentary, of interpretation in detail) calls for a method completely different from that required by a commentary on a text. In the one case, the scientific mainstay is theology; in the other case, philology' (*AP* N2,1). This is a rather unsettling argument because it disorders the distinction between the profane and the theological, a distinction on which Benjamin dwells in his theological-political fragment. As 'a commentary on reality', theology depends on the profane in order to do its interpretative work. In order to function it demands of itself a submergence into its opposite. It has to immerse itself into the profane realm of politics.

POLITICAL ROMANTICISM OR MODERNITY AS INTERRUPTION

This coincidence of opposites is the theme of Benjamin's first thesis on the concept of history. Here a despised and seemingly insignificant hunchback secretly guides the moves of the chess-playing puppet. The hunchback represents the invisible work of theology that guarantees the success of the

---

10. Carol Jacobs has noted a similar notion of identity as premised on the loss of selfhood in Benjamin's essay on the 'Task of the Translator': 'The Translatability of the text excludes the realm of man and, with him, the figure to which Benjamin's essay is devoted. The *Aufgabe* of the translator is less his task than his surrender: he is *aufgegeben*, "given up", "abandoned". This is the essay's initial irony.' (87–8)

visible actor, which is historical materialism: 'The puppet, called "historical materialism", is to win all the time. It can easily be a match for anyone
if it enlists the services of theology, which today, as we know, is small and
ugly and has to keep out of sight' (Löwy 23). The theological serves as the
hidden kernel of energy behind the automaton which is historical materialism. Michael Löwy has recently drawn attention to the romantic tradition
to which the 'the little dwarf, or the hunchbacked dwarf, as soul, as *spiritus
rector* of an inanimate structure' belongs (Löwy 26). There is, however, an
even closer connection between Benjamin's version of Marxism and his understanding of romanticism.

The secret symbiosis between entities that are apparently irreconcilable
harks back to Benjamin's doctoral thesis *The Concept of Criticism in German
Romanticism*. There he distinguishes between Schlegel and Novalis' understanding of reflection, on the one hand, and Fichte's notion of representation, on the other. The early romantics depart from Fichte in their 'cult of
the infinite, which ... divided them from Fichte and lent their thinking its
most peculiar and characteristic direction' (*SW* 1: 125–6). What characterises this romantic 'cult of the infinite'? The term infinite may be misleading
here: it does not invoke infinity as a dualistic opposite of finitude. Rather it
denotes a never-ending quest that does not exclude an encounter and engagement with anything, however profane it may be.

More important, Novalis and Schlegel's notion of infinity does not have
connotations of progress and advancement. In his thesis on the romantic
concept of criticism Benjamin already takes aim at the positivist understanding of evolutionary history. Here he prepares the ground for his later
critique of the notion of progress as developed in *The Arcades Project* and in his
Theses on the Concept of History. In his thesis on *The Concept of Criticism in German Romanticism* Benjamin makes clear that the infinite does not describe an
advance of the present and the future over and against the assumed backwardness of the past: 'To begin with, the infinity of reflection, for Schlegel
and Novalis, is not an infinity of continuous advance but an infinity of connectedness. This feature is decisive, and quite separate from and prior to its
temporally incompletable progress, which one would have to understand as
other than empty' (*SW* 1: 126). What is crucial here is the concept of 'an infinity of connectedness' which Benjamin derives from his engagement with
the critical work of early romanticism. Whereas Fichte's concept of representation is premised on the goal of completion, the romantic idea of reflection is a never-ending process which does not unfold along the trajectory of
a single line but instead branches out into an infinite growth in different directions.

Here Benjamin sketches the outline of a modernity that differs from that
of Kantian teleology, one that is not unlinear but diverse and yet interconnected. The infinite growth of difference does not eventuate in the establish-

ment of identities narrowly conceived. Rather each identity depends on its opposite. This then is the meaning of Benjamin's characterisation of infinity as the endless unfolding of interconnectivity: the one is at the same time the other, and the other is at once the one. It is this movement back and forth between selfhood and difference that shapes the unending spiral of a romantic modernity; one that upends the teleology of the modern as progress and triumph over the 'primitive' past.[11]

Spinoza's one-substance philosophy serves as the blueprint for this alternative notion of infinity that presupposes not a hierarchical teleology but a social theory of interconnectivity. Spinoza makes his understanding of connectedness abundantly clear when he writes in his *Ethics* that different parts of humanity depend on each other in a way similar to that in which God has been traditionally described as the sustaining force of human life: man is thus a God to man (*hominem homini Deum esse*) (Spinoza II: 234).

In romanticism the one-substance philosophy of the seventeenth century philosopher transmutes into, as Jean Paul Richter has floridly put it, 'the high Spinozism of the heart [*dem hohen Spinozismus des Herzens*], which values every animal, however small [*Tierchen*] and every flower, holding it fast to the heart'.[12] In his *Arcades Project* Benjamin discusses Jean Paul Richter's romantic 'Spinozism of the heart' in the context of Fourier's utopianism, which conceives of modernity not in terms of the exploitation of nature: in the Plan of March 1934 that outlines *The Arcades Project*, Benjamin thus sketches a comparison between 'Fourier and Jean Paul' under the thematic title 'Why there was no French Idealism' (*AP* 914). Benjamin opens the section dedicated to Fourier in *The Arcades Project* with the following citation from A. Pinloche's *Fourier et le socialisme*: 'The words of Jean Paul which I put at the head of this biography of Fourier—"Of the fibers that vibrate in the human soul he cut away none, but rather harmonized all"—these words apply admirably to this socialist, and in their fullest resonance only apply to him. One could not find a better way to characterize the phalansterian philosophy' (*AP* W1,1). This citation is significant in so far as it establishes a relation between Jean Paul Richter's Spinozist romanticism and Fourier's cooperative conception of modernity.

In this way Fourier's cooperative vision draws on a non-hierarchical and non-teleological understanding of humanity which the romantics developed while formulating a view of infinity that transposes Spinoza's philosophy of nature into the realm of history and art criticism. In Fourier's modern utopia the classless society of the future has its equivalent in humanity's cooperation with nature. The natural and the historical interconnect. In the

---

11. For a discussion of anthropological critique of the distinction between civilisation's progress and the backwardness of 'primitive' peoples see my work *Anthropology*.

12. 'Hielt er … mit dem hohem Spinozismus des Herzens jedes Tierchen und jede Blüte wert und am Herzen fest.' (Richter 450)

eleventh thesis on the concept of history Benjamin contrasts this roman-
tic/Spinozist notion of modernity with that of the positivist celebration of
progress and labour:

> The new conception of labor is tantamount to the exploitation of na-
> ture, which, with naïve complacency, is contrasted with the exploitation
> of the proletariat. Compared to this positivistic view, Fourier's fantasies,
> which have so often been ridiculed, prove surprisingly sound. Accord-
> ing to Fourier, cooperative labor would increase efficiency to such an
> extent that four moons would illuminate the sky at night, the polar ice
> caps would recede, seawaters would no longer taste salty, and beasts of
> prey would do man's bidding. All this illustrates a kind of labor which,
> far from exploiting nature, would help her give birth to the creations that
> now lie dormant in her womb. (Löwy 72)

Here Benjamin uses the term 'new' in a highly ironic manner. The new
merely describes the continuation of the entrenched practice of exploitation. The modernity of positivism does not instantiate an interruption that
breaks with the injustices of the past. Rather than offering a break with exploitation, modernity extends the work of abuse from the intrahuman realm
to that of nature. The modern 'progressive' exploitation of nature does not
lighten the lot of the working class. It increases it precisely because nature
occupies an inferior position within a hierarchical conception of teleology.
This is why nature resembles the lowly status of the proletariat. Fourier's
utopian conception of modernity, by contrast, offers an alternative to the
new that turns out to be nothing else but a development of the old.

Here romanticism emerges as a truly revolutionary interruption that
breaks with the continuum of history which advances the progress of exploitation. What precisely generates this break within the romantic concept of
the modern? In his thesis on the *Concept of Criticism* Benjamin focuses on the
idea of interconnection. Whereas in *The Arcades Project* he would align this
idea with Jean Paul Richter and Fourier, in this earlier work (1919) he focuses
on Hölderlin, Schlegel and Novalis:

> Hölderlin—who, without any contact with the various ideas of the early
> romantics we will encounter here, had the last and incomparably most
> profound word—writes, in a passage in which he wants to give expres-
> sion to an intimate, most thoroughgoing connection, 'They hang togeth-
> er (exactly)'. Schlegel and Novalis had the same thing in mind when they
> understood the infinitude of reflection as a full infinitude of interconnec-
> tion: everything in it is to hang together in an infinitely manifold way—
> 'systematically,' as we would say nowadays, 'exactly,' as Hölderlin says
> more simply. (*SW* I: 126)

Instead of denoting either a transcendent realm or the concept of progression, the term 'infinitude' describes the activity of reflection which es-

tablishes infinite interconnections between profane things which at first sight
seem to be isolated and thus condemned to a one-dimensional sphere of use
value. The work of reflection illuminates the spiritual/intellectual architecture of creaturely life. Whatever concerns one aspect has implications for life
in its entirety. By illuminating the hidden interconnection of what appears
to be the isolated and isolating sphere of the profane, reflection 'constitutes
the absolute, and it constitutes it as a medium' (*SW* 1: 132). How does it do so?
Reflection constitutes the absolute as medium by removing the 'restrictive
conditions' that distort profane existence as a realm of isolation (*SW* 1: 142).
Reflection confounds the distinction between the profane and the theological. In so doing it transposes use value into a sphere where it does not seem
to belong: into the sphere of the absolute.

This is why the notion of reflection is closely related to the romantic
celebration of irony. Benjamin focuses on the romantic notion of irony, because it is intrinsically linked to his understanding of incompletion: irony
puts things into question and thus prevents completion. In related but different manner, reflection mediates between the profane and the absolute and
in doing so it establishes connections between entities that appear to be opposed to each other. As has been discussed in the opening section, it is this
element of inter-connection that provokes Schmitt to single out political romanticism as the opposite (one is tempted to say 'the enemy') of his understanding of political theology. The notion of irony focuses on what facilitates
such connective work: It thrives on lack, on what is missing in any given ut-
terance.

Through irony the self appears as other. In this way the divide between
observation and theory collapses thanks to this celebration of absence. What
is absent in what is immediately observed has been traditionally associated
with theory, and theory is usually identified with the absence of observation.
Observation turns into theory when it is touched by irony and consequently
gives way to indeterminacy. The medium of reflection and observation coincide, and oppositions lose their opposing force:

> The medium of reflection of knowing and that of perceiving coincide
> for the Romantics. The term 'observation' alludes to this identity of me-
> dia; what is distinguished as perception and method of research in the
> normal experiment is united in magical observation, which is itself an
> experiment; for this theory, it is the only possible experiment. One can
> also call this magical observation in the Romantics sense an *ironic* ob-
> servation. That is, it observes in its object nothing singular, nothing de-
> terminate. No question put to nature lies at the base of this experiment.
> Instead, observation fixes in its view only the self-knowledge nascent in
> the object; or rather it, the observation, *is* the nascent consciousness of
> the object itself. It can rightly be called ironic, therefore, because in its
> not knowing—in its attending—observation knows better, being identi-

cal with the object. (*SW* 1: 148)

The indeterminacy of irony is a tool adequate not only for theoretical but also for the empirical quest for truth. Why do observation and theory coincide in Benjamin's discussion of the romantic concept 'irony'? The observer who focuses on a singular object distorts what he or she observes. This distortion is not only a question of theory but also of empirical research. The analysis of nature as developed in Spinoza's *Ethics* precludes an exclusive concern with singularity. In other words, Spinoza's one substance theory uncovers the deception implicit in a quest for singular identity. Rather singular nature is interconnected, and its specific boundaries are nevertheless indeterminate. Spinoza's one-substance constitutes a plural unity: the whole is fractured by difference, and differences are interconnected so that together they comprise the body of wholeness.

Further developing Spinoza's philosophy of nature, Goethe and the early romantics blurred the distinction between theory and observation. Those who observe nature are always already engaging with theory, because the natural world requires an ironic mode of investigation: one that never reaches an ultimate conclusion but infinitely connects one object to another. The scientist thus never truly knows the singular objects under examination. It is this lack of knowledge which Goethe and the romantics understand by the term irony: Irony qua lack constitutes indeterminacy and the blurring of singularity.

In *The Arcades Project* Benjamin applies Goethe's and the early romantics' isomorphism of theory and observation to the analysis of politics and history. He refers to Georg Simmel's study of Goethe's concept of truth. In his book about Goethe (1913), Simmel argues that the universal 'reveals itself immediately in a particular form' (57) and he goes on to quote Goethe about the coincidence of observation and theory: 'The highest thing would be to grasp that everything factual is already theory'(57). It is this coincidence which Benjamin discusses in his work on the romantic concept of criticism. It also forms the methodological basis of his analysis of the architecture of modernity as presented in *The Arcades Project*. Here Benjamin refers to the excerpt previously quoted from Simmel's Goethe study, while discussing Goethe's concept of truth as follows:

> In studying Simmel's presentation of Goethe's concept of truth, I came to see very clearly that my concept of origin in the *Trauerspiel* book is a rigorous and decisive transposition of this basic Goethean concept from the domain of nature to that of history. Origin—it is, in effect, the concept of the *Ur*-phenomenon extracted from the pagan context of nature and brought into the Jewish contexts of history. Now, in my work on the arcades I am equally concerned with fathoming an origin. To be specific, I pursue the origin of the forms and mutations of the Paris arcades from their beginning to their decline, and I locate this origin in the eco-

nomic facts. Seen from this standpoint of causality, however (and that means considered as causes), these facts would not be primal phenomena; they become such only insofar as in their own individual development—'unfolding' might be a better term—they give rise to the whole series of the arcades' concrete historical forms, just as a leaf unfolds from itself all the riches of the empirical world of plants. (*AP* N2a,4)

The observation of the architecture of modernity is always already part of the theory of modernity. The empirical world of the modern metropolis Paris is already impregnated by theory. Benjamin transposes Goethe's Spinozist analysis of nature to the study of history. Here, however, time freezes into an image. As an image it interrupts the false theory of historical continuity and progression.[13] The falseness of this theory does not remain in a self-enclosed sphere: it distorts the documentary history it supposedly represents.

This distortion is political: it establishes and celebrates the continuum of exploitation. In their distorted form history and nature transmute into a single entity. This false theory depicts exploitation as 'natural' and therefore as the not to be overturned essence of history's continuity. In the Arcades Project Benjamin breaks with this notion of both history and modernity by introducing the notion of awakening: an awakening that breaks with the continual nightmare of exploitation, which has falsely been theorized as 'natural'.

This article has shown that Benjamin defines what he understands by interruption along Spinozist lines: namely as one-substance philosophy which instantiates a break with the anthropomorphic fallacy that divides the world into binary opposites—into Schmitt's friend-enemy opposition that is the foundation of the violence implicit in political theology. Against this Spinozist background, Benjamin romantic notion of criticism emerges as an anticipation of his understanding of modernity in terms of interruption as advanced in the Arcades project. According to Benjamin the romantic notion of criticism is what Novalis and Schlegel's term hovering (*Schweben*) describes and what Schmitt has singled out as the destructive effect of political romanticism. Romantic criticism and political romanticism do not settle in one particular location. They continually endure the discontinuous. They cling to the stateless state of hovering. They do not remain in an isolated and isolating location; rather, they interconnect opposites by infinitely wandering form one place to another.

Instantiating a stateless state, romantic criticism and political romanticism are truly universal. They do not exclude anything, however 'small'

13. As Buck-Morss has acutely put it, 'The *Passagen-Werk* deals with economic facts that are not abstract causal factors, but ur-phenomena … A concrete factual representation of those historical images in which capitalist-industrial economic forms could be seen in purer embryonic stage was to be the stuff and substance of the work' (73).

or 'insignificant' it may be. Benjamin sees this coincidence of the romantic term 'hovering' and the attainment of a non-exclusive universalism most clearly depicted in Schlegel's 116th *Athenaeum* fragment: 'This grasping of the universal is conceived as "hovering" because it is a matter of infinitely rising reflection that never settles into an enduring point of view, according to Schlegel's indications in the 116th *Athenaeum* fragment' (*SW* 1: 153). In order to be truly universal, modernity needs to remain incomplete. Benjamin's romanticism is therefore modern: it hovers between binary oppositions and thus avoids the violent pitfalls of Schmitt's political theology.

4

Violence, Deconstruction, and Sovereignty: Derrida and Agamben on Benjamin's 'Critique of Violence'

Robert Sinnerbrink

Walter Benjamin's 1921 essay 'Zur Kritik der Gewalt' has been responsible for a subterranean tradition of critical thought, one that has only come to prominence in recent decades.[1] As Anselm Haverkamp points out, Herbert Marcuse, who published an introduction to the 1965 Suhrkamp paperback edition, 'was the first one ready to use this text'—some forty years after its initial publication (Haverkamp 140). More recently, Giorgio Agamben has argued that Benjamin's 'Critique of Violence' belongs to the debate between Benjamin and Carl Schmitt on the concept of the state of exception (*Ausnahmezustand*), and even that Schmitt's theory of sovereignty should be regarded as a cryptic response to Benjamin's 'Critique of Violence' (Agamben 'State' 288–9).[2] Agamben's work has contributed greatly to the renewed interest in this text, which plays an important role in Agamben's own project of theorising sovereign power and its violence against bare life.[3] In the English-speaking world, however, it was Jacques Derrida's 1990 essay 'Force

---

1. 'Zur Kritik der Gewalt' (*GS* II·1: 179–203), 'Critique of Violence' (*SW* 1: 236–52). Benjamin's essay was first published in issue 47 of the *Archiv für Sozialwissenschaft und Sozialpolitik* in 1921.

2. Haverkamp describes Agamben's *Homo Sacer* as 'the most important of all the books influenced by the "Critique of Violence" or produced in its wake' (*State* 137). See also Agamben's essays on Benjamin in *Potentialities*.

3. Andrew Norris has pointed out that Benjamin's 'Critique of Violence' essay introduces the concept of 'bare life' (*bloßes Leben*), which Agamben then develops in his own work. Unfortunately, as Norris goes on to remark, 'it is almost impossible to say what Benjamin means by this phrase' (Norris *Exemplary* 281).

of Law' that once again brought Benjamin's enigmatic text to the attention of cultural theorists and political philosophers. It seems timely then to ask how Derrida's famous reading of Benjamin's 'Critique of Violence' in 'Force of Law'—along with Agamben's recent reflections—both appear in light of this renewed critical attention brought to Benjamin's work.

As is well known, Derrida's prodigious body of work showed a marked shift during the 1990s toward increasingly explicit ethical and political themes. These included essays on the question of Europe, on apartheid, on the foundations of law, cosmopolitanism, the right to hospitality, and Derrida's long-awaited reading of Marx (via Shakespeare, Heidegger and Max Stirner).[1] Much of this ethical sensitivity and political engagement is already apparent in Derrida's famous essay, 'Force of Law: The "Mystical Foundation of Authority"',[5] delivered as two lectures in October 1989 and April 1990. This essay as a whole divides into two distinct parts: the first explores the paradoxes of 'enforcing the law', drawing on Pascal's *pensée* concerning the 'mystical foundation' of law, and developing the distinction between *deconstructible* law and *undeconstructible* justice; the second part presents a careful reading of Benjamin's essay 'Zur Kritik der Gewalt' ('Critique of Violence'), dissecting its complex layering of political, eschatological, and metaphysical themes, but also appropriating it within Derrida's project of deconstruction, indeed, within the movement of deconstruction *as* justice.

Since its publication 'Force of Law' has become a seminal text, so to speak, in critical legal studies and deconstructivist approaches to law.[6] Derrida's double gesture of aligning deconstruction with Benjamin's project, while also deconstructing Benjamin's alleged complicity with metaphysically inflected discourses of violence, has also proven very significant for the 'post-structuralist' reception of Benjamin's work. This raises the question of the relationship between Benjamin's thought and deconstruction. In what follows, I shall examine Derrida's complex deconstructive reading of Benjamin's enigmatic critique of *Gewalt* (violence, force, power), foregrounding in particular the parallel Derrida draws between deconstructive reading and Benjamin's account of pure violence. My question, put simply, is whether Derrida's deconstructive reading does justice to Benjamin's enigmatic critique of violence. In pursuing this question I argue that Derrida blurs Benjamin's Sorelian distinction between the *political general strike* (which simply inverts state power relations) and the *proletarian general strike* (which non-violently disrupts such power relations). As a consequence, Derrida criticises

---

4. 'Force of Law' (hereinafter referred to as 'Law'), *Force de Loi*. See Derrida *Other, Specters, Politics, Monolingualism, Hospitality*.

5. An earlier version of this essay appeared in *Cardozo Law Review* 11 (1990): 919–1045.

6. See the essays in Cornell et. al and the special issue of *Cardozo Law Review* 13 (1991), especially the essays by Rodolphe Gasché and Adam Thurschwell which deal specifically with Derrida's reading of Benjamin.

Benjamin's metaphysical complicity with the violence that led to the Holocaust. Along with other readers of Benjamin, such as Werner Hamacher and Giorgio Agamben, I question Derrida's critique of Benjamin's alleged complicity with 'the worst'. Derrida's deconstructive reading of Benjamin, I conclude, underplays its Marxist dimensions, privileging the theological and textual dimensions of Benjamin's thought over the political and historical.

DECONSTRUCTING BENJAMIN'S 'CRITIQUE OF VIOLENCE'

It is not surprising that deconstruction should end up with a 'problematization of the foundations of law, morality, politics' (Derrida 'Law' 8), for deconstruction has always attempted to show the paradoxes structuring the philosophical discourse on the responsible moral subject. This problematisation of law takes the form of the question: what allows us to distinguish between the legitimate force of law, the just use of force, and 'the violence that one always deems unjust?' ('Law' 6). Here Derrida's guide (above all in the second part of 'Force of Law') will be Benjamin's 'Critique of Violence', with its unstable combination, as Derrida phrases it, of 'neo-messianic Jewish mysticism grafted onto post-Sorelian neo-Marxism (or the reverse)' ('Law' 29).

Derrida's deconstructive reading of Benjamin's 'Critique of Violence' belongs to the historical, genealogical, textual version of deconstruction that Derrida outlines elsewhere in 'Force of Law' ('Law' 21). It was originally presented as part of a symposium on 'Nazism and the Final Solution', and in this respect emphasises the complicity between Benjamin's discourse on violence and other anti-*Aufklärung*, anti-democratic, critiques of liberal parliamentary democracy (especially in Carl Schmitt and Heidegger).[7] It is a 'risky reading', as Derrida admits, which raises the question of whether it is also a *just* reading, a case of deconstructive justice in action. Derrida attempts to justify this deconstructive approach by claiming that, with suitable work and precautions, 'lessons can still be drawn' from Benjamin's text for our context ('Law' 30), namely for Western liberal democracies post-1989, the epoch of triumphant global capitalism.

Derrida begins by drawing attention to the text's volatile context: the crisis of liberal parliamentary democracy in Weimar Germany but also across Europe, the failure of pacifist movements and anti-militarism, Communist agitation and the concept of a general strike, changes in the public sphere due to mass media communications, and general criticisms of jurid-

---

7. Derrida's text on Benjamin's 'Critique of Violence' was delivered as an opening address for the colloquium 'Nazism and the "Final Solution": Probing the Limits of Representation' at the University of California, Los Angeles, on April 26, 1990. The first part of 'Force of Law' (dealing with the aporias of justice) was presented in the colloquium on 'Deconstruction and the Possibility of Justice' held at the Cardozo Law School, Yeshiva University of New York, October 1989.

ico-police violence and the liberalist conception of right. Although attentive
to this context, Derrida's deconstructive reading is more concerned to show
how Benjamin's text undermines the very distinctions that it proposes in its
own argumentative movement. Indeed, Benjamin's complex critique of the
question of *droit, Recht*, right or law, invokes a philosophy of history that it at
the same time destroys. It presents the ruins of a philosophy of right, a self-
destructive or self-deconstructive text that reveals much about the fate of our
own inherited conceptions of law, violence, and justice.

The essay is organised around a series of distinctions that Derrida will
put into question. These include the distinction between two kinds of violence and their role in relation to law or right: the *law making* or *law-positing violence* (*rechtsetzende Gewalt*), which institutes law, and the *law-preserving*
or conserving violence (*rechtserhaltende Gewalt*), which maintains and insures
the 'permanence and enforceability of law' (Derrida 'Law' 31). This distinction is linked with another, though not by way of equivalence, between the
'mythic' founding violence of law (which Derrida reads as alluding to Greek
law), and the 'divine' annihilating violence of destructive law (which Derrida reads as alluding to Jewish law). Finally, there is Benjamin's enigmatic
distinction between *justice* (*Gerechtigkeit*) as the principle of the 'divine' positing of ends, and *power* (*Macht*) as the principle of the 'mythic' positing of law
or right. Derrida will argue, however, that in attempting to maintain these
distinctions as independent of each other, Benjamin will end up mirroring
the very violence and injustice that he seeks to critique. Derrida even goes
so far as to say that Benjamin's text, at certain points, evinces a vertiginous
complicity with 'the worst' (the ideological discourses that culminated in the
Holocaust) ('Law' 63). This claim has been challenged by other readers of
Benjamin, and I shall make some brief remarks on this issue in concluding
my reflections.

Benjamin's critique of violence attempts to prepare a 'critique', understood in a peculiarly post-Kantian (but also Marxist!) sense, that is, a reflective examination of the limits and legitimate use of *Gewalt* or violence as
such (meaning also force and authority). It is not a condemnation of violence
but rather a case of 'judgment, evaluation, examination that provides itself
with the means to judge violence' (Derrida 'Law' 31). Rather than inquire
into the exercise of violence, Benjamin asks the critical question concerning an 'evaluation and a justification of violence in itself' (Derrida 'Law' 32).
For both natural law and positive law traditions remain bound to the model of accounting for violence in terms of means and ends: either the natural
law justification of violence as a means to attain just ends (for example, the
right to kill in self-defence), or the justification of violence as a means so long
as it conforms to instituted law (for example, the right to use military force
to repel an invader). For Benjamin, however, these two approaches remain
within a 'circle of dogmatic presuppositions', which becomes evident when

a contradiction arises between just ends and justified means. Benjamin's critique of violence thus attempts to surpass both natural law and positive law traditions in favour of what he described as a weak messianic 'philosophy of history'—a revolutionary philosophy committed to the infinite task of redeeming past suffering.

Benjamin's critique of violence therefore examines whether *pure violence*—understood as *that which cannot be reduced to any instrumental relation between ends and means*—can legitimately establish a new order of law and right. From this perspective, the *right to strike* represents the most compelling example of a pure violence that strikes at the heart of the established legal, social, and political order. Here Benjamin refers to Georges Sorel's famous distinction, from his *Réflexions sur la violence* of 1919, between the *political* and the *proletarian general strike*. Indeed, Sorel was the first to distinguish between these two fundamentally different kinds of strike, which are 'antithetical in their relation to violence' (*GS* II·1: 193; *SW* 1: 245). This is a decisive point: the general political strike simply inverts relations of social domination, while the proletarian general strike seeks to abolish this order of social and political domination itself. As Werner Hamacher remarks in his illuminating reading of Benjamin's essay,

> for whereas the political general strike is only concerned with inverting the relation of domination, and is still based on the preservation and strengthening of state violence, the proletarian general strike aims at nothing less than the abolition of the state apparatus and the legal order maintained by it. (Hamacher 1994, 120)

The general political strike remains within the parameters of state violence, seeking to invert the relations of power; the proletarian general strike, by contrast, 'sets [*setzt*] itself the sole task [*Aufgabe*] of destroying state power' (*GS* II·1: 194; *SW* 1: 246).[8] In this respect, the proletarian general strike, as a general refusal of work, severs relations with the system of exploitation, and in doing so presents a 'non-violent means of annihilation of legal as well as state violence' (Hamacher 120). As Benjamin observes, following Sorel:

> Whereas the first form of interruption of work [general political strike] is violent, since it causes only an external modification of labor conditions, the second [proletarian general strike], as pure means, is non-violent [*gewaltlos*]. For it takes place not in readiness to resume work following external concessions and this or that modification to working conditions, but in the determination to resume only a wholly transformed work, no longer enforced by the state, an upheaval [*Umsturz*] that this kind of strike not so much causes as consummates. For this reason, the first of these undertakings is lawmaking [*rechtsetzend*] but the second anarchistic. (*GS* II·1: 194; *SW* 1: 246)

---

8. Quoted in Hamacher (120).

Here the distinction is made very clear. The general political strike is violent because it aims at altering labour conditions but remains within the legal and political order of the state, that is to say, the state's monopoly on the legitimate use of violence. The proletarian strike, by contrast, is pure political violence, understood as *pure means*; at the same time, however, it is *non-violent* in the sense that it refuses any complicity with state violence by suspending all forms of posited law. It eschews extortionate violence directed at effecting a change that can be integrated within the prevailing economic, legal, and political status quo. Instead, it advocates an anarchic suspension of state power—and the power of law—through the *refusal of work* in the name of social and political justice. It is oriented by the demand for a wholly transfigured work no longer grounded in the legal and political order of the state. In this respect, the strike does not bring about this anarchic dissolution of power but rather expresses its execution or consummation. At the same time, this refusal or withdrawal of work is a 'violent' counteraction to the injustice of state violence and its legitimation of social and economic exploitation. The pure violence of the proletarian general strike is, paradoxically, a *non-violent suspension* of the organised violence of the state and its underlying economic and social order. For Benjamin, this contrast can be understood as that between the *law-making or law-positing violence* [*rechtsetzende Gewalt*] that founds the legal and political order, and the anarchic 'pure violence' that fundamentally transforms the very nature of work and undermines the prevailing institutions of the social and political community.

At this point, however, Derrida parts company with Benjamin and proceeds to deconstruct the Benjaminian critique of violence. According to Derrida's reading, Benjamin's Sorelian-inspired endorsement of the proletarian general strike means embracing, precisely, *violence* as a legitimate means to overthrow the state. Indeed, Derrida claims that 'Benjamin clearly does not believe in the non-violence of the strike' ('Law' 34), a statement that is difficult to reconcile with Benjamin's clear separation of the *proletarian general strike*, with its pure violence that is a *non-violent violence*, a suspension of state violence, from the *general political strike*, which deploys state violence in order to invert the relations of power within the state. In class struggle, Derrida continues, the right to strike is guaranteed to workers, 'who are therefore, besides the state, the only legal subject (*Rechtssubjekt*) to find itself guaranteed a right to violence (*Recht auf Gewalt*) and so to share in the monopoly of the state in this respect' ('Law' 34). Indeed, the complete withdrawal of labour in the revolutionary *general strike* aims at the abolition of the unjust legal and political order as such.

This is the revolutionary form of pure violence that the state, as organised force of law, fears the most: it condemns as illegal the general strike that takes the conceded right to strike to the limit in order to undermine the established social-political order. As Derrida remarks, the political state fears this 'fundamental, founding violence, that is, violence able to justify, to le-gitimate (*begründen*, …), or to transform the relations of law (*Rechtsverhältnisse*, …), and so to present itself as having a right to law' ('Law' 35). This is the instituting or founding violence that Benjamin seeks to examine in his cri-tique of violence: not just the exercise of brute force but the violence that be-longs in advance to an order of right that does not yet exist (Derrida 'Law' 35). According to Derrida, the general strike is thus an important example of this founding violence, since it 'exercises the conceded right to contest the order of existing law and to create a revolutionary situation in which the task will be to found a new *droit*' ('Law' 35). The aim of this revolutionary found-ing violence, in short, is to found a new order of law and right that will ret-rospectively justify it, however much the establishment of this order may of-fend our sense of justice at the time (Derrida 'Law' 35).

We should note, however, that Derrida's reading clearly clashes with the manner in which Benjamin interprets Sorel's distinction between the *politi-cal* general strike and the *proletarian* general strike, which Derrida frequent-ly describes simply as a 'general strike,' dropping the Sorelian-Marxist ref-erence to the proletariat. Benjamin's proletarian general strike is precisely what *suspends* the violence of the political state through the anarchist-revolu-tionary withdrawal of labour. It is the proponents of the *political general* strike who, in Benjamin's view, court the danger of reproducing the violence of the political state. As Hamacher points out, Benjamin cites Sorel, who claimed that the general political strike is based upon the 'strengthening of state vi-olence', that it will prepare 'the ground for a strong centralized and disci-plined power that will be impervious to criticism from the opposition, and capable of imposing silence'; moreover, that it 'demonstrates how the state will lose none of its strength, how power is transferred from the privileged to the privileged, how the mass of producers will change their masters' (*GS* II·1: 193–4; *SW* 1: 246).[9] Far from reproducing the dangers of political suppres-sion, the proletarian general strike is, as Hamacher remarks, a 'non-violent means of annihilation of legal as well as of state violence,' one that aims, in Benjamin's words, 'to resume only a wholly transformed work, no longer en-forced by the state' (*GS* II·1: 194; *SW* 1: 246).[10] In Hamacher's reading, then, Benjamin's pure violence of the proletarian general strike marks the possi-bility of an essentially *non-violent*, anarcho-revolutionary transformation of work and of society.

As remarked above, this is quite opposed to Derrida's reading, which is concerned to show that Benjamin's critique of violence risks lapsing into a vertiginous complicity with 'the worst'. And this is not only through a questionable endorsement of forms of political violence but via a quasi-the-

9. Quoting Georges Sorel, *Réflexions sur la Violence* (5ᵗʰ ed. 1919, p. 250). Passage quoted in Hamacher (120). Translations of the passages in question can be found in Sorel (162, 171).

10. Quoted in Hamacher (120).

ological 'justification' for what Derrida identifies as the 'bloodless' violence that the Nazis would perpetrate during the Holocaust ('Law' 62). It is true that Benjamin makes some very enigmatic references to the way divine violence, as law-destroying, as expiatory, is 'lethal without spilling blood'; that God' judgment 'strikes privileged Levites, strikes them without warning, without threat, and does not stop short of annihilation.' (*GS* II·1: 200; *SW* 1: 250). Derrida famously takes these remarks to foreshadow a complicity with that which was to become 'the worst' a couple of decades after Benjamin penned his essay. Whatever the theological significance of Benjamin's enigmatic description of divine violence, however, we should recall that it is a violence that remains 'outside the law' (*GS* II·1: 202; *SW* 1: 252); that its human and historical manifestations are to be found in 'the educative power' (*erzieherische Gewalt*) which 'in its perfected form also stands outside the law' (*GS* II·1: 200; *SW* 1: 250), and also in the possibility of 'revolutionary violence, the highest manifestation of unalloyed violence by man' (*SW* 1: 252). These manifestations of pure violence, in Benjamin's enigmatic sense, do not readily lend themselves to assimilation with the horrors of the 'Final Solution'. Nonetheless, as Haverkamp remarks, attempts such as Derrida's 'to declare Benjamin's "Critique of Violence" to be a prophecy of Auschwitz' continue to generate lingering 'annihilating oversimplifications', to which Agamben's work, among others, offers a pertinent response ('State' 140).

Whatever the case, Derrida's contentious claim clearly clashes with the distinctions I have outlined and discussed above. Indeed, I would suggest that Derrida can make this criticism of Benjamin only by conflating the (Sorelian) distinction Benjamin carefully maintains between the *political* and the *proletarian general strike*, a distinction that is precisely concerned with the problem of avoiding reproducing political and state violence in attempting to overthrow or annihilate this violence. Derrida, however, will argue that Benjamin *cannot* maintain this distinction: it is always already contaminated such that the political and proletarian general strikes merge into one another, hence are mutually implicated in political violence and the exercise of domination. In short, Derrida rejects Benjamin's claim that we can distinguish 'pure violence' as the suspension of state violence, maintaining instead that pure violence and political violence are always already mutually contaminating.

Derrida then attempts to envelop Benjamin's critique of violence within the movement of deconstruction, drawing out the relation between Benjamin's pure violence and 'juridico-symbolic violence, a performative violence at the heart of interpretative reading' ('Law' 37). In other words, having first destabilised the opposition between pure violence and political violence, Derrida draws a strong parallel between Benjamin's account of the revolutionary general strike and the interpretative violence of deconstruction:

> We might say that there is a possibility of general strike, a right to general

strike in any interpretative reading, the right to contest established law in
its strongest authority, the law of the state. One has the right to suspend
legitimating authority and all its norms of reading ... for we shall see
that Benjamin distinguishes between two sorts of general strikes, some
destined to replace the order of one state with another (general political
strike), the other to abolish the state (general proletarian strike). In short,
the two temptations of deconstruction. (Derrida 'Law' 37)

Derrida thus attempts to reinscribe Benjamin's anarcho-Marxism within the project of deconstructive justice in action. Benjamin's appropriation
of the Sorelian distinction between political and proletarian general strikes
is transformed into the 'two temptations of deconstruction'. The revolutionary situation generated by the (proletarian) general strike becomes the revolutionary situation 'in every reading that founds something new and that
remains unreadable in regard to established canons and norms of reading,
that is to say the present state of reading or of what figures the State, with a
capital S, in the state of possible reading' (Derrida 'Law' 37). Deconstructive
reading as a strategy of rupture, however, is never pure but always mediated.
From this irreducibly mediated situation Derrida draws the following conclusion: 'there is never a pure opposition between the general political strike
looking to re-found another state and the general proletarian strike looking
to destroy the state' ('Law' 38).

This rather hasty conclusion (which quickly assimilates Benjamin's highly ambivalent text on violence into the always doubled strategy of deconstruction) leads Derrida to question the organising oppositions of Benjamin's
discourse on violence; to show how they deconstruct themselves in accordance with Derrida's (quasi-speculative) claim that deconstruction *is* justice.
Indeed, Derrida proposes—in what we might call an act of deconstructive
violence—that Benjamin's oppositions are caught up in a process of mutual
contamination that renders untenable the fundamental distinction between
founding or *positing violence* and *conserving* or *preserving violence*: 'I shall propose
the interpretation according to which the very violence of the foundation
or position of law (*Rechtsetzende Gewalt*) must envelop the violence of conservation (*Rechtserhaltende Gewalt*) and cannot break with it' ('Law' 38). Contra
Benjamin, for Derrida there can be no rigorous opposition between positing and conservation, only a paradoxical '*différantielle contamination*' between
the two ('Law' 38). Thus there can also be no rigorous distinction between a
general strike and a partial strike (but do we ever observe a general strike?);
for the attempt to separate revolutionary 'pure violence' from the violence of
the state—encompassing both law-making and law-preserving violence—
must always fail. Contra Benjamin, for Derrida there can be no pure violence 'outside the law'; rather, deconstruction shows that there can only be
a *différantielle contamination* at the heart of the law that, in Benjamin's phrase,
renders it 'rotten', decayed, from the start. Indeed, according to Derrida,

Benjamin ignores the fact that any originary structure involves the possibility of repetition or iteration, which renders any pure origin always already marked by the possibility of repetition. Hence it belongs to the very structure of founding or positing violence that it be iterable, repeatable, and so founds what ought to be conserved, what is promised to heritage and tradition. The distinction between positing and preserving violence therefore collapses into a *différantielle contamination* between the violence *of* law and the possibility of violence *beyond* the law.

In response to Derrida's reading, we should recall Benjamin's mention of the 'educative power' as a sphere in which pure violence, outside the law, can become manifest. Here I would point to an intriguing moment in Benjamin's text that suggests the possibility of an ethical mode of *communicative* non-violence exceeding the sphere of law or right. As Benjamin remarks, non-violent resolution of conflict is readily evident in the intersubjective relations between private persons:

> Non-violent agreement is possible wherever a civilized outlook allows the use of unalloyed means of agreement. Legal and illegal means of every kind that are all the same violent may be confronted with nonviolent ones as unalloyed means. Courtesy, sympathy, peaceableness, trust, and whatever else might here be mentioned are their subjective preconditions. (*GS* II·1: 191; *SW* 1: 244)

What to make of this moment? Derrida doesn't comment greatly upon it other than to indicate Benjamin's apparent adherence to a public/private opposition, itself in need of deconstruction ('Law' 49). It certainly represents a curious break with Benjamin's talk of law-positing and law-preserving violence. Its importance, however, lies in underlining the forms of intersubjective engagement 'outside the law' in which non-violent means are deployed between individuals. In doing so, Benjamin points, I want to suggest, to a model of *dialogical communication* with the power of suspending the violence of law or right. As Benjamin observes, it is possible to witness such non-violent suspending of conflict within the sphere of social relations over goods, in the cultural sphere of techniques, and in the hermeneutic sphere of language:

> The sphere of non-violent means opens up in the realm of human conflicts relating to goods. For this reason, technique in the broadest sense of the word is their most particular area. Its profoundest example is perhaps the conference [*die Unterredung*], considered as a technique of civil agreement. For in it not only is nonviolent agreement possible, but also the exclusion of violence in principle is quite explicitly demonstrable by one significant factor: there is no sanction for lying. (*GS* II·1: 192 ; *SW* 1: 244)

This moment of non-violent dialogical communication—beyond law and right—presents itself as one possibility, more ethical than political, for

the critique of violence. Techniques of civil agreement that are intersubjective and communicative already indicate a sphere 'beyond the law' where
the use of unalloyed means is possible. In the case of the 'conference', a dialogical situation of unconstrained communication, the exclusion of violence
is signalled by the lack of any punishment for deceptive or lying speech.
And such a possibility in turn is opened up, Benjamin claims, by the hermeneutic dimension of language: 'there is a sphere of human agreement that is
non-violent to the extent that it is wholly inaccessible to violence: the proper
sphere of 'understanding' (*Verständigung*), language' (*GS* II·1: 192; *SW* 1: 245).
Benjamin, moreover, distinguishes this ethical moment of dialogical non-
violence from the political moment of pure violence evinced in the proletarian general strike. Can these ethical and political forms of non-violence be
brought together? While Benjamin gestures towards the analogy between
pure means in politics and dialogical communication, he appears to re-
serve this dialogical non-violence for the interpersonal sphere of linguistic
communication, related forms of social intercourse governing conflicts over
goods, and the situation of unconstrained dialogue evinced in the 'conference' (*Unterredung*). Rather than development the implications of this insight,
however, Benjamin does no more than point to the analogy between the
spheres of politics and of social communication: 'We can therefore point
only to pure means in politics as analogous to those which govern peaceful
intercourse between private persons' (*GS* II·1: 193; *SW* 1: 245).

Instead of exploring the possibility of introducing dialogical communication into the sphere of politics, Benjamin's text, as Derrida observes,
takes on a decidedly theologico-metaphysical tone. Pure revolutionary violence, according to Benjamin, does not lend itself to any human knowledge
or certainty on our part (Derrida 'Law' 56). It finds its source in God, the
wholly other, the 'sovereign violence' (*waltende Gewalt*) (*GS* II·1: 203; *SW* 1:
252). For Derrida, Benjamin's relapse here into a theologically inflected philosophy of history—the historical decline from a pure origin to a teleological conclusion through revolutionary repetition—signals his complicity with
crypto-metaphysical thinkers such as Schmitt and Heidegger. But does this
also signal, as Derrida claims, Benjamin's complicity with 'the worst' (Nazism, the Holocaust)? As I noted above, the parallel Derrida draws between
Benjamin's conception of annihilating, sacrificial, 'divine' violence, and the
'bloodless' annihilation of the Holocaust, is controversial to say the least.[11]
As Werner Hamacher remarks, it should be clear that:

> Benjamin's notions of annihilation and destruction … have nothing to
> do with the corresponding propaganda terms of the so-called conserva-

---

11. As Agamben notes, the ambiguity of Benjamin's 'divine violence' can prompt the
most 'dangerous equivocations', including the 'peculiar misunderstanding' that prompts
Derrida to approximate it to the Nazi 'Final Solution' (Agamben *Homo Sacer* 63–7). Quotation on p. 64.

tive revolution, or with the 'revolution of nihilism' (as the equation of radical democratic and totalitarian politics would have it, and as some critics by now do not hesitate to insinuate with explicit references to Benjamin) (Hamacher 134).

Derrida's reading of Benjamin's alleged complicity with 'the worst' is a striking instance of the interpretative violence to which Hamacher alludes. Moreover, the parallel Derrida draws between Benjamin's messianic-revolutionary rhetoric and Carl Schmitt's *explicit* complicity with 'the worst' overlooks Benjamin's strongly critical attitude towards Schmitt's 'state of exception' as merely preserving the violence of the political and economic *status quo*. Unlike Schmitt, Benjamin's account of the strike, as Hamacher observes, does not represent the 'exception' [*Ausnahme*] to the rule of the state, to its monopoly over violence, but 'the 'exception' of any system that can still operate with the political opposition of legal norm and state of emergency' (134). Schmitt's state of exception preserves the violence of state power, grounding it in the decisionistic power of sovereignty. Benjamin's revolutionary state of exception, by contrast, would overturn this violence of the political order. As Benjamin remarks in section VIII of 'Über den Begriff der Geschichte' (translated as 'On the Concept of History'):

> The tradition of the oppressed teaches us that the 'state of exception' [*›Ausnahmezustand‹*] in which we live is the rule. We must arrive at a concept of history in accord with this insight. Then we shall see clearly that our task is to bring about the actual state of exception, and thereby we will improve our position in the struggle against Fascism. (*GS* I·2: 697; *SW* 4: 392; *Illuminations* 248–9 [translation modified])

As Agamben has observed, this passage is probably the most important one in the limited dossier comprising the debate between Benjamin and Schmitt. Agamben's reading of this passage is illuminating, however, more for what it tells us about Agamben's project than Benjamin's. According to Agamben, Benjamin's eighth thesis must be understood as modifying Schmitt's account of the state of exception presented in *Political Theology*: namely, that it defines the normal situation ('State' 293). The state of exception has now become the rule, which means that there has been an intensification of its undecidability ('State' 293). More precisely, the state of exception no longer confirms the rule; rather, it begins to coincide or blur with it (particularly if we understand Benjamin's comment in the context of the Nazi normalisation of the state of exception during the Third Reich) ('State' 193). Agamben's point here is to highlight the manner in which Benjamin and Schmitt are engaged in an esoteric debate over the relationship between pure violence and the state of exception; for Schmitt, the state of exception defines the power of sovereignty as a means of capturing 'pure violence,' while for Benjamin this 'pure violence' is always fundamentally excluded from the law.

Benjamin's distinction between a real and a fictitious state of exception, moreover, is essential in this context, a distinction that Agamben claims Benjamin takes from Schmitt ('State' 193). According to Schmitt, the fictitious state of exception is that state of siege which nonetheless maintains individual rights and freedom through the law. For Benjamin, by contrast, according to Agamben, 'the real state of exception is now opposed to a 'state of exception' (between quotation marks) that is none other than the one that, according to Schmitt, defines the sovereign' ('State' 294). Benjamin takes the fictitious status of the (currently existing) state of emergency to be indicated by its claim to be simultaneously inside and outside the juridical order (Agamben 'State' 294). The real state of exception, however, is that produced by 'pure or revolutionary violence, which has broken every relation to the law and is purely factual' (Agamben 'State' 294). In other words, Benjamin's account of the state of exception is shifted entirely *outside* the juridical order: the real state of exception is equated with 'civil war, pure violence with no relation to the law' (Agamben 'State' 294). Benjamin thus takes Schmitt to be presenting a fictitious version of the state of exception that does not ultimately break with the violence of law and the state.

For Agamben, the dispute between Schmitt and Benjamin therefore ultimately concerns a 'zone of anomie'—that which breaks with the *nomos* or law—that either must be integrated within law at any cost, via the fiction of the state of exception (Schmitt's sovereignty), or else must be kept free from any entanglement with law, ensuring the existence of violence outside the law (Benjamin's 'pure violence') ('State' 294). There are weighty metaphysical questions looming here, as Agamben observes, notably the question concerning the very meaning of the political and its metaphysical foundations: 'Why does the Western juridico-political order constitute itself through a contention over a legal vacuum in exactly the same way as Western metaphysics presents itself as a struggle over pure being?' ('State' 294). Western metaphysics and politics are both defined by a struggle over a void, a struggle for *anomie*; this is the fundamental lesson of the Benjamin-Schmitt dispute, and the inspiration for Agamben's own philosophical reflections on sovereignty and bare life.

Agamben's complex reading of the relationship between Benjamin and Schmitt calls for at least a couple of critical remarks. In Agamben's reading, Benjamin's real state of exception does not really refer to the possibility of revolutionary transformation; rather it enters into a 'zone of indistinction' with Schmitt's account of sovereignty such that sovereign power, lawless violence, and revolutionary anarchism are rendered indistinguishable. What is striking here is Agamben's elision of Benjamin's explicit conclusion, namely that the real state of exception is concerned with the struggle of (Benjamin's messianically inflected) Marxism against really existing fascism. The implication of Agamben's reading of this passage is thus to assimilate—by way of the 'zone of indistinction' analysis—Benjamin's account of pure violence to the Schmittian account of sovereignty.

Leaving the validity of this gesture to one side, it is worth reiterating that Agamben's reading of the Benjamin-Schmitt dispute repeats, from a different perspective, Derrida's elision of the Marxist dimensions of Benjamin's thesis on the real versus the false state of exception. Whatever other ambiguities remain, Benjamin clearly alludes to a revolutionary response to the conservative revolutionaries: to communism—albeit in Benjamin's peculiarly Marxist-messianic-anarchistic sense—as the actual or authentic 'state of exception' that would redeem historical suffering, and thus transfigure the wreckage of historical 'progress'. Such a real state of exception would come into being, for example, during an actual instance of the proletarian general strike as distinct from the general political strike. Here we might reflect a little further on the relationship between law-positing and law-preserving violence; these may well be mutually contaminating, as Derrida suggests, but this does not mean that the distinction between general and proletarian political strikes therefore collapses, as Derrida concludes.[12] For the means by which both strikes proceed, as I discussed above, are profoundly at odds; the former unfolds by means of an extortionate demand within the prevailing framework of law and state, the latter manifests via suspending the violence of law and of the state in favour of an anarchic transformation of work 'beyond the law'. Benjamin's actual state of exception would be this 'impossible' suspension of law and the state, a moment of revolutionary 'pure violence' that would found a new form of community 'beyond the law'.

Both Agamben and Derrida, however, elide the anarcho-Marxist dimensions of Benjamin's response to Schmitt, either by assimilating Benjamin's idiosyncratic concept of revolutionary violence to the Schmittian concept of sovereignty, or else by enveloping the Benjamin critique of violence within the 'two temptations of deconstruction'. Derrida's haste to emphasise Benjamin's proximity to fascism rather than his intimation of communism suggests a kind of interpretative violence that is troubled by Benjamin's anarcho-revolutionary politics, however ambiguous and undecidable that politics may well be. Derrida's deconstructive reading of the differential contamination between law-making and law-preserving violence evacuates Benjamin's critique of violence of its Marxist dimensions in favour of emphasising its undecidable theological aspects (gesturing towards the aporia of 'divine' or sovereign violence). On the other hand, in Agamben's reading of the 'Critique of Violence' and the relevant theses in 'On the Concept of History,' Benjamin's critique of Schmitt is assimilated to a dispute that ultimately concerns the possibility and nature of sovereignty. Ben-

12. I owe this point to Jessica Whyte, personal email communication, September 7, 2006.

jamin's references to the actual state of exception, the revolutionary transformation of law and of the state, are thus elided in favour of a discourse on
sovereignty and the violence it exerts over bare life; a move that effectively casts Benjaminian communism and really existing fascism into a perni-
cious 'zone of indistinction'. Both Derrida and Agamben can therefore be
criticised for engaging in a certain interpretative violence towards the more
enigmatic aspects of Benjamin's political thought in the 'Critique of Violence'—his revolutionary (messianic) utopianism.

By way of conclusion, we might recall Benjamin's famous parable, in
'On the Concept of History,' describing a chess automaton ('historical materialism') that can easily win the game of historical fate so long as it enlists the
services of theology, a wizened hunchback, who is small and ugly and must
be kept out of sight (*GS* I·2: 693; *Illuminations* 251). In different ways, Derrida
and Agamben unjustly invert Benjamin's fascinating image of the relationship between Marxism and theology. It is the theology of the text and the
undecidability of sovereignty that together play the winning game of chess,
while 'historical materialism', having lost the game of historical fate, is now
the wizened hunchback who must remain hidden out of sight.[13]

---

13. Benjamin's chess-playing automaton is mentioned briefly in a footnote in *Specters of
Marx* (180–1). Although Derrida aligns the deconstruction of history and politics with Benjamin's '*weak* messianic power'(*Specters* 181), he once again underplays the Marxist dimension of Benjamin's destructive appropriation of the past, the way that historical materialism should 'blast open the continuum of history'. See Benjamin (*GS* I·2: 701; *Illuminations*
254).

5

Graves, Pits and Murderous Plots: Walter Benjamin, Alois Riegl, and the German Mourning Play's Dreary Tone of Intrigue

Joel Morris

A BIT OF BAROQUE INTRIGUE

The reader of Walter Benjamin's description of baroque drama in his *Origin of the German Mourning Play* (*Ursprung des deutschen Trauerspiels*) will quickly find that he who is sovereign has never had it easy—onstage or off. At least not in the 17th century. Perhaps this is because in the case of the sovereign there was not much to differentiate the dramatic stage from the stage of history. The word *Trauerspiel*, Benjamin writes, was not only a descriptive term for a genre of 17th century baroque dramas or martyr plays, but could equally describe historic events where the sovereign, the prime exponent of history, almost serves as history's embodiment ('*Der Souverän als erster Exponent der Geschichte ist nahe daran für ihre Verkörperung zu gelten.*') (*GS* I·1: 243; *Origin* 62).[1] As the principle actor on history's stage, the sovereign himself would be called upon as a poet of sorts. Above all others, he could write his own *Trauerspiele*, what Benjamin calls an adaptation of the theatrical and the historical 'setting' (itself a theatrical term: *Szenerie*) into bombastic stage-works, however lacking in nuance such endeavours may have been. Martin Optiz even claimed that a young Julius Caesar took a turn at his own *Oedipus* (*GS* I·1: 244; *Origin* 64).

To be sure, the 17th century was not known for the tragic works of its princes. The dramatists of the time nevertheless conceived of the monarch's role in the *Trauerspiel* as the representative of history; a history completely

---

1. For the English translation of Benjamin's text, I have referred to John Osborne's translation of *The Origin of the German Tragic Drama*. In several cases I have modified the English translation to some degree; any deficiencies in the modifications are my own.

emptied of eschatology. A Counter-Reformation reaction which denied religious fulfillment to the individual, secular solutions were instead imposed
to the question of man's redemption, driving the period's theatrical forms
into ever-greater exaggerated tensions between immanence and transcendence. To compensate, the sovereign was a figure of extremes, his incarna-
tions as martyr and tyrant—the 'Janus faces' of the monarch (*GS* I·1: 249;
Origin 69)—became a detailed study in the legalities of baroque princedoms.
Threatened at any moment with catastrophes, not least of which his own
downfall, in the dramas the tyrant was represented as the holder of the
dictatorial power of decision. However, ultimate decision-making authority was not the sovereign's alone. Presented with the opportunity to enact
his commanding power, he proves himself indecisive. On the baroque stage,
Benjamin writes, political events were put through the 'painstaking analysis of the calculations of political intrigue'. Its politics regulated by plotting
machinations, 'Baroque drama knows no other historical activity than the
corrupt energy of schemers' (*GS* I·1: 267; *Origin* 88). That is, in the German
mourning play, the sovereign's was a court of dreary intrigue.

Along with the tyrant and martyr, the intriguer emerges. As courtier, as
court-advisor, it is the intriguer who is able to utilise a certain confusion of
the court and the monarch's executive power to further his own political designs. Thus he comes to control the play. In a crucial moment of his explication of the intriguer Benjamin writes:

> In all circumstances it was necessary for the intriguer to assume a domi-
> nant position in the economy of the drama. For according to the theory
> of Scaliger, which in this respect harmonized with the interests of the ba-
> roque and was accepted by it, the real purpose of the drama was to com-
> municate knowledge of the life of the soul [*die Kenntnis des Seelenlebens*], in
> the observation of which the intriguer is without equal. (*Origin* 98–9).[2]

In the intriguer's dominant position as the crucial observer of the actions on stage, he embodies an amalgamation of differing forms of cultural
and scientific mastery, from that of the organiser of the plot, the choreographer, calculator, politico, and, later in the *Trauerspiel* book, the melancholic
contemplator. An observer of the 'life of the soul', the intriguer possesses the
mastery of political gears ('*die Beherrschung des politischen Getriebes*'). He is impassioned by an anthropological and physiological knowledge which is manifest
and continues its course in the resulting dramatic confusion (*Verwirrung*)—a
terminus technicus typically characterising the German mourning play (*GS* I·1:
274; *Origin* 95). In particular, it is the intriguer's anthropological knowledge

---

2. 'Unter allen Umständen mußte der Intrigant eine beherrschende Stelle in der Ökono-
mie des Dramas einnehmen. Denn die Kenntnis des Seelenlebens, in dessen Beobachtung
er allen andern es zuvortut, mitzuteilen, war nach der Theorie des Scaliger, die hier mit
dem Interesse des Barock sich wohl vertrug und hierin Geltung behauptete, der eigentliche Zweck des Dramas' (*GS* I·1: 277).

that is important because it enables him to calculate human motivation and translate it into a Machiavellian science of politics reliant on the understanding of human emotion as its political apparatus. For this reason, human affects (*'die menschlichen Affekte'*) as a calculable, driving mechanism become 'the last piece [*das letzte Stück*] in the inventory of knowledge which had to transform the dynamism of world-history into political knowledge' (*GS* I·1: 274; *Origin* 96) and leads to a 'play of the organic life of human beings,' spatially oriented, staged in the *Trauerspiel* as a political intervention. In the calculation of organic life, it is the intriguer who is able to both observe and to communicate emotion through political action. The calculating intriguer, Benjamin remarks, is entirely intellect and will ('[*d*]*er überlegne Intrigant ist ganz Verstand und Wille'*) (*GS* I·1: 274; *Origin* 95).

Benjamin's consideration of Scaliger's theory of action and emotion underscores how the intriguer's knowledge, combined with his observations of the soul's interior life manifest in dramatic gesture, becomes a means of prescient calculation. Noting the insignificance of Aristotle's influence on their dramatic theories, Benjamin says that it was the baroque dramatists who looked to the classical influence of Scaliger's poetics for a means to emphasize the visible manifestation of affects (*Affekte*). Privileged over action or will, which had been, since Aristotle, the primary drive of dramatic plot, human affects would be the means of insight towards the knowledge of the life of the soul, and their staging would result in a necessary tendency toward dramatic, affective exaggeration.

In order to depict this exaggeration, brought about through the rising conflict between will and affect (or sentiment—*Empfindung*—Benjamin uses the words interchangeably) in the baroque's appropriation of Scaliger, Benjamin then cites another methodological influence for his critique, an influence that is not an example of political or poetic theory, but rather an art historical study that touches the dramatic, namely the Viennese art historian Alois Riegl's *Entstehung der Barockkunst in Rom* (*Emergence of Baroque Art in Rome*). 'Sentiment and will,' Benjamin writes in his example, 'lie not only in the plastic appearance of the baroque human norm in conflict [*Menschennorm im Streite*], as Riegl has so beautifully shown in the antagonism [*Zwiespalt*] between the attitude of the head and the body in the figures of Giuliano and Night of the Medici tombs, but also in their dramatic appearance' (*Origin* 99).[3] Riegl's evaluation of the development of baroque art through its architecture, sculpture and painting is fitting for what Benjamin wishes to demonstrate: the heightened, exaggerated will of the intriguer is both formed and countered by the increasing opposition of sentiment, a conflict that aris-

---

3. 'Empfindung und Wille liegen nicht nur in der plastischen Erscheinung der baroken Menschennorm im Streite—wie Riegl das so schön am Zwiespalt zwischen Haupt- und Körperhaltung bei dem Giuliano und der Nacht der Mediceergräber zeigt—sondern auch in ihrer dramatischen.' (*GS* I·1: 277)

es in the emergence of the baroque arts. With reference to Riegl's evaluation of the Medici tombs, then, the question of will in its relation to sensibility or sentiment (again, *Empfindung*) and also the specific relation of the plastic arts will become crucial for Benjamin in understanding the intriguer's political will as a relation of the viewers to the stage.

RIEGL'S TERM

The influence of Alois Riegl's work on Walter Benjamin, if relatively unexplored, is nevertheless rather well known. Riegl's observations regarding previously neglected, marginalised artworks, and his conception of *Kunstwollen* especially, have been important in particular in understanding Benjamin's early methodological strategies. Indeed Benjamin, in his essay 'Books that Remain Vital' ('Bücher, die lebendig geblieben sind'), called Riegl's seminal work *Die Spätrömische Kunstindustrie* (*The Late Roman Art Industry*) one of the four most significant books of German scholarship of the time. It is here, and in a later book on the Dutch group portrait, that Riegl is most systematic in laying out his thinking of the *Kunstwollen*, essentially a comprehensive, linear development of art historical stages, although as a theory or doctrine (as Benjamin calls it), 'artistic volition' or 'art will' remains to a large extent as enigmatic, if as 'critically suggestive', to use Michael Podro's phrase, as it was to Riegl's contemporaries.[4]

Benjamin, for his part, sees in the *Kunstwollen* the possibility of a generation realising and completing the work of the potential, if incomplete, work of its predecessor. In his 'Epistemo-Critical Prologue' to the *Trauerspiel* book, Benjamin makes explicit Riegl's importance: 'Art's highest reality is the isolated, completed [*abgeschlossenes*] work. But at times the self-contained work [*das runde Werk*] is reachable solely by the epigone. Those are the times of the 'decline' [*des Verfalls*] of the arts, of their 'will.' For this reason *Riegl discovered this term*, precisely in the final art of the Roman Empire' (*Origin* 99; my emphasis).[5] This conception may ignore Riegl's general impartiality towards any one art historical period that provided works of art that were not 'self-contained' themselves, awaiting the epigone so that they might achieve their 'highest reality'. But Benjamin is not only concerned with the *Wollen* as a methodological concept.[6] Benjamin's concern is also specifically with this

---

4. See Podro 96–7. For a more detailed account of the term's history and reception than can be worked through here, see Michael Gubser's *Time's Visible Surface*, especially 154–63.

5. 'Das höchste Wirkliche der Kunst ist isoliertes, abgeschlossenes Werk. Zu Zeiten aber bleibt das runde Werk allein dem Epigonen erreichbar. Das sind die Zeiten des "Verfalls" der Künste, ihres "Wollens". Darum entdeckte Riegl diesen Terminus gerad an der letzten Kunst des Römerreiches.' (*GS* I·1: 235)

6. This is not to diminish the importance Benjamin saw in Riegl in establishing a methodology. See also Benjamin's 1928 'Curriculum Vitae (III)':

term, a terminus that is at once terminological, a study in terms, and also a means of crucial orientation within the book on the baroque *Trauerspiel*. Orientation, that is, not merely as a citation of terms, though it is certainly that as well—the citation of Riegl's ideas giving a methodological groundwork for Benjamin's own study—but the term/terminus as a crucial spatial-temporal designation resulting in the *discovery* of a specific point of decline, the *terminus* of a *Verfall*. It is for this reason—more literally: around there, around this (*darum*)—that Riegl discovered this *term*.

As collection of lectures developed in the 1890s, published after Riegl's death and co-edited by his former student Max Dvořák, *Die Entstehung der Barockkunst in Rom* has remained for the most part overlooked both for its contribution to Riegl scholarship in general and to Benjamin's use of it in his habilitation thesis on the *Trauerspiel*. It seems, however, that if he chose the specific citation of Riegl's posthumously published lectures—a citation that appears almost as a passing remark—it is because Benjamin's concern is not only one of terminologies, but one deeply imbedded in Riegl's discovery. It is this terminus, shown by Riegl in the baroque plastic arts, that Benjamin finds so crucial to understanding the dramatic work, one that will have implications in determining the course of highest concern for the baroque mourning play: that of the singular life of the individual faced with the total secularisation of history. Further, the potential of the term *Wollen* to understand the antagonism of affect brought about by an increased *Wille* is

---

Just as Benedetto Croce opened the way to the individual concrete work of art by destroying the doctrine [*Lehre*] of artistic form, I have thus far directed my efforts at opening a path to the work of art by destroying the doctrine of the territorial character of art. What our approaches have in common is a programmatic attempt to bring about a process of integration in scholarship [*Wissenschaft*]—one that will increasingly dismantle the rigid partitions between the disciplines that typified the concept of the sciences [*Wissenschaftsbegriff*] in the 19th century—and to promote this through an analysis of the work of art. Such an analysis would regard the work of art as an integral expression of the religious, metaphysical, political, and economic tendencies of its age, unconstrained in any way by territorial concepts. This task, one that I have already undertaken on a larger scale in *Ursprung des deutschen Trauerspiels*, was linked on the one hand to the methodological ideas of Alois Riegl, in his doctrine of the *Kunstwollen* [*in seiner Lehre vom Kunstwollen*], and on the other hand to the contemporary work done by Carl Schmitt, who in his analysis of political phenomena has made a similar attempt to integrate phenomena whose apparent territorial distinctness is an illusion. (*GS* VI: 218–9; *SW* 2: 78, translation modified).

An insightful article tracing much of Riegl's influence on Benjamin, contrasted in part with Benjamin's great disappointment in the art critic Heinrich Wölfflin, is Thomas Levin's 'Walter Benjamin and the Theory of Art History'. The second half of Levin's discussion concentrates on Benjamin's 'Rigorous Study of Art' essay and its rejection by the *Frankfurter Zeitung* for the essay's perceived 'critique of the dangers of Wölfflinian formalism' as a 'categorical dismissal' of Wölfflin's work—a perception heightened by the editors' apparent lack of familiarity with Riegl's work (see esp. 81–2). Michael Jennings, in his book *Dialectical Images*, also emphasises the connections of Riegl's work to the *terminology* of some of Benjamin's early essays.

for Benjamin nowhere more explicit than in the study on the Medici tomb. For Benjamin the appropriation of Riegl's thought in the *Kunstwollen* is foremost in its significance as a term, and one that is in fact a *terminus ad quem* of the *Trauerspiel*. Thus, understanding Riegl's term, *Wollen*, as the terminus of an historical period of decline, *Verfall*, and citing the specific example of the Medici tomb, Benjamin underscores not only the increasing conflict between sentiment/sensibility and will, but also the strict immanence of the German mourning play. The stage is populated with corpses and ghostly apparitions. Because it is in the earthly portrayal of a history deprived of eschatology where the representation of emotional states vis-à-vis the intriguer's machinations are specifically set, the corpse and its location in the tomb demonstrates more fully the play of intrigue Benjamin sees unfolded on the baroque stage. Though the increased conflict of will and sentiment, the baroque stage is the space where the dark intrigue of murderous calculations is enacted and, at the same time, it is the potential terminal space of those calculations: the grave.

It is at this point, then, in referencing Riegl's study of the Medici tombs— and the fact that the study is of tombs I believe helps to account for this example—that Benjamin wishes to point out a precise instantiation of the increasing conflict between will and sentiment at the very moment when baroque art emerges. In these posthumously published notes, Riegl makes the case for Michelangelo, apart from his significant position in the Renaissance, as the 'Father of the Baroque',[7] maintaining that the artist experienced a stylistic turn (*Stilwandel*) between 1521 and 1524, precisely when he was working on the project of the Medici graves (*'denn da entstand der Entwurf für die Mediceergräber und die Laurenziana'*) (*EBK* 32). The section Benjamin cites in particular begins with Riegl's description of Michelangelo's work on the Giuliano burial tomb (*Grabmal*). Riegl writes:

> Here, at the Giuliano burial tomb 1. the architecture is removed: only three figures are there with the sarcophagus, and 2. these figures do not stand in a plane, but are divided within the space into two planes: the sarcophagus with the [two naked figures, the feminine Night and the masculine Day] forward and the wall alcove with the interred in the back. Thus the insertion of depth in the place of the absolute plane. (*EBK* 34)[8]

---

7. 'Im allgemeinen wird er zur Renaissance gezählt: Als Vater des Barockstiles gilt er überhaupt seit jeher eigentlich nur auf dem Gebiete der Architektur, und auf diesem Gebiete ist er hauptsächlich erst nach 1520 tätig gewesen mit Ausnahme der Entwürfe für diese Fassade von S. Lorenzo' (Riegl, *Entstehung der Barockkunst in Rom* 31; hereafter referred to as *EBK*).

8. 'Hier, am Grabmal des Giuliano, ist 1. die Architektur beseitigt: nur drei Figuren mit dem Sarkophag sind da, 2. diese Figuren stehen nicht in einer Ebene, sondern auf zwei Plänen im Tiefraum verteilt: vorne der Sarkophag mit Nacht und Tag [zwei nackte Figuren, eine weibliche und eine männliche, genannt Nacht und Tag (*EBK* 33)], etwas zurück

As Benjamin remarks in his citation in the *Trauerspiel* book, it is in the sculpted figures of Day and Night themselves, presented in the framework of the tomb, that there remains a crucial contradiction. The symmetry of the figures is 'strikingly moving, marked with an inner restlessness' (*'auffall-end beweglich, von einer inneren Unruhe durchzitiert'*) (*EBK* 35). This is because the figures are inverted, 'the Night appears to emerge forward from behind, the Day to remove itself to the back' (*EBK* 35),[9] giving the impression of rotation (*'Eindruck des Rotierens'*) where the parts of the figure are in movement, and yet do not stir the whole (*'ohne daß das Ganze sich vom Flecke rührt'*) (*EBK* 35). In conveying this effect there is a further heightening of contradictions: the simultaneous expression of the whole at rest while its parts are in motion. In this way, Riegl determines, perception is referred to the psychological, the emotional interior, while the composition itself refers to the physical.

Such oppositions are oriented towards the viewer, as Riegl notes in the sculpted figure of the entombed, Giuliani himself. The viewer is placed in a position where the effect of the sculpture's action, the will, is most visible: 'the will entirely evinces [the figure's] deportment, which is directed toward the beholder ... The will controls the limbs, thus the will is directed at the beholder' (*EBK* 36).[10] Yet what is striking in this orientation of the *Wille* in the figure of Giuliani is the appearance of an internal, psychological feeling that is revealed to the beholder in a glance that betrays the action of the will. This subtle glance is conveyed precisely in a *sinking* of the head that betrays the inner *Empfindung* despite the physical expression of the *Wille*:

> The almost angry face with wrinkled brow reveals that this will is broken, disturbed by sentiment. But not by a physical sentiment, an outer, sensible perception, for then it would be clearly and sharply seen. Rather it is through an inner, psychical sentiment [*Empfindung*], for the head is slightly *sunken* [*gesenkt*]. Thus here is a conflict: sentiment appears in contradiction to the will.[11] (*EBK* 36; my emphasis)

It is in this glance that the beholder of the tomb can read out what sentiment might otherwise remain concealed. This is a decisive stroke for baroque art,

die Wandnische mit der Figur des Bestatteten. Also Einführung des Tiefraumes an Stelle der absoluten Ebene.'

9. '[D]ie Nacht scheint von hinten hervorzukommen, der Tag nach hinten hinein zu entfernen.'

10. 'Seine Haltung im ganzen bekundet den Willen, sich dem Beschauer direct zuzuwenden ... Die Glieder lenkt der Wille, also der Wille ist auf eine Wendung nach dem Beschauer hin gerichtet.'

11. 'Das fast zürnende Antlitz mit gerunzelter Stirn verrät, daß dieser Wille jäh durchbrochen, gestört worden ist durch eine Empfindung. Aber nicht durch eine physische Empfindung, eine äußere, sinnliche Wahrnehmung, denn dann würde er klar und scharf ausblicken, sondern durch eine innere, psychische Empfindung, denn der Kopf ist etwas gesenkt und auch die Augenbrauen sind gesenkt. Also hier ein Konflikt: die Empfindung tritt in Gegensatz zum Willen.'

one that establishes a relation between the artwork and its onlooker.

While he does not explicate this here, we may turn to the seminal later work of his *Dutch Group Portrait* from 1902 to see that for Riegl the evaluation of the beholder as a psychological element in relation to the work of art had new implications for art theory in the late 19th century. There the problem of an artwork's autonomy from a relation to the beholder comes to fruition, as Riegl's attention to the conflicts of planar and spatial unity and the relationship of the beholder to that space (as he developed in the *Spätrömische Kunstindustrie*) come to the fore in the figures present in Dutch group portraiture. For Riegl it is there, as Margaret Olin has noted, that 'the gaze was a vehicle for a condition he termed "external coherence" ['*äußere Einheit*'], or the unification of the work of art with the beholder' (Olin 156–7). Though we must distinguish the relation of the viewer to Dutch painting from the example in Riegl's papers on baroque art, we can understand in part the psychological implications for Riegl's relation of the beholder in his later work. The face of the figure in the Medici tomb is intended to invite the look of the beholder into a unity; the beholder is linked with the sculpture in a reciprocal gaze of observation. As we see in the example above, in the tomb it is precisely in the motion of the sinking head, of the eyebrows sinking, that direct this invitation to look toward the figure's interior. What this sinking suggests is not the clear revelation of inner emotion through extreme physical pain, as examples from antiquity imply (we may think here of the famous sculpture of Laokoon); rather, according to Riegl, it is a clearly stressed inner affectation that comes outward, from the depths of the soul ('*aus den Tiefen der Seele*' *EBK* 38) which is in conflict with the figure's will, and therefore must be read out of it, in the sinking of the head. Further, for Riegl, the conflict between *Wille* and *Empfindung* in these early baroque examples is presented corporeally as a unified but nevertheless diverse movement involving not only the relations of the head and body of the plastic figure to the beholder, but of both the figure and the beholder's relations to the surroundings, that is, the grave and sarcophagus of which they are at once both a part and separate. It is in the baroque specifically that this *Empfindung* increasingly finds its new, psychological power. As Riegl says, what is new is that 'sentiment now emancipates itself in its struggle with the will. The physical in human beings divides itself; until now the material body had ruled two sides harmoniously: will and sentiment under the hegemony of the will; now however each seeks to seize power exclusively' (*EBK* 36–7).[12]

---

12. 'Das neue ist, daß nun die Empfindung sich emanzipiert, in Kampf tritt mit dem Willen. Das Psychische im Menschen spaltet sich; bisher haben beide Seiten—Wille und Empfindung—den materiellen Körper einträchtig beherrscht, unter Hegemonie des Willens; jetzt sucht jede die Herrschaft ausschließlich an sich zu reißen. Da aber der Wille früher der Herrschende war, so ist das eigentlich Neue die Steigerung der Empfindung. Die Empfindung will sich emanzipieren, um so schärfer reagiert darauf der Wille: beide

Riegl's example of Michelangelo's sculptures, with their reliance on the observer to convey *Empfindung* in its contradictory relation to *Wille*, demonstrates the connection of the body to physical space Benjamin analyses in the *Trauerspiel*. The representation of increasing reciprocal counteractions between *Wille* and *Empfindung* results in, and is made possible by, exaggerated extremes of traditional forms. In this exaggeration, whose effect Riegl describes as '*übermenschlich*', the figures strike the viewer as demonic. Specifically, the figures touch us demonically with their fractious willpower ('*sie berühren uns dämonisch mit ihrer unbändigen Willenskraft*') (*EBK* 37). It is in this sense that Benjamin also addresses a demonic effect in the intriguer. In his calculating capacity (as, for instance, '*einen Ehr-vergessenden Hof-Heuchler und Mord-stifftenden Ohrenbläser*'), the intriguer's power and will, Benjamin writes, are 'intensified to demonic proportions' ('*ins Dämonische gesteigert...*') (*GS* I·1: 276; *Origin* 97–8). The infernal intriguer balances a 'strict inner discipline and unscrupulous exterior action', his calculations always at play between the two. Having two faces—this combination of practiced faithfulness as a subject and diabolical aspirations—is in fact what Benjamin says 'awakens the mood of mourning [*Trauer*] in the creature stripped of all naïve impulses' (*GS* I·1: 276; *Origin* 98).

THE EXPONENT OF THE SHOWPLACE

German dramas, Benjamin says, could not account for such a dichotomy. Two figures were required to embody the courtier's two faces: one as intriguer and another as faithful servant. But in his explication of the intriguer's will as intensified to demonic proportions, most telling may be Benjamin's description of the intriguer as the 'exponent of the showplace' in calling Lohenstein's intriguer Rusthan, 'an honor-forgetting court hypocrite and murder-inciting ear-blower'. John Osborn's translation of Benjamin's 'Exponent des Schauplatzes' as 'representative of the setting' elides this significant word. From the Latin *ponere*, to set or to place, the exponent is literally one who 'sets outward'. We can see why Benjamin would not wish to limit the meaning to one of being representative. Like the sovereign, whom Benjamin calls the 'exponent of history', the intriguer as the exponent of the drama also serves as its embodiment. But the intriguer is an exponent in the word's double sense: not only representative of the place upon which the show/sight is directed, but also, and at the very same time, one who observes and expounds—one who directs the show by placing it outside itself. The intriguer is at once the play's audience, its beholder, and at the same time its choreographer. In this sense, the figure of the intriguer is not only intrinsic to

---

werden gesteigert. In dem Maße aber, als sich die Empfindung steigert, steigert sich auch der Wille. Daher das übermenschlich Große in der Charakteristik, die Michelangelo seinen Gestalten gibt.'

the play—the plotter or *Ohrenbläser* as merely a type of stage property—but he is also the figure through which the play and its material properties are mediated as a *Schauplatz*. Benjamin writes that the *Trauerspiel* 'has to be understood from the beholder's point of view' ('*das Trauerspiel [ist] vom Beschauer aus zu verstehen*'). The *Beschauer* 'experiences how on the stage—an interior space of feeling that bears no relation to the cosmos—situations are compellingly set before him' ('*Er erfährt, wie auf der Bühne, einem zum Kosmos ganz beziehungslosen Innenraume des Gefühls, Situationen ihm eindringlich vorgestellt werden*') (*GS* I·1: 299; *Origin* 119). We can understand this also through the figure of the intriguer. As an extreme manifestation of the *Beschauer*, it is not strictly the audience, the assembly watching the play, but the intriguer who holds the crucial position of viewership. As the *ex*-ponent of the play, the one who places outward, the movement '*vom* Beschauer *aus*' is the manner in which the interior world of feeling is to be understood, but also applied as demonic, willful design in the intriguer's political machinations. If the heightened will, through *Empfindung*, touches the audience as demonic, it is in this increased demonic display that the intriguer is the *Beschauer* par excellence. In this sense, the spectacle, the *Schauplatz* or *Schaustellung*, is to be understood *through* its beholder. But the phrase '*vom Beschauer aus*' not only describes the essential mediating ground of the drama's audience. It recognizes that the beholder, too, is a *Schauplatz*, a redirection of the show through his act of expounding. The position of beholder himself calls for observation, calls for that same penetrating look of the exponent that will extract and expound the inner life of the soul.

Further, the stage for the interior place of feeling that bears no relation to the cosmos is specifically that of the baroque court, or *Hof*. And this court, Benjamin says, is the innermost stage or showplace ('[*d*]*enn der Hof ist der innerste Schauplatz*') (*GS* I·1: 271; *Origin* 92). If, as Benjamin notes, history wanders onto the stage in the baroque drama, ('[*d*]*ie Geschichte wandert in den Schauplatz hinein*'), then it is the court, *der Hof*, in particular wherein the image of the showplace becomes the key to historical understanding ('*Das Bild des Schauplatzes, genau: des Hofes, wird Schlüssel des historischen Verstehns*') (*GS* I·1: 271; *Origin* 92). Extending this to its logical extreme, we can add to this the *Friedhof* or *Kirchhof*—the cemetery—as a key to historical understanding in the spatial manifestation of an eschatology that has been emptied of its significance, precisely because it is the baroque's staging of a history that seeks to counter the difficulties of the Reformation's promise of eschatological redemption by setting its scene, its *Schaustellung*, at the terminus of individual life: in the grave.[13] For Benjamin, this is precisely why the *Schauplatz* is the

---

13. Benjamin begins the final section on allegory ('Die Leiche als Emblem') with a citation from Lohenstein, which specifically locates the 'Kirch-Hof', as the site of the decaying human body, and its fragmentation, where its meaning can be read (*GS* I·1: 390; *Origin* 215).

terminus, its complete secularisation the *last word* of the historical unfolding of the *Trauerspiel*: '*restlose Säkularisierung des Historischen im Schöpfungsstande hat in der Weltflucht des Barock das letzte Wort*' (*GS* I·1: 271; *Origin* 92).

The determination of the baroque mourning play's *Schauplatz* as the manifestation of a non-eschatological end of the singular life of the individual is significant. While Benjamin describes the baroque Counter-Reformation's attempt to undo the paradox of individual salvation—the uncertain eschatological destiny of redemption based on the Reformation's principle of 'faith alone'—it is the *Trauerspiel* that 'immures itself entirely in the disconsolation of the earthly condition' ('vergräbt *das deutsche Trauerspiel sich ganz in die Trostlosigkeit der irdischen Verfassung*') (my emphasis). And while this 'move away from eschatology characterizes spiritual plays in all of Europe,' it is 'the senseless flight [*besinnungslose Flucht*] into unredeemed nature' that is 'specifically German' (*GS* I·1: 260; *Origin* 81). This has importance for history's representation on the stage, as Samuel Weber notes:

> Since 'history', under the antinomian impact of the Reformation, comes to be understood as the rush of an unredeemed 'nature' or 'immanence' toward an end emptied of significance, or at least rendered totally opaque, the only hope available to the baroque is to attempt to stem this forward tide by creating a space that, by virtue of its very inauthenticity, might slow if not abolish the irresistible pull toward a catastrophic *terminus*. This inauthentic locale is construed as a theatrical stage, a showplace, a *Schauplatz*. ('Storming' 173; my emphasis)

It is only here, on the historical stage set as a presentation of a sealed, interior space of emotional states, that uncontainable outside forces can be so compellingly exposed. Such forces become most essentially and intrinsically formulated in the *Schauplatz* as both a place of the intriguer's calculations and a possible grave. It is not surprising that Benjamin's brief discussion of the intrigue's gloomy tone ('*den düstern Ton der Intrige*') (*GS* I·1: 276; *Origin* 97)[14] in the German *Trauerspiel* consists of citations invoking murder-inciters and dens, or pits, of murderers, as in the quote from Gryphius: 'What is the court henceforth but a pit of murderers' ('*Was ist der hof nunmehr als eine mördergruben*') (*GS* I·1: 276; *Origin* 97). It is important to call attention to Benjamin's citation of Gryphius' play *Leo Armenius* for its combination of *Mörder* and *Grube*. The implication is that of the combination of the intriguer's calculations and the physical space of plotting and death without an eschatological end. Thus the court as *Grube*, with its associative and etymological ties to *Grab* (grave, tomb), is not only a den or pit in which the murderer contemplates and plots, but it is also the manifestation of where such plotting leads, with the sepulchral monument that holds the promise of restoring a non-escha-

---

14. It is worth noting here the significance of the adjective *düster* that is lost in English translation; it is not only 'gloomy', but dark, grim, dismal, morbid, dreary, saturnine, and sepulchral.

tological timelessness.[15] This element of the *Trauerspiel* is its essential condition. In Benjamin's vocabulary, the *Trauerspiel* is buried, *vergräbt*, immured in
the disconsolation of worldly character in its most intrinsically earthly place.
Under the condition of an eschatology that has failed, disappeared, is literally a 'fall-out' (*Ausfall*) (*GS* I·1: 259–60; *Origin* 81), the *Trauerspiel* does not direct itself heavenward, but burrows further in its earthly disconsolateness.
And it is in this burrowing, this *Vergraben*, where history enters the stage both
as and *at* the gravesite. As the melancholic contemplator, we can understand
the figure of the intriguer in the Trauerspiel with a curious German word,
as a *Grübler*, a word that holds significant implications for the combination
of the 'grave' to 'plotting' or 'contemplation', combined in the verb *grübeln*.
The intriguer is the quintessential *Grübler*, with all its literal and metaphorical resonance.[16]

---

15. While it must remain outside the range of this limited study, I find it important to
note that in the section 'Die Leiche als Emblem' ('The Corpse as Emblem'), Benjamin's
discussion focuses on allegorical relations of the body as corpse, specifically that 'the characters of the *Trauerspiel* die, because it is only thus, as *corpses*, that they can enter into the
homeland of allegory. It is not for the sake of immortality that they meet their end, but for
the sake of the *corpse*' ('*die Personen des Trauerspiels sterben, weil sie nur so, als* Leichen, *in die alle-
gorische Heimat eingehn. Nicht um der Unsterblichkeit willen, um der* Leiche *willen gehn sie zur Grun-
de*') (*GS* I·1: 391–2; *Origin* 217–8; my emphasis).

16. Though he does not specifically call the intriguer a *Grübler*, Benjamin does reflect on
the word in different contexts, especially several years after the completion of the *Ursprung
des deutschen Trauerspiels*, in his work on Baudelaire in *The Arcades Project*:
Was den Grübler vom Denker grundsätzlich unterscheidet ist, daß er nicht einer Sache allein sondern seinem Sinnen über sie nachsinnt. Der Fall des Grüblers ist der des Mannes,
der die Lösung des großen Problems schon gehabt, sie sodann aber vergessen hat. Und
nun grübelt er, nicht sowohl über die Sache als über sein vergangnes Nachsinnen über sie.
Das Denken des Grüblers steht also im Zeichen der Erinnerung. Grübler und Allegoriker
sind aus *einem* Holz. ([J79a,1]; see also [J80,2; J80a,1]; *GS* V·1: 465, 466)
Further, in Benjamin's brief discussion of the animal in Kafka's story 'Der Bau' in his 1934
essay 'Franz Kafka: Zur zehnten Wiederkehr seines Todestages', he writes: '*Sieht man das
Tier im "Bau" oder den "Riesenmaulwurf" nicht grübeln, wie man sie wühlen sieht? Und doch ist auf
der anderen Seite dieses Denken wiederum etwas sehr Zerfahrenes*' (*GS* II·2: 430).
Perhaps with its architectural undertones, a story like 'Der Bau' could be read in light of
Benjamin's comments on the presence of architecture with regards to reflection in Calderón:
Unbestreitbar allerdings bleibt, daß im XVII. Jahrhundert das deutsche Drama noch nicht
zur Entfaltung jenes kanonischen Kunstmittels gekommen ist, kraft dessen das romanti-
sche Drama von Calderon bis Tieck immer von neuem zu umrahmen und zu verkleinern
verstand: der Reflexion. Kommt die doch nicht allein in der romantischen Komödie als
eines ihrer vornehmsten Kunstmittel zur Geltung, sondern ebenso in ihrer sogenannten
Tragödie, dem Schicksalsdrama. Dem Drama Calderons vollends ist sie, was der gleich-
zeitigen Architektur die Volute. Ins Unendliche wiederholt sie sich selbst und ins Unab-
sehbare verkleinert sie den Kreis, den sie umschließt. Gleich wesentlich sind diese beiden
Seiten der Reflexion: die spielhafte Reduzierung des Wirklichen wie die Einführung einer reflexiven Unendlichkeit des Denkens in die geschloßne Endlichkeit eines profanen
Schicksalsraums. (*GS* I·1: 262)

With an image that recalls the sunken heads in Riegl's description of Michelangelo's Medici tomb, it is in the death's head of history that, for Benjamin, attests to the human being's subjection to a graceless state of sin that the observer must confront. 'Everything about history,' Benjamin writes, 'that from the very beginning has been untimely, sorrowful, unsuccessful, is expressed in a face—or rather in a death's head.'

> [I]t reveals not only the nature of human existence, but the biographic historicity of a singular human being in this, the figure of his most natural decline [*naturverfallensten*], now meaningful as an enigmatic question [*Rätselfrage*]. This is the core of the allegorical observation, the baroque, worldly exposition of the history and the world's tale of suffering [*Leidensgeschichte*]; it is only meaningful in the stations of its decline [*nur in den Stationes ihres Verfalls*]. The more significance, the more decline to death [*Todverfallenheit*], because death digs in [*eingräbt*] the jagged line of demarcation between phusis and significance deepest of all. (*GS* I·1: 343; *Origin* 166)

Indeed, if for Benjamin the knowledge of the life of the soul ('*Kenntnis des Seelenlebens*') was the actual purpose of the drama ('*der eigentliche Zweck des Dramas*'), then the grave is the essential showplace for the consideration and exposition of that knowledge. In the death's head of history, the *facies hippocratica*, as well as in the interred corpse, the beholder may see not only the physical manifestations of the very place the intrigue leads, the culminating end of creaturely existence, but also the spatial realm where the conflict between the will and sensibility may be presented and preserved as the conflict of the history of the world in its decline. For this reason, Benjamin's statement that 'history wanders onto the stage' of the *Trauerspiel* must keep in mind the stage's spatial mediation as a *Schauplatz* or 'showplace' that, as Samuel Weber says, is necessarily a 'place delimited and constituted essentially by those who witness it as an audience and as spectators, as onlookers' ('Storming' 173). The *Trauerspiel* is indeed in every sense '*vom Beschauer aus zu verstehen*'. It is in the power of political knowledge through calculated observation linked to both the scene of history and the body as corpse where such an exposition may finally be staged as both its *terminus a quo*, as a pit of murderers, and its *terminus ad quem*, as a grave.

THE SHOWPLACE-WITHIN-THE-SHOWPLACE: *HAMLET*

If the great German dramatists of the baroque were Lutherans, the denial of miracles and the dependence on 'faith alone', according to Benjamin, made the 'secular-political sphere a testing ground for a life which was only indirectly religious'. It was a grave emptied of significance. And, while there may have been, nevertheless, 'a strict sense of obedience to duty', in the great men 'it produced melancholy [*Trübsinn*]' (*GS* I·1: 317; *Origin* 138). The synthesis of the consideration of *Schaustellung* or *Schauplatz* and the termini of the plotting intriguer in the baroque's dramatic representation is nowhere more evident than in what Benjamin calls one of the greatest of the *Trauerspiele*: *Hamlet.* The Danish prince and Wittenberg student who is also a saturnine *Grübler,* Hamlet is the figure in which melancholy points to the Christian providence of redemption; redemption that the German *Trauerspiel* was never able to accomplish. For Hamlet alone, Benjamin says, is the beholder of the *Trauerspiel* by God's graces ('*Hamlet allein ist für das Trauerspiel Zuschauer von Gottes Gnaden*') (*GS* I·1: 334–5; *Origin* 158), and it is only in him that the melancholy immersion, or *sinking,* may return to a redeemed nature, for it comes to Christianity ('*Nur in diesem Prinzen kommt die melancholische* Versenkung *zur Christlichkeit*') (*GS* I·1: 335; *Origin* 158; my emphasis).

Faced with the emergency of the usurpation of the throne by his uncle Claudius, in Shakespeare's play this prince finds himself in the role of intriguer. His mind is inconstant, indecisive, saturnine, the effects of which grow into a scene of treacherous plotting. There is no more revealing moment that when Hamlet plays the chorus at the staging of his own play-within-in-the-play, 'The Mouse-Trap'. In just a few lines we see the relation of the *ex*-ponent to the *Schaustellung* that Benjamin works through in his study of the German mourning play. Watching his play-within-the-play, Hamlet explicitly sets the show of death outside itself, as the reenactment of murder. We need only observe the interaction of Hamlet and Ophelia just as the 'The Mouse-Trap' begins:

> [*Enter* Lucianus.]
>
> *HAMLET.* This is one Lucianus, nephew to the king.
> *OPHELIA.* You are as good as a chorus, my lord.
> *HAMLET.* I could interpret between you and your lord, if I could see the puppets   dallying. (3.2.244–47)

In this brief exchange we may understand more fully the significance of the Hamlet as *Beschauer*. As good as a chorus, he plays a range of roles: he is an interpreter in the sense of mediation, but also in terms of intrigue; he offers to interpret between Ophelia and her lord exactly as he is doing with the play 'The Mouse-Trap' as a *Schaustellung,* setting the scene. Yet he is also an audience member, just as Ophelia and Claudius are. An observer of the play-*outside*-the-play, Hamlet scrutinises the betrayal of sensibilities of the other audience members, Claudius especially, who themselves become players, the very 'puppets dallying' he scorns Ophelia to see. And Hamlet's exchange with Ophelia occurs at precisely the point where the player in the role of Lucianus enters the stage before them. Lucianus, nephew to the player king of 'The Mouse-Trap', is the staged intriguer and murderer, the exponent who, in the act of pouring the poison into the ear of the player king, has been plotted by Hamlet to expose Claudius' hidden *Empfindungen*. At this point in the play, Hamlet's increased will to assess whether revenge is deserved mirrors Benjamin's comment—with reference to Riegl's observations on the Medici tombs—that in the conflict between ever-intensifying will matched by intensifying feeling, the will becomes more and more broken, especially, Benjamin says, in the figure of the tyrant; that is, the tyrant as intriguer: 'In the course of his action his will is increasingly undermined by his sensibility: and he ends in madness' ('*Sein Wille wird im Verlauf der Entwicklung von der Empfindung mehr und mehr gebrochen: zuletzt tritt der Wahnsinn ein*') (*GS* I·1: 277; *Origin* 99). Though not a tyrant, the conflict appears just as well in Hamlet, whose observations demand ever-new plots to expose the king, eventually leading him into madness, however plotting or authentic it may be.

To his remark about interpreting between Ophelia and her lord, if he could 'see the puppets dallying,' the increasingly confused Ophelia responds to Hamlet: 'You are keen, my lord, you are keen' (248). Keen, that is, not only for his sharply ribald remark about the 'puppets dallying', but sharp in his observation. The sharpness of his perception is a penetrating gesture, a stabbing into the body of the observed, murder as observation and as calculation. To this comment on sharpness comes the reply:

> *HAMLET.* It would cost you a groaning to take off mine edge.
> *OPHELIA.* Still better, and worse. (249–51)

The direct link of the intriguer to the grave deepens further in Hamlet's next keen remark to Ophelia: 'It would cost you a groaning to take off mine edge'. The edge of his keenness can only be satisfied in death—the penetration of the body—a groaning extracted by a keen edge, complicated by its sexual implications. In her enigmatic reply to Hamlet's threat, Ophelia's 'Still better, and worse' summarily defines the beholder's relation to the scene. Ophelia, audience to Hamlet's calculating incisiveness, is witness to the conflict, the will battling increasing sentiment to the point of exaggerated, demonic gesture that Riegl and Benjamin articulate, and further into what she can only conceive of as the prince's madness. Finally, observed by Hamlet as audience to his play, Ophelia is at the same time audience to Hamlet's intrigue and the threatened victim of his murderous plot. It is precisely when the demonic touches the beholder that the beholder becomes aware of the violent conflict in which she participates. Hamlet, the exponent of the play, threatens Ophelia with the grave he is plotting. She may only reply, 'Still better, and worse.' Hamlet, for his part, is all the more keen—both sharp and clever—his performance all the better, his intensification towards demonic madness all the worse. It is at this moment that Hamlet is torn between the play of his life and action and that of the play he is watching, the lines of which blur dramatically when he at last turns from Ophelia in order to address Lucianus, calling on the player-murderer to set the scene so that

Hamlet's own act of murderous revenge may begin:

> *HAMLET.* It would cost you a groaning to take off mine edge.
> *OPHELIA.* Still better, and worse.
> *HAMLET.* So you mistake your husbands. Begin murtherer, leave thy
> damnable faces and begin. Come, the croaking raven doth bellow for
> revenge. (249–54)

Hamlet directs the play in every sense, calling on Lucianus to penetrate the body of the player king and thereby reveal the plot that would enable him to act against Claudius. And it is here, in this dark staging of intrigue, that the combination of the *Mördergrube*, the *Grabmal* and the *Schauplatz* predict the deathly terminus of Hamlet's plot.

6

Benjamin's Critique of Aesthetic Autonomy

George Markus

In 1928 in his *Curriculum Vitae* Benjamin described the programmatic tendency of his writings as aiming 'at opening a path to the work of art by destroying the doctrine of the territorial character of art'(*GS* VI: 218–9; *SW* 2: 78). *Gebietscharacter*—the character of a well-defined, at least relatively independent domain with its own laws or norms. A year later he defined the task of the critic as 'to lift *the mask of "pure art"*' (*GS* VI: 164; *SW* 2: 292). Always a radical thinker, Benjamin also drew the ultimate consequences from this critical idea: all attempts to make some distinction of principle between advertisement and art are inevitable fruitless and cannot but fail.

This rejection of the idea of the autonomy of art, even in that relative sense that most Marxist writings conceded, is one of the significant differences between the mature views of Benjamin and those of Adorno, the two thinkers whose legacy largely determines the tradition of critical theory for us. Their relationship certainly had the character of an elective affinity, of deep underlying concords and no less significant discords. They shared a fundamental and quite idiosyncratic premise, a particular understanding of the willed future that provided both of them with an ultimate critical standard to judge the phenomena of the present and the past. In this respect they both combined some fundamental elements of the Marxist idea of socialism with the Romantic conception of an ultimate reconciliation between man and nature beyond all utilitarian practices. No collective home for men if their world is treated as the mere collection of manipulable objects; no liquidation of the exploitation of human beings by other humans without overcoming the exploitation of nature by men. This shared conviction created between them a strong bond, in spite of all the mutual irritations that at times characterised their personal relations.

They fundamentally disagreed, however, in their understanding of the ground that so dangerously blocks the realisation of this utopia in the present, despite its material conditions being—as they both believed—at hand. This was a question that no radical thinker in the thirties could avoid. In what way do the conditions of life in late capitalism produce this effect of a 'drainage' of radical energies? In this respect their views not only differed, in a sense they were opposed to each other.

For Adorno the fundamental danger of contemporaneity consisted of the liquidation of the achieved level of *individual autonomy* that tends to undermine the core of human subjectivity. The socially 'infantilised' individuals of the contemporary world who have lost the ability to think and act on their own cannot in principle form authentic collectivities. In their insecurity, anxiety and impotence they are driven to identify themselves with the impersonal mechanisms of exchange and domination which acquire for them the character of fictive and reified communities. In this situation critical thou

ght should aim at 'the fortification of the subject', relying upon those residues of the Ego that no reification and manipulation can destroy. A society of genuinely autonomous individuals is, of course, only possible as a society of collective solidarity. However, in the contemporary world of universal heteronomy solidarity can take only anamnetic forms: the recollection of all the past and present victims of the civilisatory progress.

Benjamin, on the other hand, located the ultimate danger brought about by capitalist modernity in the progressing dissolution of all forms of *community*. This constituted the ground of his alliance with Brecht, though for Benjamin this process could not be reduced to the overt social phenomena of antagonistic competitiveness and ensuing atomisation alone. For him its most destructive aspect resided in the dissolution of the communal framework of experience itself, the regression of its conditions to the level of unconsciousness. *Erfahrung*, experience, organised by the social cadres of memory, by the interpenetration of the private and the public that endowed the course of life with a transmissible sense, is disappearing. It disintegrates: on the one hand, into *Erlebnis*, a disjointed series of incommunicable, inward events that are felt to be lived through as bearers of enigmatic, private meanings, and, on the other hand, into objective *information*, intersubjectively understandable and verifiable, but without any direct connection to the concerns of the individuals. As Freud indicated, under these conditions the decisive, usually traumatic events of life become repressed, retreating into the realm of involuntary memory, unretrievable by conscious effort and finding expression only in dreams. Similarly, Benjamin argues, the decisive, future-directed contents of collective consciousness also retreat into the unconscious, appearing only as dreams. However, the dreams of a collective do not simply exist in the form of shared mental contents. 'The situation of consciousness

... need only be transferred from the individual to the collective. Of course, much that is external to the former is internal to the latter: architecture, fashion—yes, even the weather—are, in the interior of the collective, what the sensoria of organs, the feeling of sickness or health, are inside the individual (*AP* K1,5). Collective dream images, expressing the longing of the masses for the life of genuine community, exist in objectified form. They are primarily manifested in such afunctional, seemingly only ornamental features that still attach themselves—as trivia and debris—to the objects of the world of calculative utility. Certainly, as long as these images remain unconscious, they cannot be retrieved by the individuals concerned, and are manipulable by those in power. They serve only the ends of a false, pacifying re-enchantment. If, however, even these remnants of the collective character of experience were to disappear, this would mean the catastrophic end of history: the complete loss of intersubjective understanding and of the capacity to live in the world as one's own home. In this situation the critical intentions of intellectuals can be effective only if they contribute to one end: *awakening*. That is, to make conscious these latent dream-contents, thus to render manifest the hidden signs of a radically different future in the present and its past. For only in such a way can intellectuals promote the process in which the masses take possession of their own dream, an end that only their own political action can realise.

This disagreement found a sharp expression in their respective understanding of, and attitude towards, the fundamental characteristic of artistic modernity—the *autonomy of art*. For Adorno it was the radical afunctionality of the works of art that conferred upon them the capacity to embody and articulate resistance against the contemporary world of universal exchange, in which nothing is valuable in itself. Autonomy is art's 'sign of freedom'. He, of course, fully realised the historical connection between autonomisation of art and the process of commodification. But in a good Hegelian manner he regarded autonomy as the realisation of the *telos* of artistic development, the transformation of what art always was, and aimed at transforming the 'in-itself' into the 'for-itself'. He considered it therefore 'irrevocable', and regarded all attempts to 're-function' art, whatever their political motives may be, as actually undermining its critical potential.

Benjamin, on the other hand, had an unambiguously negative attitude to the idea of autonomy, the consistent realisation of which could only result in the loss of all significance of art. He had a positive interest in those avant-garde movements that only aim to dismantle: Russian constructivism, Dada, Surrealism and, of course, Brecht's epic theatre. The obverse of this attitude is his pronouncedly negative relation to Expressionism and Neue Sachlichkeit, in spite of the Leftist commitment of some of their best known representatives, since they try to conserve the illusory claim of art to the 'extraterritorial' status of autonomy. However, the full weight of his rejection of autonomy can best be apprehended—paradoxically—from his great essays on the seminal figures of artistic modernism, of the high art of literature: Baudelaire, Proust and Kafka. For in all these cases Benjamin posits an intimate connection between their achievements and the relation of their works to the autonomy of art.

Baudelaire's is the case of successfully challenging this autonomy within autonomous art itself. He, the founding figure of modernism, was also the first to fully realise the disastrous consequences of having to create lyric poetry in a society that no longer has any mission and commission for poets—in a world where artworks are just commodities. He reacted to this situation with the destruction of the aura of his own poetry. The destructive rage that underlies the whole of *Fleurs du mal* is directed not least against an artwork offering the illusion of self-standing, harmonious totality. His allegoric imagination finds expression in the brutal transposition of intimate subjective experiences into not merely the prosaic, but frequently sordid, inorganic objects and happenings of the everyday. His poetry does not aim to manifest the hidden riches of the creative subjectivity, it gives expression to the '[h]ollowing out of the inner life' (*AP* J67a,5). This is one of the greatest achievements of his work: it makes the reader confront his self-alienation and simultaneously armours him against the reified world.

The significance of Kafka's oeuvre is, on the other hand, grounded in the necessary failure of his deepest intentions, in their unrealisability in those forms that the art of modernity offers to a writer. Kafka's novels and stories unfold as parables, but this unfolding does not mean that they bring forth a practical lesson—they unfold only in the sense of ripening into a concreteness that becomes ever more impenetrable. 'He did fail in his grandiose attempt to convert poetry into teachings, to turn it into a parable ...' (*GS* II·2: 427; *SW* 2: 808) This failure, however, did not befall him—it was intentional: '... he took all conceivable precautions against the interpretation of his writings' (*GS* II·2: 422; *SW* 2: 804). He wrote parables that offer no counsel, because they are novels whose heroes are perplexed (*ratlos*), problematic individuals. This *Ratlosigkeit*, however, is not presented by him as the outcome of their character and the circumstances of their life. It is (as in a parable) the state of everyman, the situation of the world, and therefore also of art. For the ultimate roots of Kafka's willed fiasco are not aesthetic. Its foundation is the survival of the pre-historical swamp world under the façade of a modernity that never overcame but merely repressed it. This is a world more archaic than even that of the myth. In it there were neither norms orienting conduct nor communications making self- and mutual understanding possible. In our world there seems to be a plethora of both. We have laws—but they are secret, unknown and unknowable by their subjects. What is so unknown is, of course, their abiding meaning which would give them validity. And this meaning cannot be disclosed in any form of communication, in-

cluding the arts. Thus if the latter is not to be complicit in such a state of affairs, it can disclose only this impossibility—and succeeding, it fails the aesthetic canon of art.

Benjamin's rejection of the idea of aesthetic autonomy was in a sense
rooted in a deep-seated personal aversion to all that this ideal implies and
this found a particularly robust expression in his discussion of *Proust*. Proust
was his favourite author. Proust's struggle to remember what was forgotten
in the moment it happened, since it never was truly experienced, for Benjamin both exemplifies, and in an exemplary way reacts to, the situation of
the writer in modernity. In a synthetic way the *Recherche* succeeds in restoring the extinguished capacity of experience as *Erfahrung*. Its significance lies
partly in giving 'some idea of the effort it took to restore the figure of the storyteller to the current generation' (*GS* I·2: 611; *SW* 4: 316). When, however,
it comes to the aesthetic success of this effort, Benjamin finds it disconcert-
ing. Proust's work seems to defy all the aesthetic norms of its genre: it is an
amorphous and episodistically disjointed novel, constantly alternating between heterogenous modes of representation. Nevertheless at the very end
Proust succeeds in endowing it with a closure, rendering it in a radical sense
autonomous: self-standing and self-referential. *Le Temps retrouvé* ends with the
'narrator's' decision to write the novel that the reader is just finishing reading. The ending makes the work, in Proust's words, a 'dogmatic whole'. It
thus becomes for him the embodiment of the power that art solely possesses:
to bring happiness of a 'non-egotistic type' to those readers, who through it
become able to read themselves. Now Benjamin's attitude to these claims,
which not only constitute the structuring principle of the whole but also provide the key to some of its most significant episodes (for example, the death
of Bergotte), is ironically contemptuous. They are for him loquacious reflections centring on the assumed hermetic aspect of art. 'He [i.e. Proust] writes
about the origin and intentions of his work with a fluency and an urbanity
that would befit a refined amateur.' (*GS* I·2: 639; *SW* 4: 353)

While Benjamin's rejection of the claim to the autonomy of art orients
his whole approach to culture, the grounds for this attitude are less clear, at
least in the sense that the considerations invoked by him do not seem to be
easily reconcilable.

On the one hand, he characterises the autonomy of art as a mere semblance, an ideological illusion. It mystifies art, since it abstracts from art's
social construction. It veils the fact that art by necessity stands 'in the most
intimate connection with didactical, informational, political elements', the
elimination of which would be synonymous with art's 'most frightful decay'
(*GS* I·3: 1049). Simultaneously it covers up the most elemental fact about the
art of modernity—that artworks today are *commodities* and this defines their
way of existence. The idea of autonomy not only suppresses but also provides
spurious justification for this fact. It transfigures the essentially passive atti-

tude of the consumer into the 'higher' contemplation of the recipient. With this justificatory function it serves as 'a breeding ground for asocial behavior' (*GS* I·2: 502; *SW* 4: 267) for the bourgeoisie.

At the same time, however, Benjamin often treats the autonomy of art as something real, as a *transient historical reality*, defining the social situation of modern art, which is, however, undermined today by objective processes of change. This reality is essentially that of a *loss*, the loss of any settled social function. This loss, however, is not merely an absence but is reinforced by cultural and institutional means, thereby acquiring the appearance of a gain (the freedom of art). It is stabilised first of all by those processes that destroyed the effective, community-building traditions, replacing them with the fetishistic notion of culture as the treasure house of the eternally valuable cultural goods. This transformation was accompanied by the simultaneous elaboration of a complex of ideas (creativity, novelty, beauty, etc.), systematised and justified by the new discipline of aesthetics. They claimed to offer immanent standards for the evaluation of works of art that also conferred upon them a higher, 'spiritual' significance, removed from practical life. Ultimately, under the pressure of accelerating technical and social changes, artworks became transformed into objects of a secular cult, a religion of art, for which the doctrine of *l'art pour l'art* provided a defensive theology.

These processes of change are, however, irresistible. While the development of the techniques for reproduction plays the most direct role in the ever-deepening crisis of aesthetic art, this is merely a constituent of more fundamental transformations in man's practical relation to the world. The resulting crisis has already reached the point of no return. Benjamin wrote in 1930, 'the time for aesthetics in every sense… is gone forever' (*GS* VI: 164; *SW* 2: 292). Around this time he comprehended this demise of autonomous art in a radical way. It refers not only to changes in the function of artworks and the corresponding alterations in their internal structure, but goes beyond the so conceived idea of refunctioning. The essays of this period often imply the progressive disappearance, or at least diminishing significance, of whole domains of artistic practice. In this sense he writes not only about the crisis of the novel but also that of the book which 'in this traditional form is nearing its end' (*GS* IV·1: 102; *SW* 1: 456). For this fundamental form of literary objectivation, combining a universal claim with the actual address directed at the solitary reader no longer satisfies the demands raised by the 'literarisation' of the conditions of life. These are more adequately met by forms with real mass appeal allowing the combination of the scriptural and the graphical: leaflets, brochures and placards.

From 1934 onward, however, this self-confident radicalism, relegating the aesthetic approach to art to the past, gives way to its perception as a very much present *danger*. The historical-political causes of this change are self-evident. It is, however, also connected with now situating the phenomena of

aesthetisation within a broader context. It is now seen as a general tendency observable in various areas of life under conditions of commodity production. Benjamin is one the first theorists who provided an analysis of the
aesthetisation of everyday life in modernity. In accordance with his principle to
disclose the positive in the negative itself, he underlined the hidden utopical
potential of this false aesthetic glitter, the dream-image of a radically different future concealed in fetishistic forms. This weak Messianistic power,
however, can only be made effective, if and when individuals in their mass
awakening from this secular form of mythical re-enchantment. For as wish
images merely projected upon the objects of commodity world in subjective
experience, this aesthetisation only channels utopian energies into a service,
merely perpetuating the hell of the present. It is then at this point that the
further progress of aesthetisation appears as a danger.

Under contemporary conditions the sole effective way to realise awakening is revolutionary *political action* by the masses themselves. This is the case,
not only in the sense that only such action can actually break with the catastrophic continuity of history, but also in the sense that only in the course
of such actions can an adequate collective consciousness first emerge. The
so conceived 'political' is the sole space where action creates its own self-un-
derstanding, simultaneously producing the solidaristic class as a collective
body, a new *physis*, and its adequate self-consciousness. It is the only way to
transform the amorphous, emotion-driven and reactive mass into the self-
organising class, actively pursuing the tasks determined by a collective relationship The mortal danger of Fascism arises from blocking this sole path
to awakening.

From the beginning Benjamin regarded the extension of the progressing aesthetisation of various spheres of life into the realm of the political itself as the specific and particularly dangerous characteristic of Fascism. In
1930 he had already characterised the Fascist glorification of war as 'an un-
inhibited translation of the principles of *l'art pour l'art* to war itself' (*GS* III:
240; *SW* 2: 314). As long as forces of the market restrict the peaceful employment of technology, war offers the sole space for the full utilisation of its potential. The dynamics of the productive forces under capitalism turns them
into forces of destruction, and war becomes the ultimate outlet of collective
self-affirmation, the consummation of the very principle of autonomy.

A collective, however, that can regard the possibility of mutual annihilation as the source of supreme aesthetic pleasure can only be an irrational
one. Total mobilisation for war cannot be achieved merely by means of propaganda. Fascism not only employs all the modern means of communication
to transmit messages *for* the masses. It makes the *masses themselves* the execu-
tor of its central message. This is the second aspect of the aesthetisation of
politics: the monumentalisation of the mass (cf. *GS* III: 488–9). Monumentalisation means both false aggrandisements of the mass as a fictive unity,

and its solidification *as mass* through ritualistic practices of self-presentation. Fully controlled manifestations of the mass in rallies, marches and sporting events serve to transform the mass into a spectacle, in which its members passively experience their assumed grandeur. This consolidation of the mass as mass that can only be set into motion externally and inhibits its loosening up which is the precondition of the formation of the active class in its womb. Politics becomes the realm in which the categories of idealist aesthetics find their consummation: the Führer is the creative genius capable of moulding the inert and amorphous human material into a unified totality. Mimesis, understood as mimicry, as strict adjustment to the faceless others and again becomes the means to transcend one's mere particularity and to raise one-self up to the realm of the *Volksgemeinschaft* etc. This strange affinity between political despotism at its most extreme but 'modernised' form and the ideas of aesthetic autonomy is not accidental. For although monumentalisation as a *stylistic* principle is alien to modernist art, while Fascism cannot tolerate any manifestation of artistic freedom, aestheticism itself is a particular form of monumentalisation, thereby offering a model for the extension of its principle. It transforms each great work of art into a self-standing monument, allegedly resisting all the ravages of time and demanding contemplative submission to its power from every individual.

Autonomy of art as an ideological illusion, as a transient historical reality whose time, however, has now passed, and as the model for processes of mythical re-enchantment that represent a mortal danger today—these are the diverse, perhaps even disjointed, justifications for Benjamin's rejection of this idea in general. They are, however, unified—although again not without constraints—by one of the central concepts of his late oeuvre, that of the *aura*.

This term first appears with Benjamin in early 1930, in the protocols of his experiments with hashish. He argued already with the 'theosophical' interpretation of such phenomena, conceiving it to be the extraordinary spiritual magic of rays emanating from some objects. Aura is rather an everyday phenomenon of perceiving a thing as enclosed by an 'ornamental halo' and any object can appear under particular conditions as auratic. It is, however, only in late 1931, in his first paper that systematically deals with the problem of 'technical reproducibility', his 'Little History of Photography', that he provides an explication of this term in its intended meaning—a formulation essentially repeated in the *Artwork* essay as well. 'What is aura, actually? A strange weave of space and time: the unique appearance or semblance of distance, no matter how close it may be.' (*GS* II·1: 378; *SW* 2: 518)

The so conceived aura is always predicated upon some object. It is, however, not an immanent quality of this object but a particular experiential relation of the subject to it, a form of its apperception. In auratic experience the object is endowed with paradoxical spatio-temporal characteristics.

Benjamin's formulation primarily articulates the spatial aspect involved, the perceived inapproachability of the auratised being in spite of its proximity. It does, however, equally refer to the antinomistic character of the temporality of such experiences. Such apprehension has the character of the singularity of a fleeting instant, the uniqueness of its *Now*, but this uniqueness exists in the grasp of the object as enduring beyond the passage of time. In auratic experience time itself comes to a standstill for a moment, it is the experience of the fulfilled present, the unity of momentariness and eternity.

It is in the *Artwork* essay that this conception of the aura is comprehensively elaborated—but only insofar as it is applied to traditional works of art. Their inapproachability finds its elemental and direct expression in the place which is considered the appropriate site for their exhibition: 'Do not touch' the museum commands the visitor. This normatively prescribed distance to the work is, however, not external to it. It is based upon the assumed radical singularity of the genuine artwork, its inexhaustible originality that discloses itself only in the contemplative surrender to it. It is this authenticity of the artwork that confers upon it an auratic spell as its authority. This authenticity of the work of art, the apprehension of which is restricted to the 'here and now' of direct contemplation, is at the same time the grasp of its atemporal significance and meaning. For the authenticity of the artwork, conceived as its irreplaceable uniqueness 'is identical to its embeddedness in the context of tradition' (*GS* I·2: 480; *SW* 4: 256), the tradition of 'culture' as the storehouse of eternal values. The aura of the work of art confers upon aesthetic experience, and through it upon the artwork itself, the paradoxical unity of irreplaceable uniqueness and atemporal permanence.

The auratic apprehension of the artwork as the hallmark of aesthetic experience is itself a constituent of a much broader, but historically specific, regime of perception. The auratic shell enveloping the artworks of tradition is the residue of the origin of art in *cultic-ritual* practices. What we today regard as artworks of long-gone eras or foreign archaic cultures were originally cultic objects whose sacred authority conferred upon them inapproachability by the uninitiated. Their aura had little to do with their aesthetic qualities. It depended upon their practical function in a ritual. The 'aesthetisation' of the artworks is the result of long drawn-out processes of basic changes in the way of life of human collectivities—it is a concomitant aspect of processes of secularisation, rationalisation and disenchantment, owing to which participation in ritual practices lost its ability to define social identities. Simultaneously, objects of the surrounding world lost their fixed meaning and became functional and disposable things. Works of art, enveloped by the halo of beautiful appearance, now became the auratic objects *sui generis*, their domain the last refuge of meanings not at our disposal. The sacredness of cultic objects has been replaced by the authenticity of works of art. Art became the vicar of the mythical-religious. It is this historicised conception of the aura that explicates the sense in which Benjamin regards the autonomy of art both as an illusion and also as a (transient) social reality. Autonomy, commonly understood as the freedom of artistic creativity, its essential independence from all external conditions, is a deceptive illusion. Artistic activities in modernity are always productions of some specific types of commodity. The artist may submit himself to or partially resist the demands of this segment of the market, but must always consider them as limiting conditions. Paradoxically, however, autonomy acquires an effective reality when the artwork is considered not in relation to its creation but to its *reception*. For in this respect it means the effectiveness of social norms defining the attitude of the recipient to the artwork posited as a kind of uniquely privileged object—a commodity not at the disposal of the consumer. Art is in fact autonomous, because one is institutionally demanded to treat works of art as singular embodiments of values, defined through the atemporal standards of aesthetics.

The very same processes, however, that resulted in the aesthetic auratisation of the work of art during their development inevitably lead to its shattering. The tendencies, earlier described by Benjamin as undermining the autonomy of art, more concretely appear to him as a process of *de-auratisation*. Among these tendencies the most decisive consists of the world-historical transformation of the practical relationship of humans to their material environment, the transition from the first to the second technology. In the 'Artwork' essay (Second Variant) Benjamin describes the differences between these two stages of evolution as fundamentally changing the orientation and aim of technology.

> Whereas the former made the maximum possible use of human beings, the latter reduces their use to the minimum. The achievements of the first technology might be said to culminate in human sacrifice; those of the second, in the remote-controlled aircraft which needs no human crew... The origin of the second technology lies at the point where, by an unconscious ruse, human beings first began to distance themselves from nature. It lies, in other words, in play. (*GS* VII·1: 359; *SW* 3: 107)

The realisation of the positive potential of the first technology is embodied for Benjamin in the figure of the artisan, which he characterises in *The Storyteller* with an apparent nostalgia. The traditional artisan was still embedded in the community, whose needs he serviced with his wares. His fluid, continuous activity was directed at the realisation of some meaningful and useful end. In comparison with him the individual actor of the second technology represents a figure of dehumanising alienation. Merely a member of the anonymous crowd of the city, he is without communal ties. His labour at the machine consists of the endless repetition of the same shock-like movements, determined by the objectified system of factory organisation and machinery. The end product of his work is beyond his purvey and control.

Nevertheless, Benjamin ascribes an emancipatory potential to this second technology. It is not an inorganic addition, when, in the midst of what seems to be a lament over the decline of the craft of storytelling and of craftsmanship in general, he makes a quite unexpected remark: 'And nothing would be more fatuous than to wish to see it as merely a "symptom of decay", let alone a "modern symptom" ' (GS II·2: 442; SW 3: 146). For it is the sway of the unquestioningly accepted tradition that integrated the artisan into his community and determined his activity. His skilful hand may have left the mark of his individuality upon the product, but only because he learned in practice to vary imperceptibly the traditional routines of fabrication, adapting them to the given singularity of the available materials and the requested end-product. It is the fixed meaning and the given particularity of the object that still determined the subject, kept him under its spell.

In comparison, second technology opens up revolutionary possibilities. '...[T]o describe the goal of the second technology as "mastery over nature" is highly questionable, since this implies viewing the second technology from the standpoint of the first. The first technology really sought to master nature, whereas the second aims rather at an interplay between nature and humanity.' (GS VII·1: 359; SW 3: 107) It not possible to reconstruct this technological utopia of Benjamin here. However, three points are clear. Firstly, such a technology creates a new subject: a collectivity that is rationally organised, whose activity is not restricted to the mere coordination of the habitual actions of the encompassed individuals. Capitalism can realise its full potential only in destruction that brings home the truth: a rational collectivity can only be organised by collective ratio. The perspective of awakening is that of the rational *self*-organisation of the new collective bodies, a post-organic teleology of human existence.

Secondly, this technology also imposes new demands upon the individuals constituting the collective body. It demands from them a new type of 'motor innervation' and 'the decisive refunctioning of the human apparatus of apperception' (GS I·3: 1049). Instead of being directed at the apprehension of the singularity of what is familiar, perceptual awareness now is characterised by a heightened attention ('the presence of mind') to the unexpected and the new, comprehended in their generalisable, repeatable traits.

Lastly, the dynamic character of this technology demands not simply new habits, but habituation to the formation of ever-new habits. This implies an experimenting attitude to the objects that shatters their stable meaning, which in the past regulated the means of utilising them. Benjamin does not regard this as a constituent of an exploitative relation to nature. Tearing natural objects out of the context of their fixed use also leaves the object free to react to the ever new conditions and thereby more fully disclose its nature. It actually creates a room for the inter-play of the subject and object as the promise of the second technology.

It is from this perspective that the phenomenon of aura is treated in the 'Artwork' essay. Second technology, even under capitalist conditions, strips all objects of pre-given meaning. What it destroys in this way is the power of tradition, fetishistically regarded as natural—it disenchants the world. Changing the means of human apperception, this creates an irresistible tendency to de-auratise. Art was the sole domain of practice that resisted this tendency. The auratic works of art presented, and to a degree still present, the last refuge of the cult. For the connection between the cultic-ritual and the artistic practices is not merely a genealogical one. Cult is the paradigmatic form in which an unchallengeable tradition can immobilise the meaning of an object, and thereby also the way it is to be handled. The auratic art of early modernity, co-existing with the emergence of the second technology, is the cult's last inheritor. It therefore provides a *model*, how the radical consequences of this fundamental change in practices can be kept within limits, making it harmless for the existing system of domination—a model of the *re-enchantment* of the world through its aesthetisation. Advertisement, fashion, display, the cult of novelty endow the world of commodities with an aesthetised lustre. This reconciles the individual-as-consumer with this world, offering a seeming re-assertion of his or her unique personality—by making the choices among mass produced commodities the affirmation of one's own taste. The aesthetisation of politics then makes the individuals as members of the monumentalised mass enjoy their own submissiveness through mass displays as the ultimate, total work of art. While within the realm of art itself aura crumbles under the impact of spontaneous processes of de-auratisation, its manipulative extension to everyday life and politics represents a danger capable of blocking the realisation of the radical consequences of second technology.

In the 'Artwork' essay the decay of the aura is ultimately presented in a positive light—the task of critical intellectuals, it seems, consists of fostering this spontaneously on-going process. However, in some of his other writings, Benjamin formulates a more complex relation to auratic experience. In them he indicates that de-auratisation ought not to mean the wholesale disappearance of all such relationships to objects. These ideas are most fully elaborated in his last paper on Baudelaire and his later notes in the Baudelaire section of *The Arcades Project*.

In his essay 'On Some Motifs in Baudelaire' Benjamin explicitly invokes the definition of aura as 'the unique appearance of distance'. The experience of inapproachability, however, partly receives a different interpretation. Benjamin now relates it to the incapacity of voluntary, discursive memory to access the data of *mémoire involuntaire*. Aura is then characterised as 'the associations which, at home in the *mémoire involuntaire*, seek to cluster around an object of perception' (*GS* I·2: 644; *SW* 4: 337), associations having the character of repressed wish images. This changes the very meaning of auratic distancing. '...The distant (*die Ferne*) is the land of wish-fulfilment' (*GS* I·3: 1178). This desire is internal to the very act of perception. 'Inherent in the gaze ... is the expectation that it will be returned by that on which it is bestowed. Where this expectation is met ... , there is an experience (*Erfahrung*) of the aura in all its fullness' (*GS* I·2: 646; *SW* 4: 338). The loss of aura in *this* sense, an unchecked de-auratisation of the world would therefore mean also its complete dehumanisation. A world in which even human eyes would not reciprocate our gaze but respond to our look with the glassy emptiness that in Baudelaire characterises the eyes of female satyrs and nymphs, such a world would be inhuman, even deadly. The allure of *sexus* could perhaps still be retained in such a world but *eros* would not even be concievable in it. It may allow the satisfaction of needs but would not know what is meant by desire. In *The Arcades Project* Benjamin formulates the consequences of such an unrestrained de-auratisation with particular force: 'The decline of the aura and the waning of the dream of a better nature—this latter conditioned on the defensive position in the class struggle—are one and the same. It follows that the decline of the aura and the decline of potency are also, at bottom, one' (*AP* J76,1—translation partly modified, G.M.).

Actually it is this positive aspect of the aura that also makes possible its transformation into a danger. For in a world in which the progress of technological rationalisation can be fully realised only in the growing effectiveness of wars of annihilation, auratic experiences, produced by re-enchantment, however manipulative they be, still respond to an inextinguishable desire. This is the human desire for a world that can be our home, and for a life possessing intrinsic meaning. Aura in its positive function is essentially the perceptual manifestation of those *correspondences*, the experience of which alone can offer the bliss of happiness that transcends the satisfaction of pre-given needs. This idea of correspondences (partly under the name of 'non-sensuous similarities') was central to Benjamin's early philosophy of language and to his conception of mimesis. To make such correspondences genuinely re-experienceable, this is, in his view, the great *positive* achievement of Baudelaire's poetry and of the novel of Proust.

In the Baudelaire essay Benjamin succeeds in bringing the negative and the positive aspects of aura—as the distance of inapproachability, on the one hand, and the reciprocating gaze of the perceived object, on the other—under a common formula that discloses the shared experiential structure underlying both these phenomena, evaluated as to their significance in radically opposed ways. 'Experience of the aura thus arises from the fact that a response characteristic of human relationships is transposed to the relationship between humans and inanimate or natural objects.' (*GS* I·2: 646; *SW* 4: 338) This formulation, on the one hand, directly refers to Marx's conception of fetishism as the 'personification of things'. Just as for Marx the fetishism

of commodities expresses the domination of the reified conditions of production over the labouring subject, auratic distancing for Benjamin expresses the domination of the reified tradition over the perceiving subject. With
Benjamin, however, the same formula covers also a radically different possibility: endowing the experienced object with the capacity to respond spontaneously to one's desires. This keeps alive the faith in the utopian possibility
of a better nature, a nature whose components became liberated 'from the
drudgery of being useful' (*AP* H3a,1). Aura in this sense provides us in the
present with the lived experience of a promise. It is the promise of a possible future, to which even the idea of a free interplay between the subject and
the object could no more be applied. In such a future of bliss there would be
a fully mimetic-communicative relation between man and nature and this
does not allow any strict distinction between the initiating role of the questioning subject and that of the autonomously reacting/answering object.

Benjamin's formula thus discloses the common structure of all auratic
experiences, whether of fetishistic-negative or of redeeming-positive character. It also makes clear that their opposed significance does not primarily depend on their intrinsic qualities as experiences, but rather on the way
they are integrated into the historical regimes of perception and social imagination. The second Baudelaire essay thus seems to bring his discourses
concerning the aura to a consummating synthesis. However, it also raises
questions about this very success. Is this attempt to unify the two opposed
meanings of the aura truly consistent? In particular, can one genuinely interconnect what Benjamin regards as the two aspects of Baudelaire's singular achievement? On the one hand he underlines the negative-destructive
character of this oeuvre, represented by the allegorical intention that perme-
ates the *Fleurs du mal*, destroying all intimacy with things and liquidating not
only the aura of the poet, but that of poetry in general. On the other hand,
he emphasises its celebratory aspect, retrieving those hidden correspondences that underlie the positive experience of the aura, assembling 'the days of
recollection into a spiritual year' (*GS* I·2: 641; *SW* 4: 335).

To this question Benjamin himself gives a clear answer. These two aspects are not truly connected—*not in Baudelaire*.

> The crucial basis of Baudelaire's production is the tension between an
> extremely heightened sensitivity and an extremely intense contempla-
> tion. This tension is reflected theoretically in the doctrine of *correspond-*
> *ances* and in the principle of allegory. Baudelaire never made the slight-
> est attempt to establish any sort of relations between these two forms of
> speculation, both of the greatest concern to him. (*GS* I·2: 674; *SW* 4: 177)

Benjamin himself, however, leaves no doubt that this is a limitation of
Baudelaire, for these two tendencies must and can be unified. 'If it is imagination that presents correspondences to the memory, it is thinking that con-

secrates allegories to it. Memory brings about the convergence of imagination and thought.' (*GS* I·2: 669; *SW* 4: 171)

This laconic formulation raises anew, however, the question of consistency. Is this faith of Benjamin, certainly underlying his whole late oeuvre,
itself coherent? Does memory figure in this formulation in the same sense?
To answer this question we need to pay closer attention to the central practical idea of his philosophy, the idea of awakening.

Benjamin, so it seems, assumes two different understandings of what is
involved in awakening as the practical condition of the realisation of a future that alone can save us from catastrophe. Awakening, on the one hand,
involves the actualisation of the full potential of the second technology, by
removing the barriers that capitalism imposes upon its utilisation. It implies
the creation of a new type of community—the rational community of human agents, self-organising, emancipated from the authority of dead tradition, freely accepting and following shared ends dictated by collective ratio,
and thus constituting a new *physis*, a new collective body. It means therefore
the consistent rationalisation and de-auratisation of the world that transforms also the relationship between humans and nature, creating an interplay between the subject and the object in which both retain their freedom.
The collective subject, through its interventions and experiments, freely poses rational questions to nature and the object freely reacts to, answers them,
according to its own nature.

On the other hand, however, there is another conception of awakening,
prima facie irreconcilable with the first. It refers to a transformation that
hardly can be effectuated by the intentional actions of the self-conscious
class. It requires some process able to actualise the repressed contents of the
collective unconscious that persist only in the individuals' involuntary memory. Awakening then brings these hidden shared contents of the unconscious
into the reach of awareness, transforming them into community building
new tradition. This is a tradition that does not command but redeems, redeems precisely that what never could have been part of culturally codified
traditions. It redeems the collective desires and wish-images, the forgotten
future in the past, reaching back to archaic times, of which the individuals
were and are aware only in the form of mute suffering and anxiety. Such an
act of re-collecting is, however, only possible because there are hidden correspondences between humans and nature, independent of all human intervention. Nature, whose cosmic processes produced us in our anthropological characteristics, cannot but also favour us. 'So there must be something
human in things which is *not* put there by labor' (*Br* 2: 849; *SW* 4: 413), writes
Benjamin in May 1940 in a letter to Adorno. This is attested on occasions in
the positive experiences of aura, which awakening makes a matter of collective experience. It re-auratises the world in an act of secular re-enchantment
as the ultimate emancipation from mythic fear.

These are certainly strikingly different conceptions. If Benjamin nevertheless draws them together, this is not an act of confusion—he is aware of their incompatibility. Nothing expresses this more clearly than that other fundamental idea of his philosophy which is most intimately related to the task of awakening, an idea that can only be formulated by an oxymoron: *profane illumination*. This necessarily raises the question concerning the meaning, the profane meaning of his Messianism—a problem which cannot be adequately treated as a mere appendix to some more specific issue, but neither can be avoided, since it fundamentally orients Benjamin's whole approach and his place within critical theory.

The hunchbacked dwarf of theology is always there to accompany Benjamin's commitment to Marxism with its determinist approach to history. And in this respect the formulation of the first thesis in his *On the Concept History* presents us with an unresolved ambiguity (see *GS* I·2: 691–704; *SW* 4: 389–400). Is this theology simply to serve historical materialism by throwing light upon the ultimate source on those revolutionary energies which keep this automaton in motion till its fulfils its function, realises its own end? Or is this Messianistic faith in redemption true guide, which alone is capable of defining this very end, actually directing the seemingly purely automated (i.e. strictly determined) movement of history toward a socialist future, the ultimate inevitability of which is assumed by many adherents of historical materialism? (This dilemma clearly parallels the indicated ambiguity in his conception of awakening.)

Benjamin does not in the text resolve this ambiguity, which is all the more disturbing since the two propositions seem to exclude each other: one cannot assert both. It is, however, just what Benjamin does, for in his understanding they are not incompatible at all, if related to their proper context, which immediately clarifies also the relation between them. For a redeemed future cannot arise without the conscious collective activity of the exploited class, driven to revolution first of all by the impossibility of satisfying its basic needs and elementary human interests under the present conditions of capitalism. It is this radical transformation of the second nature, that is, of the whole organisation and structure of social life, which alone would allow the development and realisation of the full positive potential of second technology, whose utilisation is both arrested or made to serve the ends of destruction by the forces of market and the drive for profit. Only the free social self-organisation of all producers can put an end to that exploiting attitude to nature which always brings with itself the danger that the ultimately untameable cosmic forces will destroy the possibility of human life on Earth. Only the intentional actions of the revolutionary class, realising the radical aim of social emancipation, creating a society that is nothing but the rational and free, self-governing collectivity of all producers as a new *physis*, only these can open an unlimited space for the genuine inter-play between such a collectivity, on the one hand, and autonomous nature, on the other.

There is, however, still something beyond this great emancipatory project and equally beyond that which the revolutionary class as a rationally and intentionally collective can do and achieve. A redeemed future can never be realised without our conscious collective efforts, but it still cannot be achieved by them alone, for no intentional human doings can make the Messiah come. Even the free inter-play between the collective body and nature, made possible only by the revolutionary transformation of society as our second nature, preserves the division between the initiating, questioning subject and the sovereignly responding nature. It still does not fulfil our deepest, unconsciously shared hope and desire: for the blissful life of happiness, in which all distinction between production and play disappeared. For only *play* allows the realisation of a mimetic-communicative relationship between all participants, not admitting any distinction between them concerning their functions and capacities. And only play is a deeply satisfying human activity, independent of considerations of any drudging utility. We humans as bodily individuals are beings with needs demanding satisfaction, just as we are productive beings. A redeemed future as a life of happiness presupposes a full correspondence between our needs, desires, intentions, productive ends and all those objective conditions—social, material and natural—surrounding us upon which our full satisfaction depends. This is possible only if there is a radical change in first nature, in the essential character of the relation between the bodily individual and the whole objective environment of its life. It presupposes a better nature, spontaneously coming to satisfy our deepest desires, not because we have somehow mastered it, but because it favours us. This alone can create such a correspondence between the capacities and desires of the individual and the objective conditions of his or her life, in which neither side can be conceived independently of the other, because they are constantly adjusting to each other in a playful mimesis. Only under such conditions can a future be conceived that not only satisfies all needs, but also offers the bliss of a fully meaningful life. The emancipatory transformation of second nature, which can only be realised through revolution as the intentional act of the conscious class, is the most fundamental precondition of such a future. It alone, however, cannot create such a state of bliss, nor can even guarantee its arrival. This ultimate transformation can only—this seems to be Benjamin's final conviction—happen to us as a favour of nature: the Messianistic fulfilment of our inextinguishable collective dream.

7

Framing Pictures, Transcending Marks: Walter Benjamin's 'Paintings, or Signs and Marks'

Andrew Benjamin

'Experience is the uniform and continuous multiplicity of knowledge.'

Walter Benjamin

OPENING

Initial access to Benjamin's early writings on painting is provided by a letter to Scholem written on the 22nd October 1917. Benjamin's letter was written in response to an earlier one in which Scholem outlined an approach to Cubism (Benjamin refers to the now lost letter as 'Ihren Brief über Kubismus'). For Scholem that approach was clearly intended to have greater extension (*Briefe* 388–96). Benjamin is responding to a philosophy of painting sketched by Scholem and which would generate an account of all specific types of painting. Scholem's formal analysis using notions of line, colour and their subsequent combination is insufficient for Benjamin. An insufficiency arising not just for formal reasons but because the elements that were given as an attempt to address art misunderstood the relationship between the internal world of painting and externality. The latter, externality, is described by Benjamin in the letter as the painting's 'sensuous object' (*sinnlichen Gegenstände*). Benjamin's response is to suggest that what is needed is to bring painting into the realm of language. Only then would it be possible to deal with particularity. The reference in the letter to language and thus to the primacy of the word is intended, as Benjamin makes clear, to evoke his early work on language.[1] However, it also opens another related path and that is to his doctoral dissertation on Romantic criticism, and thus to a different conception of the word, namely 'prose'. Another possible line to pursue therefore is the relationship between language and prose (*Sprache* and *Prosa*).[2] It is essential to hold the register of prose in place.

Evoking language and allowing that evocation to be thought of in terms of prose is to link art work to that which provides it with an essential part of its conditions of possibility, namely criticism. Criticism is one way of naming the relation between prose and art work. Naming—the act—which should be understood within this context as criticism, has a constituting power.[3] Rather than identifying the process merely as criticism, precisely because criticism will have a constituting power, it can be repositioned as 'becoming criticism'. Henceforth, criticism would no longer be there as an addition to art's work. On the contrary it is that through which the object becomes the work of art. What is intended by the expression 'becoming criticism' is twofold. Both aspects are related. In the first instance it identifies the object of criticism in terms of an ontology of potentiality. While criticism constitutes the work of art as art, the act of constitution involves pure potentiality. (It is precisely this aspect of the object that will re-emerge in terms of 'nameability' at a later stage.) A pure state that is explicable in terms of an infinite of potential. In relation to pure potentiality any one act of criticism—an act resulting in interpretation—is finitude. The second aspect emerges here precisely because there cannot be an identity, let alone a complementarity, between pure potentiality and finitude; the finite is itself to be understood therefore as continually becoming; in the sense of the continuity of interpretive acts, each one finite and therefore complete and yet present within a set up that is itself continuous.

Finitude—the act of interpretation—is the interruption of continuity. There is a further sense therefore in which finitude involves the continuity of the discontinuous. Precisely because what is named is at work—art work as an activity rather than an already determined object—the name then cannot just locate the work of art, as though art work was its explicable in terms of mere empirical presence. Were that to be the case then the work would be assumed to be no more than a simple static entity. Contrary to an insistence on stasis, the position that then emerges is that art work is consti-

---

1. The first major instance of that work is the paper, 'On Language as Such and on the Language of Man' (*GS* II·1: 140–57; *SW* 1: 62–74.) I have offered an interpretation of this paper in my *Philosophy's Literature*.

2. The following discussion of prose needs to be interpreted as an attempt to take up and the work through Benjamin's treatment of prose in 'The Concept of Criticism in German Romanticism' (*GS* I·1: 7–122; *SW* 1: 116–200 (in particular *GS* 100–109; *SW* 172–8). In sum, the argument is that prose (in the guise of criticism), rather than leading to the work's dissolution, is that which allows the art's work an afterlife.

3. I have developed aspects of this argument in my 'Literary Potential'.

tuted through a specific act of naming. Naming would no longer be the simple identification of the object. Rather naming occurs within and as part of becoming criticism. And yet, this act, precisely because of its differentiation from the medium that it constitutes, breaks art's possible hold on the idiosyncratic. In other words, though at this stage such a claim is no more than a conjecture, the inherently disjunctive relation between art and prose rather than leading to the work's undoing, is that which allows on the one hand a conjunctive dimension in which the art's work comes to be stated within and as prose, and yet on the other hand the disjunctive connection holds art's aleatory presence in play by refusing a coextensivity between media, thereby allowing art its articulation within that potentiality which occasions interpretation. (Interpretation as finitude.) Art remains—remains what it is in its relation of distance to prose—while simultaneously art comes to be what it is insofar as it allows for the introduction of prose. Moreover, the interplay of distance and relation forestalls the incursion of philosophical idealism by opening up a link between art and writing within which what is staged is art's coming to presence as art—a coming to presence realised within becoming criticism, as opposed to that presence having the Idea (or an Ideal) as its guarantor.

The structural presence of this form of distinction is evident in a range of Benjamin's early writings. In another context, in a short discussion of landscape, he argues that,

if a painter sits in front of a landscape and 'copies' it (as we say), the landscape itself does not occur in the picture; it could at best be described as the symbol of its artistic content. (*GS* VI: 36; *SW* I: 95)

For Benjamin, the use of the term symbol identifies the distinction between different 'conceptual realms'. What Benjamin is arguing for—and this is an argument which can be read as directed at Kant—is a distinction between what he calls 'natural experience' and the experience that is linked to knowledge. The former is the conception of experience that is developed by Kant in the *Critique of Pure Reason*, the conditions of possibility for which are established in the 'Transcendental Aesthetic'.[4] The first is a conception

4. Benjamin's relation to Kant raises a series of complex questions. Two paths need to be pursued. The first is Benjamin's explicit confrontation with Kant in a range of early papers. The second is to trace an implicit distancing of Kantianism through Benjamin's continual engagement with 'experience'. The allusion to Kant in this paper forms part of this second approach. In sum, the argument is that what the 'Transcendental Aesthetic' cannot take into consideration is the necessary historicity of experience and the complex subject positions that experience necessitates within modernity. The retention of Kantianism has to be understood as bound up the retained effective presence of immediacy. The critique both of Kantian aesthetic theory (as is evidenced, for example, in the conception of Beauty in *The Critique of Judgment*) and the 'transcendental aesthetic' in *The Critique of Pure Reason* forms a fundamental part of the development of a philosophy of art. The latter demanding a reconceptualisation of the ontology of art work as opposed to locating that

of experience that is articulated within a structure of immediacy, the latter
is one that ties knowledge to experience. Within in it form will always be
that which is becoming determinant, i.e. form as a process of forming rather
than an already established and determinant end result. As will be argued
the distinction between immediacy and forming, and thus the distancing of
immediacy that it occasions is necessary in order to give an account of affect
that is linked to knowledge as opposed to an account of affect that takes immediacy as its point of departure. (Here it should be added that if there is a
difference between the philosophical position that insists on the primacy of
art work and it is precisely this position that informs the approach taken in
this context to Walter Benjamin, and Benjamin's own then it resides in a resistance to the link on which Benjamin insists between art and epistemology.
In lieu of that link epistemology cedes its place to ontology. While there is a
concomitant repositioning of art—a repositioning in which there is a shift in
emphasis from meaning to art's workful character—the move to the ontological allows Benjamin's own claims about criticism to acquire a more appropriate philosophical expression.)

Prior to pursuing these possible openings it is essential to stay with Scholem's letter to Benjamin. On one level it would seem that Scholem's evocation of painting's constitutive elements—given in the three-fold division
noted above—would open up the possibility of rethinking the hold of generic determinations in favour of the object. The difficulty for Benjamin
is that the way this state of affairs is presented assumes an immediate correspondence between internality and externality. If there is a necessity for
mediacy then it does not lie simply in the impossibility of immediacy—after
all a certain version of the history of the symbol is comprised of such possibilities—on the contrary it lies in the way the object exits. In other words,
though to employ a language that is not Walter Benjamin's, and to relate it
to the methodological point made above, it lies in the relationship between
the ontology of the art object—in this instance painting—and its becoming
an object of experience. More is at stake therefore than the mere refusal of
the opposition between the inside and the outside.

Here, of course, it is not experience as end in itself, rather it is the experience demanded by art's work. Throughout Benjamin's writings the possibility of experience as such—in part a possibility that is the legacy of a re-
sidual Kantian epistemology whose critique, for Benjamin, is a necessary
point of departure—gives way to a complex relation in which Benjamin's
own reflections, initially on art and then on cultural objects in general, re-
works experience both in relation to the object as well as in terms of experience's historical possibility. Moving from a Kantian conception of possibility to one more centrally ground in Benjamin's work is not just to introduce

---

work within a subject's immediate experience of an object. (The latter comprises aesthetics par excellence.)

an historical sense of experience but also to recognise that such a possibility is inextricably bound up with a reconfiguration of the relationship between knowledge and its object. These concerns create the setting in which to turn to Benjamin's short though demanding text.

The paper in question, 'Über die Malerie oder Zeichen und Mal' ('Painting, or Signs and Marks') was written in 1917 (*GS* II·2: 603–7; *SW* I: 83–6).[5] While remaining unpublished during his lifetime it nonetheless provides an important point of focus for any treatment of Benjamin's overall concern with art.[6] Painting obviously re-emerges as a topic in the famous essay 'The Work of Art in the Age of its Technical Reproducibility'. In addition, there is a review of an exhibition of Chinese painting that was held in the Bibliotheque Nationale during Benjamin's stay in Paris (*GS* IV·1, 2: 601–5). While Benjamin's ostensible concerns were with the effects of photography, references to painting have a sustained presence. In the context of 'Painting, or Signs and Marks' two specific areas of concern are opened up by the text's move to painting. The first, as already intimated, pertains to the way in which language and art come to be connected. The nature of that connection—a connection in which holding to the particularity of art on the one hand and language on the other—transforms both the relation and its constituent elements. The second element concerns the text's ostensible area of concern. Precisely because the text ends with a discussion of painting—painting as a delimited and specific area—this allows for the more general concern of the relationship between specific art forms and criticism to become the focus of attention rather than either a too generalised description of art, as though specificity were no more than a secondary characteristic, or to too hasty a slide between technical innovation and novelty. (The latter, once positioned within a philosophical concern with art, is the conflation of chronological time and the 'now' resulting in the positing of the new. With such a move innovation and experimentation become no more than the banality of the 'new'.)

---

5. One of the most sustained recent discussions about this paper occurs in the context of an important examination of the relationship between Benjamin and Carl Einstein. See Haxthausen (particularly 63–8).

6. There are, in addition, a series of early unpublished papers that touch equally on the concerns of painting and colour. They can for the most part be found in *GS* VI: 109–29. Howard Caygill has incorporated this paper into the development of his more general interpretation of Benjamin, which is based in part on reading these early papers as part of a sustained encounter with Kant. (See *The Colour of Experience*.) While the path that Caygill opens insofar as it concerns Kant is undoubtedly correct, whether the retention of an opposition between the transcendental and the speculative is the most productive way of reading Benjamin is a topic too vast to be pursued in detail here. The project in this instance involves staying with the detail of the paper itself and to allow that detail to open up concerns that move in a direction other than the provision of an overall account of Benjamin's project.

BENJAMIN'S 'PAINTING, OR SIGNS AND MARKS'

While it may yield a task almost as long as this brief work itself, it is none-theless essential that the detail of its formulations be noted. While empha-sis will be given to painting (*Malerei*), it emerges from a consideration of the mark (*Mal*). The text starts by invoking the 'realm of signs'. Within it, the 'line' has different meanings. These differing possibilities include ' the writ-ten line' 'the graphic line' and what he refers to as 'the line of the absolute sign'. The latter form of line is described as 'magical'. What is meant by this designation will be of fundamental importance. This line is not defined by what it represents. Its magical nature is not given by a relationship between the external and the internal. It is magical 'as such' (*als solche*). Here, both the object and its projective quality—its having that quality is, of course, part of its magic—both form part of the object. It is as though the object now has a thickness. No longer the presentation of an outside, it then registers as more than a simple surface. This move to a definition in terms of an 'absolute'—an 'absolute' as given beyond any simple oscillation between an inside and an outside—will continue to be of real significance. Benjamin does not con-sider either 'geometric' or 'written' lines. He moves straight to a discussion of the 'graphic line'. The importance of this form of line is in how it comes to acquire its identity. Its emergence, in contrast to 'area' (*Fläche*), has for Ben-jamin both metaphysical as well as graphic significance.

The graphic line marks out an area and as such becomes its background. Reciprocally, of course, a graphic line exists in relation to the background though equally in its differentiation from it. Background therefore has a fundamental meaning for 'drawing' (*Zeichnung*) because it is sustains iden-tity. While the significance graphically of 'background' cannot be denied, of equal importance is what Benjamin refers to as the metaphysical dimen-sion. This has to do with the conferring, thus securing, of identity. Benja-min writes that '[t]he graphic line confers an identity on its background' ('*Die graphische Linie verleiht ihrem Untergrunde Identität*') (*SW* 1: 83; *GS* II·2: 604). Of greater significance, especially in relation to the rethinking of the surface is the following comment:

> The identity of the background of a drawing is quite different from that of the white surface [*weißen Papierfläche*] on which it is inscribed. We might even deny it that identity by thinking of it as a surge of white waves (though these might not even be distinguishable to the naked eye). [*even-tuell mit bloßem Auge nicht unterscheidbarer*] (*SW* 1: 83; *GS* II·2: 604)

What is of real note in this formulation is that this difference may not be evi-dent to the eye. In other words, despite having a graphic result, it would not have simple graphic presence. Surface is more than a literal surface. With-in drawing—thought by Benjamin in terms of 'the pure drawing' ('*die reine Zeichnung*')—surfaces cannot be reduced to the status of blank white space. A way of understanding what Benjamin means by the metaphysical can be located in the distinction between simple graphic presence and what is not given to the eye. While not expressed in these terms it would be as though the metaphysical came into play at the moment in which mere physical presence was transformed into material presence. (A materialist account, one that allowed for matter to be operative, will hold itself apart from the philosophical problematic of empiricism. The next part of the text is on the 'absolute sign' (*'das absolute Zeichen'*). Its significance lies, in part, in what Benjamin describes as its antithetical relation to 'the absolute mark' (*'das absolute Mal'*). It is in connection to the latter that painting (*Malerei*), almost as a voiced presence, emerges.

Signs have a 'spatial relation' and refer to persons. Examples of the absolute sign include the sign of Cain and the one that the Israelites put on their door to ward of the angel of death during the Tenth Plague. The spatiality of the sign is given by a form of distance. The sign is other than what it signifies. What is signified, however, is a specific type of person; equally, it has significance for specific persons. Distance therefore has a two-fold dimension. The sign is always doubly other. The antithesis lies in the distance since it introduces a realm of representation. What will identify—on a metaphysical level and thus not just visually—the mark is the closure of this space and thus the compression of the structure of distance that representation demands. Further evidence for this distancing emerges from Benjamin's description of the sign as 'printed' on to something. It can only exist therefore on a surface. The mark on the other hand 'emerges'. Benjamin goes on to argue that the 'mark appears on living things'. There is no distinction therefore between its appearing and its being what it is; hence, there cannot be a distinction between the mark and the absolute mark. For Benjamin, 'the mark is always absolute and resembles nothing else in its manifestation' (*'und ist im Erscheinen nichts anderem ähnlich'*) (*SW* 1: 84; *GS* II·2: 605). Examples of the mark—blushing—not only indicate a relation to guilt but can also, as in the case of Belshazzar's feast, appear as the 'warning of guilt' and thus as its sign. To that extent the sign and the mark are coterminous. Past and future are elided in this moment. Not only is this the province of G-d, it also indicates that extent to which there endures a magical quality. He then adds— and this will serve as the introduction of painting (*Malerei*)—that this temporal simultaneity, and its 'meaning' do not delimit 'the medium of the mark' (*'das Medium des Mals'*) (*SW* 1: 85; *GS* II·2: 606).

The delimitation of meaning—its limit as the point of orientation—is the opening to painting. What has emerged with the mark, indeed what maybe be said to characterise its presence—and here the characteristic in question is essentially metaphysical—is the mark's self-referential nature. The self-referential has an opening out; an opening already identified in the possible confluence between sign and mark. In the case of the instances given by Benjamin, the example noted above was Belshazzar's feast, it was this movement that brought the mark into the province controlled by G-d. In the case of painting there will be a similar correspondence with the divine. In this instance it will not be the refusal of a distinction between the past and the future—a temporal event that can, for the Benjamin of this early text, only be G-d's province—but the connection between the act of naming and the conferring of identity. The human imitates the divine by naming. Naming becomes a form of creating. Two elements of this formulation will have to be pursued. The first, as was noted at the outset, is that art is constituted. It has therefore neither a natural existence nor one located within history if history is understood to be no more than the continuation of time, chronology as the naturalisation of historical time. Art is created by its being named. (The creation has a history.) Its being named as such occurs within and as the act of criticism. Secondly, criticism necessitates that incorporation of this 'higher power'; necessitates it and, to a certain extent, is it.

Benjamin begins his treatment of painting by invoking the distinction, originally drawn in this context by Scholem in his letter, between colour and line. The setting is the opening line in which the 'image/painting' (*das Bild*) is described as having 'no background' (*keinen Untergrund*) (*SW* 1: 85; *GS* II·2: 606). The absence of this form of ground—clearly as a literal presence—reintroduces what was alluded to earlier as a thickened surface. Even though the example given is from Raphael, Benjamin's argument that the distinctions of colour within one of his works is not brought about by the use of a 'graphic line' is an argument with greater extension. It is worth noting Benjamin's actual formulation. He writes that, '[t]he reciprocal demarcations of the colored surface (the composition) [*der Farbflächen (Komposition)*] of a painting by Raphael are not based on graphic line' (*SW* 1: 85; *GS* II·2: 606). To which he then adds that the 'essence' (*Wesen*) of compositions of this type have 'nothing to do with the graphic' ('*mit Graphik gar nichts zu tun*') (*SW* 1: 85; *GS* II·2: 606). The significance of the formulation lies, in the first instance, in the identification of the coloured surface with the image 'composition'. In the second place, however, it yields a further instance in which the focus of concern becomes the surface. Prior to taking up the above mentioned identification between coloured surface and composition, it is essential to note the refrain of the surface.

The two points that have already been identified are the following. In the first instance, it is that the graphic line attains identity by the way it can be contrasted with a 'surface/area' (*Fläche*). The reciprocity between surface and line is fundamental since the surface is now no longer a simple background. Equally, of course, the graphic line holds itself apart from a simple surface. It forms its own surface in marking it out. In sum, therefore, the surface—not the literal surface but the essential surface—is a construct of art's work. The second point stems from the argument, already cited, in which Benjamin differentiates between '[t]he identity … the background of a drawing' has ('*Die Identität, welche der Untergrund einer Zeichnung hat*') and its inscription on a 'white surface' ('*weißen Papierfläche*') (*SW* 1: 83; *GS* II·2: 604). Both of these moves are, to use Benjamin's terminology, 'metaphysical'. They work beyond the hold of the eye insofar as they cannot be equated with literal presence. In addition, they are preparatory to any more direct approach painting. (Painting as art work.) They clear the way by allowing the concepts proper to an account of painting to emerge.

What is opened up here is a concern with the surface that works beyond any reduction to literal presence. (Hence, there is an accord with what was identified earlier as a 'thickened surface'.) Now there is the 'coloured surface' i.e. the composition itself. What is for Benjamin 'astonishing' about this state of affairs is that a composition cannot be equated with the 'graphic'. Moreover, a composition—remembering of course the reciprocity, if not identity, between composition and 'coloured surface'—is not an 'illusion' (*Schein*). In other words, it is neither semblance nor mere appearance. What then is it that appears? The image (*Bild*) comprises more than an organised collection of marks. (Hence, in more general terms, an image is the result of technique, marks the result of the technical.) The proof of this proposition resides, for Benjamin, in the negative supposition, namely if it were only marks then the 'composition would be 'impossible to name' (*zu benennen*). Two points therefore: firstly, a picture can be described such that it is no more than marks. And yet, secondly, there is something else. The 'picture'(*Bild*) is linked to 'something that it is not' (*auf etwas das es nicht selbst ist*) (*SW* 1: 85; *GS* II·2: 606). What this 'something' is, is given within naming. This other element is language. (Identified earlier as prose and thus as writing.) The composition—the coloured surface—transcends any reduction to marks, it overcomes the marks themselves—overcoming them by incorporating them.

Composition creates the possibility of naming. (A point that will acquire greater clarity in the later discussion of Rembrandt's *The Feast of Belshazzar*.) What is introduced is a 'higher power' (*einer höhern Macht*) (*SW* 1: 85; *GS* II·2: 607). Prior to taking up the question of how this power is to be understood, the nature of its presence needs to be noted. This power is neutral. Placed within the mark it resides there without threatening the mark (*Mal*). While not the same it inhabits the mark because it is 'related' to it. After presenting these moves, clarifications that situate this 'power', Benjamin then defines it. Within this definition, what is introduced is the constituting force of naming. As has been indicated, within the name—naming as process—prose comes to be fundamental to art work.

> This power is the linguistic word, which lodges in the medium of the language of painting, invisible as such and revealing itself only in the composition. The picture is named after the composition. [*Das Bild wird nach der Komposition benannt*]. (*SW* 1: 86; *GS* II·2: 607)

The marks and the overall composition bear the name. The painting comes to be what it is through the act of naming. And yet, it is not as though any work can be named—or merely named, if naming is no more than identifying—hence, the need to distinguish, radically, between the formal presence of graphic lines and 'composition'. (Graphic lines, in the end, are inextricably tied up with immediacy and thus with a certain conception of aesthetics as opposed to a philosophy of art.) This allows for an understanding of the history of painting that is no longer bound by iconography but by the relation between the mark and word. The question then is how is the presence of 'word' to be understood. What conditions the introduction of prose? There are two aspects involved in answering this question. The first pertains to necessity. What can be described as the necessity of the work to be named. Composition coming into its own through the transcendence of the mark, or at least through the transcendence of the reduction of the mark to its literal presence, a move effected by the act of naming. The second is a claim; *in extremis* a right. These two elements are brought together directly following the point noted above that the 'picture/image' (*Bild*) is named after the composition.

> From what has been said, it is self-evident that marks and composition are the elements of every picture [*jedes Bildes*] that claims the right to be named. [a claim on 'nameability' or *Benennbarkeit*] A picture that did not do this would cease to be one and would therefore enter into the realm of the mark as such; but this is something that we cannot imagine. [*keine Vorstellung machen können.*] (*SW* 1: 86; *GS* II·2: 607)

Central to this formulation is the argument that 'pictures' make a claim on being named, where that claim pertains to a quality of the composition rather than naming as an arbitrary designation. In order to make this position consistent with the one developed by Benjamin in relation to translation and language, the argument needs to be that 'nameability' is a quality of the 'picture' in precisely the same way as 'translatability' is a quality of language. Translatability is that which allows for translation. Benjamin formulates this position in the following terms:

> Translation is a form. To comprehend it as a form, one must go back to the original, for the laws governing the translation lie within the original, contained in the issue of translatability. [*Übersetzbarkeit*]. (*GS* IV·1: 9; *SW* 1: 254)

'Translatability' as a quality therefore involves at the minimum that which inheres in the original, not, however, as a literal presence but as a potentiality. The precondition is that this quality cannot be reduced to literal presence if the latter is understood to be a conception of meaning that can be equated with ostensive definition. Translation is then the actualisation of a work's potentiality. Translatability is that which allows for a work to live on through the discontinuous continuity of its being translated. Translatability allows a work to have 'afterlife'. The connection to nameability emerges at this precise point. The continuity of the work's being named—a possibility allowed for by the work—is, again, the discontinuous continuity of its presence as an object within criticism. It must always be discontinuous. Continuity would be the end of the work's life. That end, whether it appear in the guise of the reduction of criticism to the interpretive equivalent to ostensive definition or the incorporation of criticism within a theory of truth (the truth of epistemology as opposed to the truth of ontology), is precluded because of the ontological preconditions for 'nameability'. That precondition, one equally at work within 'translatability', is potentiality. Potentiality allows for criticism. Criticism releases a work's potentiality. The release occurs within the interplay of continuity and discontinuity that, in this instance, defines the relationship between art and prose.

REMBRANDT'S ABSOLUTE MARK

A way of taking up this relationship is to return to the example given by Benjamin, namely the reference to Belshazzar's feast. Benjamin, as was noted, is clearly referring to the Book of Daniel (5: 1–30). In painting, within the medium's own history, the reference could have been made more precisely; namely, it would have been to Rembrandt's painting *The Feast of Belshazzar.* Here this 'event' is staged pictorially. Perhaps, it could be argued, what is staged is its painting.

The words written by the divine hand are there to be read. They warn of an impending disaster, but neither standing for it nor symbolising it. They are that warning. Within the painting Belshazzar is surrounded by treasures taken from the destruction of the Temple in Jerusalem. It is as though there is an important shift in temporal stature. The future is not present as a possibility. Its actuality is stated. The reign of the Babylonian kings is at an end. The work of time has a greater exigency, exerting a more demanding hold, due to the complex temporality occasioned by the presence of the hand that writes. In order that this point is developed is the painting central.

Within the painting wine pours from a goblet. Beneath the wine is the outstretched hand of the servant. Above that hand Belshazzar's hand and arm frame the words written by the hand that appears. The hand that writes. Lines of hands having been drawn in parallel. It is as if the surface contained four parallel lines marking the place where arms and hands would come to be placed. Perhaps they were marked out in advance. Even if they were in the work, now as becoming art work and as such transcending marks, there is a different form of presence. The question therefore concerns this transcendence; a transcendence that has its essential corollary in the re-emergence of the mark as the site of technique. (A site given by the

mark having been attributed an operative quality rather than a representational one.)

The narrative of the Book of Daniel, or at least the appropriate verses,
needs to be located in (and as) the painting. Invited to the Babylonian court
because of his interpretive powers, Daniel came to occupy a unique position. Unique in that context though in the end it is a position that opens
up to a type of generalisation. Belshazzar surrounded himself with seers.
The task was to interpret signs. Daniel, who displayed exceptional skills
when it came to the interpretation of dreams—dreams and signs were themselves domains in which both interpretational conflicts and limits could be
played out—was already positioned at a distance from the court. Within
this setting—the court feasting—a disembodied hand appears. Appearing
and writing are coterminous. They exist in, and as, the instant. While the
writing is taking place—a taking place the registration of which is, in part,
the painting's work—the wine goblet is overturned. The wine captured at
the moment of its being split defines the instant. And yet, as the goblet is
overturned at the moment—and it is that moment, moment as the instant,
since the wine is yet to leave fully the goblet and thus still to land on the car-
peted floor—the final letter is being written. (While it is interesting to note
that Rembrandt has misunderstood the source and confused two Aramaic
letters—that is, the *zayin* with the final *nun*—as yet this does not impede the
establishing of the instant.) Nonetheless, what must be questioned is what is
being written. A question that, as will be suggested, turns around the relationship between writing and time. (However, not writing and time in the
abstract. What occurs is their presence as painting.) As the absolute mark
what is being written resists, or should, its incorporation into the structured
oppositions that identify either the symbol or the sign. Hence the questions:
Who reads? What is the experience of knowledge? Note that these question
arise from the particularity of the painting.

The letters themselves can be read. Being read is, of course, their transformation from mere marks to words, in a sense their prosaic transformation. However, they cannot be read if the reading conventions of either Aramaic or Hebrew are followed—that is, reading right to left. Nor can they
be read if the convention is simply reversed; that is, reading from left to
right. The problem of reading these letters becomes therefore the already
inscribed presence of the move from immediacy to the conjoining of knowledge and experience. They cannot be read immediately. Moreover, that is
true both in terms of immediacy as a temporal term thus equated with the
temporality of the instant, and in regards to the suggested absence of the
conceptual. Overcoming the instant is the allowing of knowledge, the introduction of which is predicated upon the space opened by the process of criticism. Criticism becomes knowledge. (While the point will be made again, it
should nonetheless be noted that the opening in question could not be sim-

ply posited. It has to be located within the work. The process of its being located is inextricably bound up with what has emerged thus far in terms of
naming and criticism.)

The letters in the painting can only be read if they are approached from
the right and the read vertically. The source of the transformation is Me-
nasseh ben Israel's *De Termina Vitae* (1639),[7] a text that repeats the ordering
suggested by both the Talmud and the Midrash. That suggestion was itself
advanced in order to account both for the Babylonian's lack of comprehension as well as Daniel's ability. The inability to decipher the letters—the impossibility, that is, of their immediate comprehension—would have been a
state of affairs in which the letters would have come to have been equated
with their graphic presence. The overcoming of that twofold position means
that not only are the letters no longer identified with their literal presence,
at the same time there would have been a transformation of that presence
on the part of Daniel. As such, the marks were subject to another act of constitution. The marks were able to be named by allowing them to become
prose, a becoming in which initially they literally became prose, though
they became prose because of a response to an object that demands to be
named—a call for naming, thus occurring as a response to the necessity for
naming inherent in art's work.

What needs to be noted is the consequence of that transformation of the
temporality of the instant. To begin with the instant has to be understood
as pure immediacy: immediacy as the now of a happening. Immediacy is
not literalised since immediacy must be literal: that is, unmediated. In the
painting the instant is the wine falling from the goblet. Paint captures, holds
and thus presents that moment. It is presented as the instant. Perhaps its presentation occurs in an instant. And yet, what of the moment after—the moment after the instant but within the work? It is as though in the evocation of
the instant as a moment the painting announces another one. It is both the
force, though more exactly the actual possibility of another moment, one occurring after but still within the work, that shatters the hold of the instant. (It
is as though it enacts the shattering of the conventions of the line in which it
was trapped between the sign and the literal.) However, the question of the
further moment, an addition that still forms part of the original (thereby defining the original as a site at work, working within its becoming art) would
be merely speculative if it could not be given material presence. What is presented materially is not just a site that has to become prose, more is in play.

The question of the additional moment—an after-effect that defines a
complex origin—is not an invented addition. It can be located in the pres-

---

7. For an important discussion of the relationship between Rembrandt and Manasseh
ben Israel in which there is a discussion of Belshazzar's Feast see Zell (59–72). The preceding discussion of the painting draws on Zell's analysis. However, the implications advanced are different.

ence of Belshazzar's arm. His arm in framing the words not only identifies the locus of the disembodied hand, it causes the move between the four
hands—the parallel lines—to mark, within the same space, different spatial-temporal locations. They can be held together visually only if the instant is privileged. The overcoming of the instant is not its denial, rather it
is its inclusion into a larger economy. What that means in this context is not
allowing the falling wine to define the temporality of the painting's comprehension while, of course, holding the wine within the painting now positioned within becoming criticism. That economy, while demanding prose—
demanding that a work incorporates the complex presence of the interplay
of identity and language—brings with it something other than the reduction
of the work to a literary narrative. While the complication of the site of orig-
ination demands prose there will always be a found(er)ing and disjunctive
relation between the site that makes a claim to naming and the process of
criticism. In other words, even though there is the demand to be named, the
inherent disjunction between prose and art work—a disjunction sustained
ontologically by the distinction between potentiality and finitude—allows,
as was noted earlier, a work its afterlife.

   In sum, it is the move away both from the temporality of the instant
and thus also away from the insistence within aesthetics on immediacy that
opens up painting. Here it occurs because of having to hold together that
which cannot be defined by the instant. What occurs is an opening and thus
an opening up which is art's work. This reframes the point already noted by
Benjamin that art is connected 'to something it is not'. To which it should
be added that it is precisely that link that allows art to come into its own.
What is allowed for by that opening, and which occasions it, is criticism.
The content of criticism pertains to how the relation between the instant
and that which could never occur immediately—that is, knowing both how
to read what is being written and thus working through their consequences.
The opening up—an opening in which it becomes possible to locate knowledge—is allowed for by the ontology of art's work defined in terms of potentiality and criticism as the occasioning of art's relation to prose.

cities and images

8

Interiority, Exteriority and Spatial Politics in Benjamin's Cityscapes

Peter Schmiedgen

Within modernity two primary conceptions of the subject have held sway. On the one hand liberal individualism and indeed also its contemporary neo-liberal descendants posit an atomic subject as the appropriate *telos* of the modern project and on the other Marxist and also some anarcho-socialist traditions have posited a collective social subject as the ultimate *telos* of the modernisation process.[1] In Benjamin's cityscapes these two conceptions of the modern subject are of interest primarily because of the ways in which he explores the modern city as a site of disambiguation and rationalisation of social space through either privatisation and atomisation (in the case of Berlin and Paris) or collectivisation (in the case of Moscow) of built space and hence also atomisation or collectivisation of the subjects who dwelt within these spaces. Built space is also a space of subjectification for Benjamin in this sense. What we see in the process of being 'disambiguated' are the ambiguous lines between public and private space that characterised the barely modern city of Naples in Benjamin's assessment.[2]

This process of disambiguation is not just reflected in the built structure of the city (although it might be as in the case of the 'Hausmannisation' of Paris in the early 19th century), but also in the normative assumptions about for whom built space exists and about how individuals and populations will

1. Lukác's *History and Class Consciousness* and also Gramsci's *Prison Notebooks* are the most exemplary classical sources of this kind of position.

2. Although these cityscapes are temporally dispersed, I am nevertheless reading them as presenting a series of interconnecting phenomenologies of interior space, exterior space and their interconnections. This seems to be a justifiable strategy given the continuing 'grip' of these categories upon contemporary experience. Thanks to Charles Rice for raising this question.

be distributed through it. In contrast with the cities of both capitalist and socialist modernity, in normative terms Naples is a city which appears to explode out of its architectural seams. Family, and hence private, life happens
in apparently public places, and cafes are almost indistinguishable from the
crowds which provide them with business. Although importantly for the argument to come, there is still nevertheless an ambiguous zone which divides
the public from the private and the individual from the social collectivity
in Naples. However, it is far from clear for whom built space exists. Its usage is ambiguous and subject to chance and there appears to be only a weak
normative framework to define the boundary between interior and exterior
space. In contrast, in Paris and Berlin as Benjamin understood them, built
space exists either for the sake of the private individual, or the individual
family, whilst in the case of Moscow built space exists for the sake of the collectivity. There are strong normative frameworks in action in these cases
which either exclude certain activities from specific spaces or which specify
that only specific activities can be carried out in specific spaces, in specific
ways.[3] Erotic activity is the most obvious of these proscribed activities, although it is also clear that even sleeping in the stairways of apartment buildings, as Benjamin observed some Neapolitan children doing, would have
marked one out as homeless in relation to bourgeois Berlin.

However, in spatial terms the world in which we live is no longer the ra-
tionalised world of Weberian bureaucracy, Simmelian urban sociology and
Baudelairean urban poetry which formed the background of the narrative
of spatial modernisation which I am exploring here. I would argue that in
the contemporary Western world our experience of being-in-built-space has
become once again somewhat more like the experience of those who inhabited the porous modernising spaces of Naples.[4] It is once again unclear for
whom or for what purpose built spaces primarily exist. Do they exist for the
sake of the private individual, for the sake of the collectivity, or indeed for
the sake of one's employer, or maybe even more generally are they simply

---

3. In this sense, Benjamin is also as concerned with who occupies which interiors and
the ways in they occupy them as with the construction of built space itself and hence the
division between interior and exterior. This interest in the ways in which both interior and
exterior spaces are inhabited is at the heart of both his reflections upon the transgressive,
or anti-bourgeois modes of inhabitation characteristic of the *flâneur*, the rag picker and the
collector, and of his equally important meditations on the undisciplined pre-bourgeois
creativity of the child as collector and explorer prior to the impact of the domesticating
adult bourgeois world. For more contemporary examples of closely related ways of inhabiting the urban and the rural environments see Agnés Varda's wonderful documentary *The
Gleaners and I* (2000) and its sequel (*The Gleaners and I: Two Years Later*, 2002). Needless to say
Benjamin's own discourse is also expanded upon by a number of recent contributions to
queer and feminist theory. See for example Mark Turner's *Backward Glances*, in which the
queer male cruiser is critically contrasted with the heterosexual *flâneur*.

4. See Zygmunt Bauman's useful reflections upon the relationship between spatial and
technological mobility and class stratification in 'Tourists and vagabonds'.

capital itself? Although in the past activities such as gleaning, or public sex, may already have brought into question the hard line drawn between public and private, there is a sense in which this is done even more forcefully in our world by the use we now make of communications technology. Even though I work at home and hence also within a supposedly private space, I am always able to be in contact with colleagues and friends, via instant messenger, file sharing, email, text messages, web cams and of course old-fashioned voice communication as well. The private is only ambiguously private. The walls of the self are already perforated by the other. The telephone is no longer in the back hallway, as it was for Benjamin, but in the back pocket of our jeans (*SW* 3: 350; *GS* VII·1: 391).

But the public sphere is also now only ambiguously public as well. Having left the walled space of my house I can surround myself with the privacy of my iPod and have access to work colleagues and friends who are not within the spatial perimeters of the buildings or spaces I now occupy through the use of wireless communications technology. The consequences of this situation are that subjectivity is no longer as simple to negotiate, or indeed disambiguate, as it was when Benjamin was writing. The bourgeois subject is no longer simply the subject who forms around him- or herself an almost impenetrable material and ideological cocoon composed of walls, furniture, possessions, urban geographic boundaries and the hard earned scars of bourgeois education. The bourgeois subject is a subject who is in fact already in question for us in spatial and social terms.

THE BOURGEOIS INTERIOR

In order to make more concrete the argument I have only abstractly sketched in my introduction, I will first briefly discuss some of the more concrete features of bourgeois interior space as Benjamin understood it. The two main points I will concentrate on are firstly, the tendency for the bourgeois interior to be a space within which subjectivity is always forced, in at least some ways, to be in the closet about itself and secondly, the tendency of bourgeois interiority to attempt to internalise the other and hence the exterior, albeit in a non-allergenic and domesticated form.

In 'One-way street' Benjamin compares the self to a house with a cellar (*SW* 1: 445; *GS* IV·1: 86). However, unlike the sanguine images of Descartes' meditations upon the refounding and rebuilding of the house of the self, Benjamin implies that the cellar of the self is a location within which we will find not only the traces of unreflective and irrational action in need of rational reform, but also interred 'antiquities' that we cannot simply rationalise away and which will not fit into any neat order of the self. He implies that below the social façade which we have carefully moulded in order to be acceptable to others, we will find a field of messy, irrational truths which we have systematically tried to forget or exclude from consciousness.[5]

This sense in which bourgeois interior space is closeted space is emphasized to an even greater effect in "Betting Office" (*SW* 1: 484–5; *GS* IV·1: 144). Political conviction, financial situation, religion and perhaps most of all eroticism each find their own closets in this airless space. Public eroticism is left as the preserve of the proletariat and of course, although Benjamin only gestures towards it, of the prostitute, or the sexual outlaw.[6] So the bourgeois interior is a space of cellars and hidden closets as well as presentable public areas or, as Goffman argues in *The presentation of self in everyday life*, back and front of stage areas; places to hide and places to perform before others in public, or semi-public areas. It is a space of both hypocrisy and proud display.[7] The closet contains the historical and psychogenetic disasters that we have all left behind ourselves in the process of becoming publicly presentable bourgeois subjects.[8]

Initially the child knows the bourgeois interior as just such a space of hiding places and hence also by implication of hidden places (*SW* 1: 465–6; *GS* IV·1: 115–6). Becoming a bourgeois adult is not just about closeting the socially indigestible, but also about forgetting that anything was hidden in the first place. Once again we see the sense in which for Benjamin the bourgeois interior functions as a mask which covers a field of 'dirty' secrets; the dirty secrets which are the messy, untotalisable truth of the self. Only the child, not yet fully the victim of the hypocrisy and ways of being of such bourgeois spaces, is able to comfortably find his way into the cracks and interstices of the carefully constructed surface of adult bourgeois subjectivity.[9] Indeed Benjamin implies in his reflections upon the school that it is through the process of 'education' that the unkempt love which the child has for the irrational, the incoherent and the socially unacceptable is eliminated (*SW* 2: 601–3; *GS* VI: 473–5). The child is subject there not simply to the materiality of the bourgeois interior but also to the ideology of bourgeois rationality and efficiency. In the school the airless bourgeois interior also becomes an ideological 'timetable cage' (*SW* 2: 602; *GS* VI: 473).[10]

But what then are the qualities of the 'public' rather than the hidden

---

5. On which see also the politico-historical reflections of the 'On the Concept of History' (*SW* 4: 389–400; *GS* I·2: 691–704)

6. See ch. 6, 7 and 8 of Chauncey on private space, sexual freedom and class.

7. See Michael Warner and Samuel Delany for more contemporary reflections upon spatial closeting of queer populations.

8. It is just this process of identity management that Benjamin is interested in more politico-historical terms in the 'On the Concept of History'.

9. Just indeed as queer men find their ways into the cracks and interstices of the urban fabric. See Betsky on this.

10. And so in a sense the child plays hide and seek within the bourgeois interior. Endlessly trying to evade the grasp of bourgeois rationality/hypocrisy in its attempts to educate him.

surfaces of the bourgeois interior from Benjamin's point of view? In 'Mano-
rially furnished ten room apartment' Benjamin brings to light two important points about the public side of bourgeois interior spaces (*SW* 1: 446–7;
GS IV·1: 88–9). Firstly, in the very wording he uses he underlines the ways in
which the bourgeois interior is in fact always the interior of capital itself. The
title of the fragment suggests the words of the real estate agent as he markets
the latest hot new property. Further to this Benjamin also points out that the
interior is a place where the master of the house can have '… orgies with his
share certificates …' (*SW* 1: 447; *GS* IV·1: 89). Note that it is not the mistress
of the house who has orgies with the share certificates. This is both a capitalist and a patriarchal space.

However, the surfaces and the fields of objects and furnishings within
which these 'orgies' are enacted are also important to Benjamin's analysis.
This is a space which is filled with the traces of the cultural other. Whilst the
sexual alterity of the prostitute is consigned to the streets, and other sources
of shame to the closet, the traces of the cultural other are proudly displayed
here. The economic orgies of the master of the house are carried out on a
stage which has been set with Persian carpets, ottomans, hanging lamps
and even the almost faux masculinity of a Caucasian dagger. The Western
bourgeois interior contains the traces of the other and yet it is a domesticated
other; an other who does not unsettle the calm surface of Western bourgeois
sexual and economic hypocrisy. This multiculturalism which plays at being
open to the other, but only in safe and domesticated forms, must surely still
be familiar to us in the post-multicultural Australia of the early twenty first
century, where multiculturalism now appears to mean little more than an
appreciation of culinary diversity.

A final point that is also important to note is that these interiors, unlike
the interiors of the collector and the child, are marked by a certain completeness (*Moscow Diary* 26; *Moskauer Tagebuch* 39). They are indeed the decorative equivalents of the violently totalising, 'pretentious, universal gesture
of the book' which Benjamin already decries in the very first section of 'One-
Way Street' (*SW* 1: 444; *GS* IV·1: 85). Bourgeois interiority is all about covering over the evidence of the closeting, editing and systematising required to
produce the glossy public surfaces of the bourgeois interior and the subject
who occupies it in the first place.

THE POST-BOURGEOIS INTERIOR

Having briefly considered Benjamin's reading of the atomised bourgeois interior I will now discuss his comments on the domestic interiors of post-
bourgeois Moscow. Although these interiors are of course not dominated, as
those of Benjamin's Berlin childhood were, by the imperative to construct
and present oneself as an essentially bourgeois capitalist, patriarchal sub-

ject, they are also not in the end understood by Benjamin to be wholly liberated spaces either. Indeed they bring along with them their own pathological tendencies.

As I argued earlier, the bourgeois interior is for Benjamin an interior which strives for the appearance of both completeness and fullness, insofar as it is a field of surfaces and things available for the general inspection of guests and hence a stage for the performance of the bourgeois self before others. The subjectivities and intersubjectivities who inhabit such spaces see themselves as being complete unto themselves and hence as private individuals, or private groupings who have only external and contingent relations with other subjects, or families, rather than as subjects who are always already amongst others in ways which cannot and ought not to be fully controlled or eliminated. It is this very tendency towards the reification of the privacy of bourgeois interior space into a conception of the self as simply a social atom that the organisation of living space in Moscow militated against from Benjamin's point of view. As Benjamin asserts in 'Moscow', 'Bolshevism has abolished private life' (*SW* 2: 30). In Moscow it is the imperatives of the socialist collective mediated through the organs of the bureaucracy, the press and political channels, rather than the imperatives of the singular bourgeois capitalist subject which take precedence. The state as the representative of the collective is master in Moscow, just as the autonomous capitalist subject is in Berlin.

Apartments that were previously for only one family, as he goes on to further assert, were filled with eight families. The interiors of such spaces become for Benjamin more like camps than homes. They are not there to be lived in, but are rather only available for fleeting camping trips between political meetings. The streets and the collectivity which fills them have in a sense almost effaced these spaces as interiors and hence also the independent identities of the subjects who inhabit them.

These interior spaces are, as Benjamin asserts in a number of places, emptied out. The pretentious conspicuous consumption of the bourgeois interior and indeed also its tendency to be the place in which the bourgeois subject strives to preserve the traces of the self in a private museum, are replaced here by rooms which contain only limited amounts of furniture (*Moscow Diary* 26, 31; *Moskauer Tagebuch* 39, 47; *SW* 2: 30).[11] The wall as a solid boundary between oneself and the potentially threatening, or corrosive alterity of the urban crowd is replaced here with the curtain that previously only covered over the window of the bourgeois interior. In post-bourgeois Moscow the curtain is not a covering for an 'eye' which has been pierced through the hard shell of bourgeois interiority, but rather the only means at hand to separate oneself in a semi-permanent way from the other campers

---

11. On traces and preserving them, see 'The Paris of the Second Empire in Baudelaire' (*SW* 4: 25–6; *GS* I·2: 548–9) and Convolute I of 'The Arcades Project'(*GS* V·1: 281–301).

who share one's living space.

The sparse furnishings to be found within these interiors are themselves moved, according to Benjamin, every week, and indeed that appears to be the only concession made to the individuality of the occupants (*SW* 2: 28–9; *Moscow Diary* 36; *Moskauer Tagebuch* 54). The occupants of these rooms have become comrades and hence also individuals who have only a very limited right to display their individual wealth, cultivation and respectability through the spaces they inhabit. Needless to say the weekly alteration of the interior decorations and furnishings must indeed have militated against the tendency towards the reification of interior space motivated by the more static bourgeois interior. There is simply no space in these 'emptied out' interiors for the hypocritical closetedness of the bourgeois capitalist subject and indeed Benjamin observes that along with these uncloseted interior spaces come children who have a decidedly emancipated quality about them as well, unlike those children who are subject to the ongoing violence of bourgeois education (*Moscow* 183; *SW* 2: 27).

However, the assault on bourgeois privacy does not stop with the collectivisation of interior space either. In Moscow, Benjamin tells us, there are no cafes to be found (*SW* 2: 31). This is important here for the following reasons. In Benjamin's reflections upon the *flâneur*, cafes are understood to be akin to 'observation posts' within which the *flâneur* stops to rest and observe (*SW* 4: 27; *GS* I·2: 551). He withdraws briefly from the crowd into a less corrosive, semi-private space. On the other hand in Benjamin's analyses of his own psychogenesis, cafes are islands of semi-privacy within which the young Benjamin and his political friends can gather to begin the process of articulating their own adult subjectivities in spaces freed at least to some extent of the interfering gaze of the parental world ('A Berlin Chronicle' *SW* 2: 606–9; *GS* VI: 480–4). In both of these examples, cafes function, to use Benjamin's own words, as 'strategic quarters'. (*GS*, VI: 481). They are locations within which the subject can stake out a momentary and semi-private position within the ongoing battle with the urban crowd, without having to withdraw completely into the more restrictive bourgeois interior itself. The absence of these kinds of spaces in the Moscow of Benjamin's analyses means that there was available in Moscow neither interior domesticity, nor exterior semi-privacy. There are indeed almost no spaces within which the subject can cultivate his or her own individuality or singularity independent of the impact of the surrounding social collectivity.

However, there was not simply a lack of spaces within which individuality or individual subjectivity could be cultivated within Moscow. In reading *Moscow Diary* it is impossible to miss the ways in which the organisation of living space made it impossible for Benjamin to pursue his romantic intentions in relation to Asja Lacis. Leaving aside the fact that Lacis herself, at least as she appears in *Moscow Diary*, appears to have been a decidedly prickly individual in her dealings with Benjamin, it is nevertheless also the case that on many occasions Benjamin was not able to spend private time with her because of either his or her roommates. Benjamin's ill fated attempts to find private space within which an erotic or romantic intersubjectivity could be further articulated between the two exemplifies a further negative attribute of post-bourgeois interior space in Moscow. Just as the atomised bourgeois interior is a closeted and de-eroticised interior, so also is the collectivised post-bourgeois interior in its own way. In the bourgeois interior the erotic must be closeted in order to create a good impression and to put on a good face, but in the post-bourgeois interior individual erotic needs must give way to the housing needs of the collectivity.

The ultimate consequence of the collectivisation of interior living space and the absence of even the semi-privacy of the cafe is that the post-bourgeois modern interiors of Moscow are spaces which in Benjamin's terms militate with ferocious effectiveness not only against bourgeois capitalist subjectivity, but also against the kind of individual critical intellectual and cultural activity and indeed also intersubjective erotic relations that are required in order to stop societies from simply becoming dominated by totalitarianism, or as ultimately happened in the Soviet Union, Stalinism. In both the spaces of Moscow and those of bourgeois capitalist modernity the attempt to disambiguate urban space, and hence also urban subjectivity, effectively effaces the ambiguous lines between the public and the private that characterised the modernising city of Naples. In so doing, however, they also effaced the need to endlessly reflect upon, negotiate and re-negotiate the boundaries and borders between the individual subject and the social collectivity.

LATE BOURGEOIS POROSITY

In the final section of my paper I will briefly return to the location and indeed the city which I have argued was the beginning of Benjamin's narrative. In a sense one can view the two ways of being in the city and of being in urban interior/exterior space which I have just outlined as two extreme poles of a dialectic of interiority and exteriority within the ambiguous field of modernity itself. Benjamin's analyses emphasise for us the failure of both of these projects for the disambiguation of the modern social and spatial field. What I would like to argue is that in fact in the wake of the failure of these projects, we ought rather to turn towards the more fluid and radical conception of social porosity initially exemplified by the modernising space of Naples as a more plausible way of understanding the ambiguities of contemporary late-modern or post-modern modes of urban socio-spatial inhabitation.

In contrast with either bourgeois Berlin, or Socialist Moscow, both of which embody either one or the other extremes of interiority or exteriority, in Naples one sees what is in effect neither an effacement of the interior by the exterior nor of the exterior by the interior. Instead one sees an interpenetration and play of spatial and social opposites. According to Benjamin, in Naples day and night, noise and peace, outer light and inner darkness, and street and home all interpenetrate (*SW* 1: 420). But this interpenetration of opposites is neither a dialectical *Aufhebung* which somehow reconciles whilst maintaining opposites nor simply a totalising effacement of one opposite by the other, but rather it is an inconclusive and never-ending play of the opposites with each other around and across ambiguous and uncertain borders. In Naples built space provides a network of spaces within which unforeseen constellations of people and activities can come into being and in which a definitive functional, or temporal ordering of built space is avoided (*SW* 1: 416).

During the day the domestic interiors of Naples emigrate out onto the streets of the city. People work as they sit on chairs in their front yards and hang their kitchen utensils from their balconies (*GS* IV·1: 314–15; *SW* 1: 419–20). On the other hand, Benjamin also notes that the interiors of these spaces are as densely filled with a disorganised horde of possessions as are the streets of the city itself (*SW* 1: 420). At night, because these rooms are also often over-filled with people and provide insufficient bedding, there are often children in the streets at midnight or even at two in the morning (*SW* 1: 420). Rather than sleeping in their beds during the night children instead sleep in any space that is available during the day. We are told that it is as common to find children sleeping at midday on a stairwell or behind a shop counter as anywhere else, at any other time (*SW* 1: 420). And in fact in this city of interpenetrating opposites children are also often given refuge within the families of neighbours, when situations arise that make it difficult or impossible for their own parents to care for them (*SW* 1: 421). Families themselves interpenetrate without simply coalescing within these urban spaces.

The cafes of Naples are also important spaces from Benjamin's point of view. Unlike Moscow, there are indeed cafes to be found in Naples, however, the ways in which they function as spaces of semi-privacy is in important respects distinct from the ways cafes function in Berlin and, as Benjamin explicitly notes, Vienna. The cafes of Naples are not in any sense like the outposts of bourgeois subjectivity and indeed bourgeois interiority which the cafes of Benjamin's youth and the literary cafes of Vienna were. Benjamin suggests that Neapolitan cafes are more like people's cafes, they are not able to provide for more than a fleeting break from the swirling crowds and they certainly do not provide the extended observational, or even discursive, spaces to which he compares them (*SW* 1: 421).

Needless to say there is a sense in which these analyses of Neapolitan social space are at least to some extent analyses of urban poverty and deprivation. Without wishing to suggest that poverty or deprivation are good things, I nevertheless still wish to argue in conclusion that there is a strong analogy between the kinds of fluidity and interpenetration of work space and time, private space and time, and public space and time to be found in the Naples of Benjamin's analyses, and similar phenomena in our own late or post-modern context. As a result of flexible employment practices and also of the impact of the electronic and mobile communications technologies we now make so much use of, we also inhabit spaces that are in important senses porous. Nevertheless this porosity is not of exactly the same kind as the porosity of Naples. In fact, to refer back to the previous discussions of bourgeois and post-bourgeois subjectivities and interiors, it seems that in fact we now live within what can only be described as a kind of late bourgeois porosity. We have not regressed to a pre-bourgeois mode of social life so much as come to live within a new bourgeois mode of existence. The porous social spaces which we inhabit do indeed allow us to form different and new constellations of people, spaces and practices with remarkable fluidity and yet it still remains a porosity which is premised upon the singular bourgeois subject and firmly embedded within neo-liberal capital. These new constellations are only able with great difficulty to be for the sake of anything other than capital itself. Needless to say it is also true that we do not live in entirely uncloseted interiors now. Often enough the porous bourgeois subject, equally at home in built or virtual space is also a subject who has withdrawn into an electronic or virtual closet to some extent, rather than into the cellars or hiding places of Benjamin's own reflections.

Unlike Benjamin's recollection in 'Berlin childhood around 1900' that the phone was carefully hidden in the back hallway, for us the communications technology is always firmly embedded in the heart of our interior spaces. The contemporary porous bourgeois subject is always already pierced, marked and scarred by the communications technologies which fill our interiors. There is no longer an unblemished or unscarred surface which the bourgeois subject can present to or use as a defence from the others. These scars and piercings are in the end the scars and piercings which neo-liberal capital itself causes in its endless scarification, incision and domination of the late modern bourgeois subject. Just as Benjamin's Moscow dwellers before had only curtains and not walls, so also are we in some senses condemned to a life behind the curtain. However, our curtains are made of technology rather than fabric, and the dominating force is not a soviet bureaucracy but rather neo-liberal capital. A more emancipated world requires not that we transcend this porosity itself, but rather that we transcend, or at least regularly re-negotiate, the limits placed upon porous subjectivity and space by neo-liberal capital.

9

Time Without End: Exploring the Temporal Experience of Wong Kar-Wai's *2046* Through Walter Benjamin

Jo Law

INTRODUCTION

In this article, I present an analysis of Wong Kar-Wai's films focusing on his 2004 work, *2046*. I do so through the works of Walter Benjamin, particularly his works on German mourning plays.[1] I argue that Wong Kar-Wai's films can be explored through Benjamin's analysis of the *Trauerspiel* and suggest that Wong's tales of missed opportunities, repetition, regrets, lamentations, and mis-recognition extend the modern form of mourning plays. I contend that rather than merely being an affirmation of melancholia, Wong's *2046* takes an extra step beyond mourning to glimpse at the present from both within and without time.

My analysis uses the model of Benjamin's immanent critique to access the truth content (*Wahrheitsgehalt*) of Wong's works through material content (*Sachgehalt*) of their production process, structural and narrative content. The relationship between material content and truth content is an important one in Benjamin's model of critique. Material content is sometimes described as appearance or mortal, while truth content is hidden and ascribed the quality of immortal. The relationship between the two is binding but not necessarily oppositional. Benjamin establishes that material content can be a symbolic representation of the truth content; critique then extracts the truth from the material form. However, he also asserts that this is not always so, especially in Goethe's works. In *Elective Affinities* (*Die Wahlverwandshaften*), material and truth content are inseparable. If material content is extracted

---

1. Benjamin, Walter. The Origin of German Tragic Drama.

from the work in attempt to reveal the truth content, whatever remains becomes insignificant. When appearance is destroyed so too is the truth. It is not a matter of 'unveiling' for the veil is integral to both appearance and truth. In Goethe's novella, truth, like 'the immanence of death in life cannot be symbolically expressed[, i]t can only be shown' (Caygill 50–1). Likewise, the truth content of Wong's films is bound to their material content. They succeed in embodying and conveying what 'cannot be symbolically expressed' through an interplay between symbolic and allegorical forms.

The task of this essay is to examine the truth content of Wong's films in regard to time through their material content without rending the former insignificant. A key to this is to arrive at an understanding of how Wong succeeds in making the elusive temporal experience of modernity perceptible—a condition Ackbar Abbas, referring to the problem of meaningful depiction in Hong Kong, describes as 'the more you try to make [experience] hold still in a reflective gaze, the more it moves under you' (6).

I tackle this argument by first examining the temporal structure of Wong Kar-Wai's films through their structures and the processes of his filmmaking. This analysis will be further contextualised by a brief exploration into the relationship between time and modernity as guided by Benjamin, Peter Osborne, Marc Augé and Ackbar Abbas. Based on the groundwork established, I build on the argument that *2046* can be interpreted as a modern mourning play with reference to the works of Howard Caygill and Stewart Martin. Lastly, I show how in the case of *2046*, Wong offers glimpses of hopes of breaking out of the endless repetition of modern temporality.

THE STRUCTURE OF WONG KAR-WAI'S FILMMAKING

Time plays a central role in Wong Kar-Wai's films. His conceptual exploration, formal experimentation and the practical solutions to problems encountered in production have become undistinguishable. His practice is based on an evolutionary process of creating permutations of instances, extensions to previous experiments, and re-configuration of existing narratives. *Ashes of Time* presents convoluted tales of lost loves and forgotten friendships told over layers upon layers of dream time, lived time, past times and future times. The rhythmic, circular, epic quality of the final work is largely due to the number of transformations it underwent during a difficult and over-extended production. As Wong simultaneously re-wrote and re-shot parts of the film, actors changed roles, characters appeared and disappeared, plots dissolved and re-formed. *Chungking Express* was shot, edited and completed using spare stock and equipment during the momentous editing task of *Ashes of Time*. Originally conceived as a composite of three stories, *Chungking Express* retained only two segments with the third mutating into a stand-alone release, *Fallen Angels*. Completed films are also open to reconfiguration. References to characters, events and instances from earlier films are drawn out, re-configured and re-presented in later ones. The life of the character Mimi/Lulu (Carina Lau Ka-Ling) from *Days of Being Wild* continues in *2046*; the main protagonist of *In the Mood for Love*, Chow Mo-Wan (Tony Leung Chiu-Wai), is given a new lease on life in the 2004 film.[2] Strategies such as these expand the depth of Wong's films to create permutations of the same instances, so that, as his cinematographer Christopher Doyle remarks, 'All Wong's films are like CD-ROMs, full of endless possible versions, and certain "virtual realities"' (n.pag.).

The dynamic relationships between narratives, characters and forms are facilitated by the interaction between the script and filmmaking process. Wong's scripts are structured and complete, but this structure is used as a scaffold within which he builds the film's narrative and character development. It is during filming and editing that decisions, such as how long a shot should last, which scene should follow the last, what narrative path to develop, are made. Rather than acting to illustrate a script, the filming and editing processes allow new meaning and narrative possibilities to be generated. In Wong's approach to filmmaking, the script acts as a 'rough' map to give direction to the act of filming, the meaning the work holds is *discovered* as the film is made. Doyle remarks that what 'feels right' ends up being what is followed (n.pag.). He recounts:

> Wong says that it's only as he edits the film that he finds the meaning of much of what we have shot. We didn't really know what certain details or colours or actions meant at the time. They anticipated where the film would take us. They were images from the future at that time that we've only just arrived. (n.pag.)

This evolutionary and generative process of creating scenarios, imagery and editing structure also gives form to Wong's 'style'.[3] This is particularly important in the construction of temporal experiences in the works. Doyle describes the process of how a particular scene was shot in *Happy Together*:

> 'Is this part real or imaginary?', I ask William [Cheung, Art Director/Editor]. We're on our own again today, Wong's still working out whether this part is a flash forward dream sequence or the last stop on Tony's [the character, Lai Yiu-Fai] physical and spiritual journey and another possible end of the film. We have no idea which image should be what,

---

2. Rather than treating the later film as a sequel, it is more useful to think of the later film as a permutation of the existing story or an experiment that re-invests in the same central character. The transformation of the protagonist, Chow Mo-Wan, from a quietly spoken, mild-mannered, sensitive young man to a sly, decadent, deceitful playboy is so total as to remain a little unconvincing.

3. I have placed the word 'style' in quotation marks to emphasise that the look and feel of the film owes to the process of making rather than a consciously prescribed 'look and feel'.

so we shoot it both ways. All we know is the real parts are to be shot on the real film stock, the same one we've used in the rest of the film. While the flatter, less saturated stock we've been forced to replace our depleted original stocks with will represent an imaginary view. (n. pag.)

The evolution of the script, characters and narrative during production creates gaps that are bridged or widened to suggest new directions and possibilities. 'Loose ends' are not ignored, surplus footage is not simply abandoned, often being re-interpreted and re-explored, at times placed at points in the films strategically—to bridge gaps or to create them. Discontinuities play an important role in Wong's films.

Memories are central to the generation of meanings in these discontinuities. Multiplying narrative threads and intersecting timelines criss-cross Wong Kar-Wai's films forming intricate webs of *mémoire involuntaire*. Hints of past events (fictional or sometimes factual) that may trigger the audience's memories are littered throughout the film in numerous ways.[4] In *2046*, the exquisite *coeng-sam*[5] is most reminiscent of *In the Mood for Love*. Bai Ling's (Zhang Ziyi) room recalls that of Yuddy's (Leslie Cheung) in *Days of Being Wild*. Dialogue is also laden with references that point to other narrative events.[6] The taxi scenes in *2046*, in particular, deliberately repeat and recall former reincarnations in previous scenes and *In the Mood for Love*.[7] Gestures, movements and poses reiterate throughout. Music used in preceding films (such as the theme tune from *Days of Being Wild*) immediately conjures up images and feelings from other stories, other times. In this way, *2064* presents a heavily convoluted set of memories on the verge of suffocation.

Music is a key element and provides an underlying structure for all Wong's films. Initially envisaged as three operas, musical thematic and tempos remain a central compositional element in *2046*. The accompaniment of music pieces with the major characters or narrative threads, namely *Siboney* with Bai Ling and *Casa Diva* (from the opera *Norma*) with Chow's unrequited love for Wang Jing-Wen (Faye Wong), act as variations to the *2046 Main Theme* by Shigeru Umbebayashi. The *Main Theme* functions as a rephrase, bringing the viewers back to a starting point. This musical structure is reflected in the narrative. The title, *2046*, stands for a city, a room, a state of

---

4. In particular the political unrest in Cambodia in 1963 and the 1966 and 1967 riots and civil unrest in Hong Kong.

5. I have used Cantonese phonetics here instead of Mandarin pinyi, since *coeng-sam* is a colloquial Cantonese term commonly used in Hong Kong to refer to this traditional dress. The formal term is *Keipo*.

6. The old method for unburdening your secret concludes *In the Mood for Love* and opens *2046*. The reference to the 'legless bird legend' first appears in *Days of Being Wild* as its central thematic. Its mention in *2046* recalls the story in the former film.

7. This also echoes a taxi scene with the two characters, Lai Yiu-fai and Ho Po-wing, set in Bueno Aires in *Happy Together*.

mind, a memory, a life event, a past, a place where nothing ever changes. In Chow's novel of the same title, 'everyone who goes to 2046 has the same goal, that is to find his/her lost past'.[8] Chow searches for Su Li-zhen (Maggie Cheung, *In the Mood for Love*) in 2046 in order to relive his past, to regain the missed opportunity to ask her whether she loves him. Chow, like all other characters in the film, is in love with his past and is unable to move on. In a frozen present, he is caught in repetitive loops of affairs and fruitless relationships. His liaisons with three women, Black Spider/Su Li-zhen (Gong Li), Bai Ling, and Wang Jing-Wen, offer him the chance of redemption in the possibility of change, but his inability to severe with the past means he remains imprisoned in 2046.[9] At the end of each affair, he returns to the same starting point.

There are two recurring locations in the film that epitomise a (non-) place where things never change. The night-club (or dance hall) Chow visits when he returns from Singapore is like metaphorical stage-set where people meet and perform their social stereotypes: the playboy, the hostess, the socialite, the entertainer. Like being on a social merry-go-round, characters slide pass each other between the tall red curtains, momentarily reconnecting their tenuous relationships through a smile, a wave, a touch, before moving on.[10] The restaurant Chow frequents is a similar non-place where the passing of time is meaningless.[11] The close-up of the restaurant set is non-distinct, the background gives no clue of time or place—it could be anywhere, anytime. Over the years that Chow goes there, things remain the same. In the restaurant scene that concludes Chow's break with Bai Ling, bodies waltz through the narrow thoroughfare, the *Main Theme* returns on the audio track orchestrating the bodies in graceful slow-motion as the camera tracks slowly backwards in the crowded space.[12] The camera frames the

---

8. My own translation of the Cantonese dialogue.

9. The naming of characters in Wong's films borders on the arbitrary. He prefers to use very ordinary and commonplace names. For example, the character names, Lai Yiu-fai and Ho Po-wing, in *Happy Together* happen to be the names of two of his crew members. Names like Su Li-zhen have a traditional ring in their ordinariness. Wong takes advantage of their commonplace quality by reusing the names. Characters named Su Li-zhen appear in *Days of Being Wild*, *In the Mood for Love* and *2046*; the two characters played by Maggie Cheung in the two earlier films could be the same person in different times—1960 and 1962. Whereas there are two Su Li-zhen in *2046*, Maggie Cheung's and Gong Li's character, both are romantically involved with Chow.

10. Fredrico Fellini employs a similar metaphor in *La Dolce Vita*.

11. Chow puts on birthday banquettes in this restaurant in order to get out of paying rents, repaying debts, or simply to make some money. Guests to such formal functions are expected to offer gifts to the host in the form of money. Chow sends invitations to his landlord and says that the invitation is in lieu of his rent—deducting the amount of rent he owes from the value of the gift.

12. This echoes similar scenes in *In the Mood for Love* when Su Li-zhen walks into the living room, bringing cigarettes for her husband. Through a doorway, we see the neigh-

figures tightly as they jostle pass one another exchanging intimate glances. There are pauses at key points in this sequence—fleeting moments of recognition as Chow and Bai Ling pass each other. Chow narrates: 'Sometimes we crossed paths but we pretended not have seen each other. Although it seemed a pity, it was probably for the best'.[13] The slow motion and repetition of the theme music sets these scenes apart from the main narratives imparting a heightened sense of time in suspension. Like a gramophone record revolving on an old turntable, the repetition intensifies the moods generated in the scene. Scenes like this repeat themselves as if existing outside lived time—like a memory or a dream.

Like a variation on a theme in music composition, Wong's films present different explorations or expressions of the same thematic. In *Two Poems by Friedrich Hölderlin* (1915) Benjamin defines the core or quintessence of a poem as the 'Poetic': 'the "sphere" [that] encompasses the "poetic task"', which in turn is 'both immanent and external to a poem' (Caygill 36). In Friedrich Hölderlin two poems, Benjamin locates the same Poetic and asserts that the two poems were configurations of the same poetic, namely the idea of death in life. The first version explores death in life in that if courage is to defend life from death, then beauty can only be a consolation. The second version approaches the concept differently: if courage is to take life through death, that is, to accept death as a necessary part of life, then life becomes beauty. In a similar way, Wong Kar-Wai's stories have the same quintessence, but each is a different attempt at tackling the task of expressing the temporal experience of modernity.[14]

Wong is upfront about the repetition, complex references, and re-departures from the same theme in his films. He describes *2046* as a conclusion to his works to date or perhaps a resolution of his long-term obsession with 1960s Hong Kong. When speaking about this setting, Wong recalls:

> I came to Hong Kong from Shanghai in 1963. For me, the Hong Kong

---

bours playing a game of mahjong. Su sits near the doorway by her husband's side. Chow Mo-Wan's wife enters the small space. Su stands up against the door as she let Chow's wife through the narrow gap into the room shortly followed by Chow leaving the room. The movement with which the bodies slide pass each other, gracefully negotiating each other's space, is slowed down, exaggerated and juxtaposed to the rhythmic rumba music. The movement of the bodies, stretched out in time, appear to dance.

13. My own translation.

14. The stories in Wong's films can also be compared to the narrative structure of Marcel Proust's *In Search of Lost Time* (*Á la Recherche du temps perdu*), where the thematic of love, friendship, and time recur throughout the narrator's remembrance of his life. As he reflects on this life at the end of the novel, he notices that events in his life form patterns. His consuming love affair takes the model of Swann's affair with Odette; his experience echoes that of the older man. Similarly, we find these patterns in Wong's characters—repeating and echoing their pasts or the pasts of others. In this way, truth content is explored and re-explored in different works.

then is a very memorable place, as if even the sun shone brighter, and radio waves permeated the air ... But memory has its own ways of modifying the past. At that time, everything seems slow. I did not intend to accurately recreate the 1960s [in *Days of Being Wild*], I just wanted to realise
some of my own memories of this past. (Ngai 27, my own translation)

Rather than interpreting Wong's works as the realisation of repressed
memories, it would be more useful to ask whether Wong himself, like his
characters, is trying to make sense of the relationship between his memories
and the constantly shifting, flowing, experience of his now. The transformation of time is central to this project.

TIME AND MODERNITY

In Peter Osborne's exposition on global capitalist modernity in 'Non-places
and the spaces of art', he asserts that modernity is primarily a schema from
which both the term's usage to label a period in history and its expression
as a social formalism are derived. These secondarily applications are essentially set in temporal relation to 'the new'. The new not only severs the future from the past and the present, but also defines the past and the present
through negation. At the same time, for the new to be meaningful, it must
also cease to be different. The new thus becomes merely repetitious. In this
way, the modern experience of temporality losses its finiteness; instead of
ending with the apocalypse, the end of time is forever delayed without the
possibility of redemption. Borrowing Benjamin's angel of history, Stewart
Martin describes this modern temporality in relation to capitalism:

> [T]he passage of time is experienced as perpetual destruction. This
> functions as theological-archaic correspondence to the abstract labour
> time of capitalist accumulation; the endless horizon of surplus value un-
> veiled as wreckage unto oblivion. (19)

The temporal experience of modernity is intrinsically linked with capitalism. Osborne argues that capitalism's more recent manifestation as a global hegemony gives rise to a new spatial model that inherently changes the
temporal logic of modernity. Through the globalisation of capitalist economy, the ubiquitous modernity can no longer be periodised by terms such as
'late' or 'post' because it is clear that it is not coming to an end (modernity
seems to have multiple beginnings but no ends). Temporal coding of modernity (such as colonisation, imperialism and the Cold War) gives way to the
'distribution of temporal differentiation at a global level'. In other words,
the multiplicity of modernity (for instance, models or stages of capitalist
economies in different countries or regions) is contained within a global social space. Departing from the temporal logic defined by 'the new', parallel
'timelines' run within one global spatial order. Historical and geo-political

definitions give way to movement of the capital (through systems such as
transportation, trade economy, and information and communication technologies within the globe) in shaping this global spatial order. This is a more
intense form of modernity characterised by the proliferation of non-places.

Here Osborne extends Marc Augé's conceptualisation of non-places as
found in *Non-Places: Introduction to an Anthropology of Supermodernity*. Augé quali-
fies non-place negatively as 'a space which cannot be defined as relational,
or historical, or concerned with identity', or as Osborne summarises, as 'a
form of space characterised by abstraction' (187). To utilise this concept in
more concrete terms, Osborne refines this definition as 'the product of the
dialectic between space of place and space of flows' (189).

The epicentre of Wong's films, the city of Hong Kong, exists within this
dialectic. The experiences found in the works are ones of global capitalist
modernity. In the one hundred and fifty years of British colonial rule Hong
Kong transformed from a fishing village, trading port, manufacturing and
export centre, into a centre for economic and cultural exchange. The arrival
of refugees and migrants displaced by the Sino-Japanese War (1937–45), the
Chinese Civil War (1946–49)[15], the Great Proletarian Cultural Revolution
(1966–76), and the Vietnam War (1959–75)[16], and the departure of residents,
most notably after the 1967 riots and the signing of the Sino-British Joint
Declaration in 1984, have all contributed to a sense of continuously accelerating change. The experience of transience culminated in the territory's
1997 change of sovereignty from a British Crown Colony to a Special Administrative Region of the People's Republic of China. The city continues to
transform itself with its streams of returning expatriates, temporary foreign
workers, newly affluent tourists and new migrants from the mainland cross-
ing the city's gates everyday. In this city, continuous flows of people, capitals,
goods and information disrupt the nature of time and turn the experience
of time into one which , in Martin's words, 'is never fulfilled and always incomplete, in debt to past or future value' (21). Time resides in the dialectic
between space that is Hong Kong and the space of its flows.

It is no coincidence that Marc Augé begins his thesis on non-places with
Roissy Airport. To Augé, the traveller's space is the archetype of non-place
where identity fails to establish itself, a condition he defines as 'supermodernity'. He claims that three types of 'accelerated transformations' give rise to
supermodernity (24). Firstly, the excess of time is brought about by an over-
abundance of seemingly significant incidents, which by their sheer density,

---

15. Following the victory of the Chinese Communist Party in October 1949, the number of people departing China for Hong Kong was so great that the Chinese government
banned its citizens from leaving its borders on 30 April 1950. The Hong Kong government
also enforced China's policy of stopping Chinese refugees from entering the territory.

16. Great Britain declared Hong Kong as the first port of refuge for Vietnam war refugees in 1975.

robs events of meanings (Augé 28). Time is thus displaced as an intelligible marker in our perception of the past. Secondly, his description of the over-abundance of space echoes that of Paul Virilio, arguing that modern tech-nologies, from astronomy and space exploration to terrestrial transportation and communication, have reshaped our spatial perception of the world. Not only the scales and speeds we perceive have multiplied, the references with which we make meanings have also proliferated. Thirdly, the 'individualisa-tion of references' necessitates 'the multiplicity of average individuals' where the 'average of individuals' is simply 'an abstraction' (Augé 38).

In the context of Hong Kong, these excesses cumulate into what Ackbar Abbas calls 'dis-appearance'. He writes:

> [D]is-appearance here does not imply non appearance, absence, or lack of presence. It is not even non recognition—it is more a question of mis-recognition, of recognising a thing as something else. (Abbas 7)

Superimposing Augé's framework of three accelerated forms of super-modernity onto the cultural conditions of Hong Kong, we see the three spe-cific factors at work.[17] Firstly, the excess of time is heightened by the speed of change in the city. Each layer in the rapid turnover of place and product occurs at different speeds relative to one another resulting in asynchronici-ty.[18] Secondly, the overabundance of space is a consequence of Hong Kong's ephemeral cityscape and marketplace. For example, the continuous shifting of shorelines through reclamation alone necessitates a constant revision of maps. Thirdly, 'individualisation of references' takes the form of symbolic abstraction, which disconnects representations from their relation to actual existing situations. The spatial and temporal reference points provided by fixed definitions, such as the term 'to return and to belong', or the 'East–West' binary, continue to dictate how actual space and time are interpreted, yet as reference points they no longer adequately delineate the actual exist-ing social, cultural, and physical conditions of Hong Kong in a meaningful way.[19] These three accelerations make the conditions of Hong Kong elusive to grasp and problematic in its representation. Wong Kar-Wai's films chal-lenge these un-representable conditions by eluding to the different experi-ences of time through scenarios.

Two O Four Six is a film about a promise.[20] This promise refers to the '50 years without change' guaranteed by both Chinese and British politicians on the advent of Hong Kong's change of sovereignty in 1997, making 2046

---

17. See the introduction in Abbas (1–15). Although Abbas writes of the three conditions as outlined here, he does not do so with reference to Augé.

18. Also see Virilio (18).

19. 'To return and to belong' was a term used to denote Hong Kong's hand-over of sov-ereignty in 1997. *Huigui* can also be translated as 'to return where one belongs'.

20. I have translated this literally from how the title is spoken in Chinese.

the year this promise expires. In the face of fear, uncertainties, and anxieties, the promise of '50 years without change' was offered as an assurance, or
perhaps a consolation.[21] This is particularly absurd given the rapid changes
Hong Kong has continuously undergone since its colonisation in the late 19th
century. If '50 years without change' can be offered as a kind of assurance,
what kind of comfort does this promise bring and at what cost? As Wang
Jing-Wen in the film asks, 'Is there anything in this world that will never
change?'. 'Fifty years without change' is time without end.

In supermodernity, time has become a commodity, an abstract but nevertheless actual thing that can be bought, sold, and exchanged. Chow tells
Bai Ling, 'I don't have anything except plenty of time'. He proposes that
everyone's surplus time can be borrowed and repaid. Likewise, relationships
can only be temporary transactions.[22] Bai Ling is offended by the thought
that people are simply 'time-fillers' for Chow, but she too fills her time until
'the right person comes along'. Connections can only be temporary, everyone waits for love but it does not come. Chow frequently offers himself the
consolation: 'Love is a matter of timing'. Finding love has become the only
promise of salvation, but like a reunion with God, this too has been forever
deferred. In Wong Kar-Wai's films, love provides a key to connection, but
the hyper-capitalistic conditions of excessive remembering and the reluc-
tance to forget render this impossible. Chow's love has no future; his present
is a frozen repetition because he cannot leave his past.

The overabundance of events marking time produces multiple asynchronous temporalities. In the film, Chow writes '2047'—a story of asynchronous temporal disjuncture. It tells the story of a man, escaping from
2046, aboard a high-speed train. In what seems an interminable journey, he
falls in love with an android cabin attendant, but their asynchronous speeds
prevent their connection. By filming the movement of the actors' slow action
at half-speed (12 frames per second) and running the final composite runs
at normal speed, these scenes convey the asynchronous reality. No matter
how many times the man conveys his feelings for the android she does not
respond. The barman explains that the long journeys have taken their toll
on these androids and their mechanisms are wearing out. They are in decay and their reactions are inevitably delayed: 'They might want to laugh,
but the smile will be too slow to come. They might want to cry but the tears
won't well up till next day.' These asynchronous temporalities produce inef-

---

21. This broadly refers to the conserving the city's political, legal, cultural and social
systems.

22. As suggested by his statement in narration: 'I learnt to make the most out of these
social situations. These relationships last only as long as the morning dew, but who cares?
What, in the world, last forever?'. The frequent use of vernacular phrases, 'fung cheung jok
hing/ fengchang zuoxing' means handling a situation and making fun; 'mou seui ching
yan/ wushui qingren' describes lovers who part as the morning mist disperses.

fective mourning.

MOURNING

Developed from the trajectory laid down in his earlier 1916 essays, 'The Happiness of Ancient Humanity', 'Socrates' and 'On the Middle Ages', Benjamin's habilitation thesis, *The Origin of German Tragic Drama*, tackles a frequently asked question about the mourning plays (*Trauerspiel*): what is being mourned? This question is approached first by comparing the concept of happiness in ancient classical civilisation with that of the Christian era.

Benjamin argues that in ancient Greek culture, happiness is understood to be the victory endowed by the gods. Tragedy, like happiness, fulfils destiny that is willed by the gods. It is within this completion and fulfilment where the absolute resides. In comparison, in Christian mourning absolute is removed in the later era where God is no longer accessible, destiny is prolonged, and fate is incomplete. In Christian times, the experience of time itself is transformed as Caygill summarises:

> [T]ime is open-ended; God is remote, and the completion of time in the advent of the absolute has both already happened in the birth of Christ and is eternally deferred in the Last Judgement. In the mourning play, the organising principle is not completion in and of time, but repetition ... (53–4)

Central to the transformation of the nature of time in mourning plays is the shift in 'forms of consciousness and experience' to the modern. Benjamin links early modernity to the prevalence of Protestantism and the emergence of capitalism. Extending from Max Weber's *The Protestant Ethic* (1904) and *The Spirit of Capitalism* (1904), Benjamin does not argue that capitalism is a result of the Protestant faith, but rather capitalism itself became a religion (as argued in his 1921's 'Capitalism as Religion', *SW* 1: 288–91). The concept of capitalism as religion provides the context for mourning plays, where fulfilment (or reunion with God) is forever deferred. It is the loss of complete-able time (or fulfilled fate) that is mourned in these dramas. This is reinforced by the comparison of the deep structural differences between the German mourning play and Greek tragedy. While tragedy actively fulfils time, the actions in mourning plays are 'inauthentic' and 'empty'. The writers of the *Trauerspiele* were witnesses to the temporal transformation brought about by early capitalism.

Wong's films take the forms of mourning plays, albeit in the contexts of supermodernity and hypercapitalism. The experience of an endless, repetitive time is played out in his works through a deliberate play on temporality. The use of inter-titles to mark times and dates in *2046* is one example where filmic language and image are employed to create an asynchronous tension between experienced time and told time. 'December 24th 1966', 'De-

cember 24th 1967', 'December 24th 1968', and 'December 24th 1969' act like
a metronome marking various points in the unfolding narrative. However,
just as these inter-titles tell time they also deliberately lie about time. Two
scenes, in particular, accentuate the tension between experienced time and
told time by juxtaposing shots of stillness with suggestions of rapid passing
of time. At the end of '2047', long shots and close-ups of the android staring
dreamily outside the train intercut with the intertitles: 'one hour later', 'ten
hours later', 'a hundred hours later', 'a thousand hours later'. It is as if she
ceases to function and remains there for a thousand years. When attempting
to change the ending of '2047', Chow sits at his desk, pen poised. As the pen
hovers above the page the surrounding light changes from light to dark to
light. The same intertitles flash up to announce the passing of time—a hundred hours have passed. The markers of time cease to be meaningful.

This hellish repetition and endless waiting manifests as senseless utterances in the language of lamentation and mourning. Caygill writes, 'For
Benjamin, the mourning play evokes this lament for the loss of significance
or the removal of the absolute through an intensified question of loss.' (54)
When Chow first encounters Wang he hears faint muttering in the next
room. Peering through the wall partition, he sees Wang pacing back and
forth repeating in Japanese, 'Yes, I will come with you', 'Yes, I understand',
'Let us go'. These are answers to her lover's last request: 'Leave with me'.
She remained silent as she watched him leave and now her replies come late.
Like the androids in '2047', her responses are out of time, discordant, fragments with no meaning. Her senseless utterances mourn for lost time, endlessly repeating in empty time.

The material content of the German mourning play is largely characterised by the actions of the sovereign and the intriguer, and the dialectics
that occur between the two roles. The sovereign, who by definition has absolute power, is powerless in the face of unfolding events. He is melancholic,
indecisive and consumed by his mourning of the past. He is unable to make
meaning, while his dialectic opposite, the intriguer, destroys all meanings.
'The sovereign freezes the present and the future through a mourning for
meaning that has been forever lost while [the intriguer] consumes past and
present in an ecstatic destruction of any attempt to arrive at meaning.' (Caygill 60) This dialectical opposition is the underlying structure or 'the principle of construction' of the mourning play.

In *Happy Together*, the two roles take the forms of Lai Yiu-Fai (Tony Leung Chiu-Wai) and Ho Po-Wing (Leslie Cheung). The two lovers are stranded in Buenos Aires. On the verge of yet another break-up, Ho asks Lai to
start over again. Lai is the sovereign; he is seemingly in control. He finds
them a place to live; he takes odd jobs to raise money for the airfare home;
he pays the rent; he takes care of their everyday needs. Ho is the intriguer:
he is a destroyer. He steals; he hustles; he is unfaithful. He mocks his lover's

devotion with his infidelities. Lai tries to control Ho but is powerless to stop him from leaving despite hiding his lover's passport. Just as Lai resolves to move on, Ho returns, beaten and broken. Lai nurses him back to health. They start over again only to end up in the same dead-end. In *2046*, the roles become less distinct. Chow is both the sovereign and the intriguer. As an author he has absolute power over his characters. He says, 'I felt total control in my fictional world'. Yet when asked to alter the ending of '2047', he remains frozen, unable to write a single word. In reality, his actions mock his true intentions. He abandons his present and future in order to mourn for the past where the only meaningful relationship for him exists. Although desperate for authentic connections, he destroys his own attempts at building meaningful relationships.

EXTRA-TEMPORALITY OF 2047

Chow writes two stories in the film: '2046', a newspaper serial that tells the story of men and women who strive to find the place, 2046, where they can retrieve their lost memories and relive their pasts; and '2047', a gift to Wang Jing-Wen that tells of a man escaping from 2046. The former is a story of hellish repetition, obsessive remembering and despair; the later is a story of struggle, overcoming dejection and hope. At the film draws to an end, Chow leaves Bai Ling for the last time, the camera tracks slowly left to follow him across the hallway, down the stairs, and into the night. On screen, an intertitle flashes up, 'He did not turn around. It was as if he boarded a long, long train, in the boundless night, towards a hazy future'.[23] Like a coda to the main phrase, Chow catches a taxi, but this time he sits in the back, alone and with no companion. 'How long does it take to leave 2046? No one knows,' writes Chow, 'For some, it is relatively easy; for others it will take tremendous will.'[24] Chow realises that 'there can never be substitution in love' and he will never find his lost love in 2046, in the place where nothing changes. It will take Chow tremendous will to put the past behind him, but the existence of '2047' alludes to the possibility of breaking out of the endless loop—to stand outside of time albeit momentarily.[25]

While Wong uses symbols of an aestheticised romanticism to mark out generic time, he also presents allegories in the form of narratives that exist outside of time in order to uncover the underlying meaning of the lives that exist within time. He combines the use of symbols and allegories in his works. The symbol makes a finite image infinite by 'freezing the moment'; in

---

23. My own translation.

24. My own translation.

25. Like the many allegories in the film, the meaning of '2047' is manyfold. It is the story Chow has written for Wang, it is the room he lives in, and most importantly it is the first year after the promise 'fifty years without change' expires.

allegory, whilst the difference between appearance and essence is marked, 'all meanings are subject to time' (Caygill 59). According to Caygill, Benjamin presents their 'dialectic reversal' in *The Origin of German Tragic Drama* that:

> When allegory turns upon itself, the occasion for mourning becomes one of affirmation, a celebration of the finitude of the thought of finitude. This is not a return to a symbolic affirmation of the presence of the eternal in the finite, but an allegory of the finitude of the finite. (61)

Mourning and melancholy are tied with the incompleteness of time. By allowing symbols and allegory to act on the same stage, finiteness returns to time through allegory. Benjamin pays particular attention to the extension of mourning in the later modernist works in 'distorted recognition' in memory or 'aura'. In *In Search of Lost Time*, the narrator's epiphany allows him to identify the extra-temporality of unconscious memories, he writes:

> [T]he being within me who was enjoying this impression was enjoying it because of something shared between a day and the present moment, something extra-temporal, and this being appeared only when through one of these moments of identity between the present and the past, it was to find itself in the only milieu in which it could live and enjoy the essence of things, that is to say outside of time. (Proust, 176)

When confronted with the effects of aging shortly after his epiphany, the narrator is reminded that for experiences to be meaningful they also need to be lived within time, within the passing of time.

In 'Some Motifs on Baudelaire', Benjamin employs Baudelaire, Freud and Proust as guides to unearth the nature of modern experience. Using Freud's 'Beyond the Pleasure Principles' and establishing a connection between shocks and the formation of the unconscious memory, Benjamin construes that to live with the constant distraction of modern life, everyday occurrences are only 'processed' at the level of the merely lived through (*Erlebnis*) rather than formed fully as experience (*Erfahrang*). He asks: if the aura, which stands outside of time, which is necessary to access the unconscious memory to enable experience, is destroyed by the new (and he argues that it does)—how then is experience possible in modern times?

The formation of modern experience relies on navigating through the shock to allow conscious and unconscious memory to come together. This convergence results in the modern condition of memory (Martin 22). Proust's works combine *mémoire voluntaire* with *mémoire involontaire* to produce experience. The destruction of the aura is compensated by 'correspondences' that simultaneously deflect and absorb shocks into the unconscious. Allegories (used in Baudelaire's poetry) and montage both play crucial roles in accessing unconscious memory and leading to its convergence with conscious memory in the generation of experience. Benjamin writes that in

Baudelaire, 'significant days are days of completing time … days of recollection … not connected with the other days, but stand out from time. As for
their substance, Baudelaire has defined it in the notion of *correspondences* …'
(*Illuminations* 177).[26] In Martin's words: 'The correspondences exit the negative temporality of the new, accessing time outside of history, a completed
time' (Martin 22).

Wong offers us a story of Hong Kong embedded in the audio track of *2046*'s
concluding credits. Woven in with the theme music are 'the radio waves
that permeated the air' evoking moments of the city's history: Hong Kong's
first television broadcast, its recovery from the ruins of war, its rise in the
economic miracle, Margaret Thatcher's ominous foretelling that, 'Hong
Kong will maintain its economic systems and way of life for fifty years
after the first of July, 1997'.[27] Through his films, Wong presents us with the
unchanging symbols that stand for Hong Kong with the decaying allegories
that evoke its experience. The films allow us to glimpse outside of time,
borrowing Martin's words: 'exit[ing] the negative temporality of the new,
accessing time outside history, a completed time', in order to overcome love,
loss and mourning to live within time.

---

26. On Some Motifs in Baudelaire, p. 177.

27. The impression that radio waves permeating the air is one of Wong's first memory of
Hong Kong when he arrived there from Shanghai in 1963. See Ngai (27).

10

Experience and Play:
Walter Benjamin and the Prelapsarian Child

Carlo Salzani

> The gracefulness of children does exist, and it exists pri-
> marily as a kind of corrective to society; it is one of those
> 'hints' we are vouchsafed of a 'happiness as yet undisci-
> plined'.
>
> Benjamin to Adorno, 7 May 1940

In 1951 Adorno published *A Berlin Childhood around 1900*, a thin volume of Benjamin's childhood memories; his first work to appear posthumously, it was a commercial failure. Today it is one of the most popular of his works with non-academic audiences, but probably for the wrong reason: it is generally considered a sophisticated and elegant collection of childhood memories, to be filed under the section 'autobiography'. It should rather be situated within a wider theoretical frame, that of a life-long interest in the figure of the child. This was not merely an ephemeral liking for the world of childhood; rather, the child holds a central theoretical place within Benjamin's project: it stands for a concept of experience, as opposed to the hollowed-out experience of the modern bourgeois adult and is therefore a figure of and for redemption and revolution. 'Experience' is a central concept in Benjamin, from his early writings for the student journal *Der Anfang* through to *The Arcades Project*, and the question of the child constantly accompanies it, albeit often implicitly or in a minor tone. Nevertheless, 'experience' is also an ambiguous notion in Benjamin, locked into the antinomy between the yearning for a lost 'authenticity' and the celebration of the dawn of a new era, an ambiguity best represented by the image of a Janus-faced Benjamin, looking si-

multaneously to the past and into the future. In this dialectic, the child usually stands for the fullness of experience of lost times, but there are also hints
that connect it with the 'fresh start' of a mechanised, *non-innocent* modernity.
I will here attempt to explore this dialectic, analysing the figure of the child
in Benjamin's work through the lens of the notion of experience.

EXPERIENCE AND YOUTH

The pillars upon which the concepts of experience and childhood are founded are Benjamin's peculiar notions of perception, language and *physis*, and
their origins are to be sought in the writings of his student years, the 1910s.
Here the child itself does not appear, but the attributes that later make it a
figure of redemption are nonetheless defined. A few biographical facts are
crucial: Benjamin's encounter, as a boarder in Hermann Lietz's school in
Haubinda, with the educational reformer Gustav Wyneken; his first publications in the student journals *Der Anfang* and *Die freie Schulgemeinde* (the second
edited by Wyneken); his involvement in what is known as the *Jugendbewegung*,
or student movement, including his participation in student organizations
such as the *Freie Studentenschaft* (Free Students' Unions), the *Sprechsaal* (speech
hall) and the *Abteilung für Schulreform* (Department for School Reform). These
facts cannot be analysed in depth here.[1] What is important for the present
argument is that in these years, and through the involvement with the *Jugendbewegung*, Benjamin shaped and defended an idea of youth (and experience)
Irving Wohlfarth defines 'the guiding "idea" of his life'. Youth precedes the
'Fall' into bourgeois adulthood, it is still idealistic and heroic, capable of
spirituality and nobility, and is thus 'the metaphysical age *par excellence*', in a
sense, a 'prelapsarian' age (Wohlfarth 164). The writings of these years are
full of rhetoric and tacky idealism,[2] but their notion of a prelapsarian youth,
modified, purified and transformed, will remain at the core of Benjamin's
interest in the child.

For example, in the short piece 'Experience' (*Erfahrung*), published pseu-
donymously in *Der Anfang* in 1913, Benjamin counterposes to (bourgeois)
adult experience understood as an 'expressionless, impenetrable, and ever-
the-same' mask devoid of any spirit, a 'different experience' (*eine andere Erfahrung*), youth, which is 'the most beautiful, most untouchable, most immediate because it can never be without spirit while we remain young'. The

1. For detailed accounts and analyses see for example Brodersen, Imai (35–47), Wohlfarth
(160–72).

2. See for example 'Die Freie Schulgemeinde' (*GS* VII·1: 9–15); 'Lily Brauns Manifest an
die Schuljugend' (*GS* III: 9–11); 'Die Schulreform, eine Kulturbewegung' (*GS* II·1: 12–16);
'Die Moralunterricht' (*GS* II·1: 48–54); 'Ziele und Wege der studentisch-pädagogischen
Gruppen an reichsdeutschen Universitäten' (*GS* II·1: 60–6); 'Die Jugend schwieg' (*GS* II·1:
66–7); 'Studentische Autorenabende' (*GS* II·1: 68–71); 'Die religiöse Stellung der neuen
Jugend' (*GS* II·1: 72–4).

adult 'philistine' devalues the youth's experience, making it into a 'time of sweet youthful pranks, of childish rapture, before the long sobriety of serious life'. But where the philistine's experience is the anaesthetised, comfortable 'eternal one of spiritlessness', 'the youth will experience [*erleben*] spirit, and the less effortlessly he attains greatness, the more he will encounter spirit everywhere in his wanderings and in every person' (*GS* II·1: 54–6; SW 1: 3–5).[3] This piece introduces two terms, for which in English only 'experience' is available as a translation, key words running through all of Benjamin's thought: *Erfahrung* and *Erlebnis*. Their connotation is not constant in Benjamin and varies with the years and the contexts; I will repeatedly return to this difference.[1] In the juvenile 'Experience', *Erfahrung* is the philistine mask of a science-based (Kantian or Neo-Kantian) experience, blind to the higher values of the spirit, which remain *unerfahrbar*, 'inexperienceable'.

The same notion is reiterated in the 1914–15 fragment 'The Life of Students': what distinguishes student life, Benjamin writes, 'is the will to submit to a principle, to identify completely with an idea', whilst 'the concept of "science" or scholarly discipline [*Wissenschaft*] serves primarily to conceal a deep-rooted, bourgeois indifference' (*GS* II·1: 76; *SW* 1: 38). The need to establish a higher concept of experience, different from the merely scientific in Kant and the Neo-Kantian school, is central to the more mature 1918 'On the Program of the Coming Philosophy'. To take the principles of experience (*Erfahrung* is the term used throughout the fragment) from the sciences, Benjamin writes, means to reduce it to 'naked, primitive, self-evident experience' as the only kind possible (*GS* II·1: 158; *SW* 1: 101). Benjamin calls for a re-foundation of the concept of experience through a re-foundation of the conditions of knowledge, in order to overcome the pragmatist division of object and subject and achieve 'the sphere of total neutrality' in regard to them. This will, in turn, lead to the discovery of an 'autonomous, innate sphere of knowledge in which this concept in no way continues to designate the relation between two metaphysical entities' (*GS* II·1: 163; *SW* 1: 104). Religious experience is important here because it transcends the subject/object

---

3. All references to Benjamin's works are made parenthetically in the text. All references to *The Arcades Project* are to the convolute number. For the other works, references are provided both to the German text of the *Gesammelte Schriften* (hereafter cited as *GS*), and to the English translation of the *Selected Writings* (hereafter cited as SW).

4. Both terms can be rendered as 'experience', but, etymologically, *Erlebnis* refers to the verb *leben*, to live, and hints thus as something 'lived', sometimes with temporal and spatial limitations—'a single, noteworthy experience', explain the translators of the Harvard edition (SW 2: 267n)—, other times with a negative, vitalistic and irrationalist emphasis (see 'On Some Motifs in Baudelaire'). *Erfahrung* contains instead *fahren*, to travel, and refers at times to that kind of experience learned from life and travels over an extended period and that can be narrated (see 'The Storyteller'), at other times to a more authentic concept of experience (see 'On Some Motifs in Baudelaire'). A thorough exposition of this concept can be found, for example, in Weber.

dichotomy in the revelation of an ontological truth and is thus the basis of a concept of experience Martin Jay argues 'might justly be called noumenal or ontological' (Jay 147). This can be achieved 'only by relating knowledge to language', since 'a concept of knowledge gained from reflection on the linguistic nature of knowledge will create a corresponding concept of experience which will also encompass realms that Kant failed to truly systematize' (*GS* II·1: 168; *SW* 1: 108). The notion of experience here rejects both the Kantian *Erfahrung*, the empirical experience of the scientific subject, and the Diltheyan *Erlebnis*, the inner experience of the contingent and pre-rational subject. Founded upon a knowledge autonomously beyond the subject-object terminology—Jay defines it as 'mythical' (148)—it is central for the child of the later writings, as is the focus on language.

The 1916 fragment 'On Language as Such and on the Language of Man' is thus fundamental. Here, in a strongly anti-Saussurean argument, the 'name' is identified as 'the linguistic being of things' and therefore the true knowledge of the thing. The Adamite act of naming depends on how the language of things is communicated to the namer: it is thus not 'creative', but 'receptive', and in it 'the word of God shines forth' (*GS* II·1: 150; *SW* 1: 69). What matters for the discussion of the child is the relationship between language and nature after the Fall. When God's word curses the ground, the 'muteness' of nature begins, 'which is what we mean by the 'deep sadness of nature'. This muteness and profound melancholy come from the fact of being named 'not from the one blessed paradisiacal language ... , but from the hundred languages of man, in which name has already withered'. Things no longer have 'proper names' (*Eigennamen*), but rather, in the language of men, they are 'overnamed' (*überbenannt*) (*GS* II·1: 155; *SW* 1: 73). Only the child, in the later writings, will be given access, through its prelapsarian condition, to the 'secret password' (*geheime Losung*) of the language of nature (*GS* II·1: 157; *SW* 1: 74).[5]

This conception of nature, which will remain a constant throughout Benjamin, is profoundly Romantic, precedent and opposed to the objectifying and exploitative attitude of scientific/productive observation. Romanticism was the greatest influence on Benjamin in these years and was never merely superseded by either Marxism or Baudelairean modernism. Rather, it will 'merge' with them and persist, as a subterranean but powerful current, in the later writings.[6] The section of his doctoral thesis, *The Concept of*

---

5. For a thorough analysis of the question of language in Benjamin see Menninghaus; see also Bröcker.

6. On Benjamin and Romanticism see for example Bullock, and Hanssen and Benjamin. Freud's influence on Benjamin is also important, but as far as the figure of the child is concerned, it seems that the Romantics' suggestions of childhood as mythical, prelapsarial innocence and wholeness are not touched by the Freudian notion of a 'perverse' and 'polymorphic' childhood. The concept of 'innocence', which Freud dispels and is instead

Criticism in German Romanticism (1919), entitled 'The Early Romantic Theory of the Knowledge of Nature' is fundamental to the analysis of the child.[7]
The knowledge of the object, according to this theory (based principally on
Novalis), is 'immediate [*unmittelbar*] in the same high degree as only perception can be; and the readiest grounding of the immediacy of perception likewise proceeds from a medium common to the perceiver and the perceived'.
That is, this immediacy presupposes a partial 'interpenetration' (*Durchdrin-
gung*) of subject and object: knowledge proceeds from the self-knowledge of
the object, which, through 'observation' (*Beobachtung*), is called into 'wakeful-
ness' (*wachgerufen*) 'by one centre of reflection (the observer) in another (the
thing) only insofar as the first, through repeated reflections, intensifies itself
to the point of encompassing the second'. Observation is thus the 'evocation
of self-consciousness and self-knowledge in the things observed. To observe
a thing means only to arouse it to self-recognition' (*GS* I·1: 60; *SW* 1: 148). It
has 'magical' (also called 'ironic') character, which consists in the observer's
quality of 'getting nearer to the object and of finally drawing it into himself'.
Observation—and this is fundamental—*does not put questions to nature*:

> [i]nstead, [it] fixes in its view only the self-knowledge nascent in the ob-
> ject; or rather it, the observation, is the nascent consciousness of the ob-
> ject itself. It can rightly be called ironic, therefore, because in its *not know-
> ing* [*Nicht-Wissen*]—in its attending [*Zuschauen*]—observation *knows better*,
> being identical with the object. It would thus be permissible, if indeed
> not more correct, to leave this correlation generally out of play, and to
> speak of a *coincidence of the objective and the subjective side in knowledge*. Simul-
> taneous with any cognition of an object is the actual coming-into-being
> [*Werden*] of this object itself. For knowledge, according to the basic prin-
> ciple of knowledge of objects, is a process that first makes what is to be
> known into that as which it is known. (*GS* I·1: 61; *SW* 1: 148, my empha-
> ses)

This mode of 'attending' to the object without questioning it, this 'not-knowing' that 'knows better', the ability to listen to the 'secret password' of the
language of nature, will be named the 'mimetic faculty' in his later writings
and will become the prerogative of the child.[8] Mimesis and prelapsarian

---

the core of the Romantics' 'cult of childhood', will remain the central feature of Benjamin's
child. On Freud's influence on Benjamin see for example Rickels (142–53), and Cohen
(passim).

7. A very Romantic notion of nature can also be found in the 1914–15 fragment 'The
Metaphysics of Youth', especially the section 'The Diary'. See *GS* II·1: 96–103; *SW* 1:
10–6.

8. Where these questions receive a systematic treatment is in two important fragments
of the 1930s: 'Doctrine of the Similar' (January–February 1933) and 'On the Mimetic
Faculty' (April–September 1933). Similarity is here identified not only as a characteristic
of nature, but also as a peculiar capacity of human beings, the 'once powerful compulsion
to become similar and to behave mimetically', whose school' is children's play: it is

language thus form the basis of the experience of the child and remain key concepts throughout Benjamin's work.

ON BOOKS AND CITIES

The birth of his son Stefan in 1918 represented a turning point for Benjamin: he not only started a collection of children's books,[9] but also began to take an interest in the world of childhood and to consider it a topic for intellectual analysis. His analysis starts from the children books: the 1918–21 short 'Notes for a Study of the Beauty of Colored Illustrations in Children's Books' extends the observations of the 1914–15 fragment 'A Child's View of Color' into the analysis of colourful illustrations. The problem of perception (*Wahrnehmung*) is a focus for Benjamin's interest in these early years, and child's perception interested him because it is not yet developed and structured into a system of correlations and reflections. The child's receptivity is therefore 'pure' (*reinen Empfänglichkeit*), insofar as it is 'directed at the world' (*GS* VI: 111; *SW* I: 51), in the sense of observation theorised by the early Romantics. Coloured illustrations awaken a sort of Platonic anamnesis in the child, 'for whom picture books are paradise'. 'Children,' Benjamin writes, 'learn in the memory of their first intuition. And they learn from bright colors, because the fantastic play of color is the home of memory without yearning (*sehnsuchtlosen*), and it can be free of yearning because it is unalloyed' (*GS* VI: 123–5; *SW* I: 264–5). This intuitive learning is the 'secret password' adults have forgotten (in their yearning[10]) and that gives access to the lost paradise.

The 1924 review essay of Karl Hobrecher's *Alte vergessene Kinderbücher* and its 1926 companion piece 'A Glimpse into the World of Children's Books'

'everywhere permeated by mimetic modes of behaviour, and its realm is by no means limited to what one person can imitate in another. The child plays at being not only a shopkeeper or teacher but also a windmill and a train'. The canon of what Benjamin calls 'nonsensuous similarities' [*unsinnliche Ähnlichkeiten*] though, is to be individuated in language: Benjamin reiterates here his concept of language 'not as an agreed-upon system of signs' but as fundamental onomatopoeic, and thus imbued with a fundamental 'magical aspect'. Language is the 'medium into which the earlier perceptual capacity for recognizing the similar had, without residue, entered to such an extent that language now represents the medium in which objects encounter and come into relation with one another' (see *GS* II·1: 204–10, 210–13; *SW* 2: 694–8, 720–22). On these concepts see Opitz ('Ähnlichkeit' 15–49).

9. As Scholem writes, 'the collection was really launched by Dora's enthusiasm for the genre. Dora also loved legends and fairy tales. She and Benjamin made each other birthday presents of illustrated children's books until at least 1923' (66). When they finally divorced in 1930 Dora kept the collection.

10. 'For adults, the yearning for paradise is the yearning of yearnings [*die Sehnsucht der Sehnsuchten*]. Not the yearning for fulfillment, but the yearning to be without yearning' (*GS* VI: 124; *SW* I: 265).

are both important: in these two pieces Benjamin not only reiterates his ideas on colour and perception (in almost exactly the same words), but also introduces some fundamental concepts that will remain central. First, he argues that when reading books and most of all their images, children 'inhabit' (*wohnen*) them: they annul the distance between the subject and the object, complete the books by filling them 'with a poetry of their own'; they 'inscribe [*beschreiben*] the pictures with their ideas' (*GS* III: 20; *SW* I: 411). In the second piece, the child is described as penetrating (*eindringen*) 'into those pages, becoming suffused, like a cloud, with the riotous colors of the world of pictures'; he 'overcomes the illusory barrier of the book's surface and passes through colored textures and brightly painted partitions to enter a stage on which fairy tales spring to life' (*GS* IV·1,2: 609; *SW* I: 435). With a final reference to Goethe, Benjamin describes colours as 'the intuitions of fantasy; in contrast to the creative imagination', which 'manifest themselves as a primal phenomenon [*Urphänomen*]'(*GS* IV·1,2: 613; *SW* I: 442).

The second important and recurrent motif is that

> children are particularly fond of haunting any site where things are being visibly worked on. They are irresistibly drawn by the *detritus* generated by building, gardening, housework, tailoring, or carpentry. In waste products they recognize *the face that the world of thinGS turns directly and solely to them*. In using these things, they do not so much *imitate* [*nachbilden*] the works of adults as bring together, in the artefact produced in play, materials of widely differing kinds *in a new, intuitive relationship* [*in eine sprunghafte neue Beziehung*]. Children thus produce their own small world of things within the greater one. (*GS* III: 16; *SW* I: 408, my emphases)

This passage will be reproduced word for word in 'One-Way Street' under the title 'Construction Site'. It introduces the observation that children, unlike bourgeois adults, are not attracted by the world of the untouchable and fetishised commodity, but by *detritus* and *waste*: like the ragpicker, they collect the detritus and put them together in new relationships, that is, new *constellations*. Like the ragpicker, they thus redeem things from the fate of the commodity. But, unlike the ragpicker, in refuse they also gain true access to the world of things, which can communicate their divine 'names' 'directly and solely' to children (cf Gilloch *Myth* 86ff; Richter 212ff). Another important point is that children's activity, play, is not an 'imitation' (*Nachbildung*, copy or replica) of the work of adults, but is rather distinct, autonomous and creative in its own terms. Finally, a recurrent motif is the accusation that bourgeois pedagogy is too 'infatuated with psychology', reflecting adults' anxieties and fashions rather than pursuing a true fulfilment of childhood (*GS* III: 16; *SW* I: 412). These intuitions come together in the radio talk 'Children's Literature' (1929), one passage of which is especially important for this argument. The anti-cumulative notion of *Erfahrung*, aired in the juvenile 'Experience', returns here with regard to reading: it is compared to 'nourishment' (*Ernährung*), which is not merely the cumulative act of eating, but a process of 'absorption' (*Einverleibung*): 'we do not read to increase our experiences,' Benjamin writes, 'we read to increase ourselves' (*GS* VII·1: 257; *SW* 2: 255).[11] This is the child's approach to reading, different from, and uncomprehended by, the psychologised bourgeois model of education.

The other important locus for the figure of the child in the writings of the 1920s is his city portraits. Here the child is no more than an 'extra', but the connections child-city-memory and child-city-experience, so important for the Berlin *mémoires* of the 1930s, are established here. In 'Naples' (1925), children don't live the 'protected' bourgeois life of the German north, but 'experience' the porosity of the city, the 'interpenetration' (*ineinander übergehen*) of everything with everyone that forms new and ever-changing constellations: they wander the streets late at night, are acquainted with sex and almost 'exchanged' among relatives and neighbours (*GS* IV·1: 307–16; *SW* 1: 414–21). 'Moscow' (1927) is probably the most important of his city portraits: the child is here connected with the newcomer or the stranger or, better, the stranger is *like* a child in the city. 'The instant you arrive,' Benjamin writes, 'the childhood stage [*Kinderstadium*] begins. On the thick sheet ice of the streets, walking has to be relearned' (*GS* IV·1: 318; *SW* 2: 23). The experience of the city is for the newcomer as new and unbiased, that is, *unmediated*, by previous knowledge, as is that of the child.[12] In another passage, a further important distinction is made: now it is the Muscovite who is like a child, 'closely mingled [*gemischt*] with people and things', whose gaze is a 'tender, swift brushing along stones, people, and horses', whereas the western European plays the role of the adult, whose gaze is 'condescending' (*von oben herab*) and who enjoys 'superiority' and 'dominance' (*GS* IV·1: 331; *SW* 2: 33). These distinctions will remain a constant theme in the later writings: whereas the adult's relationship with things is one of distant separation, condescension, superiority and dominance, the child is unpretentiously 'mingled' with them in a tender acquaintance, which represents a higher level of knowledge and experience. That is why, as Benjamin writes in 'Marseilles' (1929) and repeats in 'The Return of the *Flâneur*' (1929), to know cities 'one must have been a child in them' (*GS* IV·1: 362; *SW* 2:234). In order to achieve this redemptive level of experience the adult must become a stranger in the city and re-learn the 'childhood stage'.[13]

---

11. For a detailed analysis of Benjamin's writings on children's literature see for example Doderer. For an analysis of Benjamin's radio talks see Mehlman.

12. Thus, 'the city turns into a labyrinth for the newcomer … The whole exciting sequence of topographical deceptions to which he falls prey could be shown only by a film: the city is on its guard against him, masks itself, flees, intrigues, lures him to wander its circles to the point of exhaustion' (*GS* IV·1: 319; *SW* 2: 24).

13. Gilloch particularly insists on this point, drawing from the observations put forward by Peter Szondi. Szondi emphasises the category of 'distance', which defamiliarises the city and allows the newcomer to see it with the eyes of a child: the child sees the city 'at first

Books and cities come together in 'One-Way Street' (1928), where strongly avant-gardist and Brechtian tones politicize the act of reading, in the form of criticism, and make of it a semiotic experience of the city. 'One-Way Street' is a collection of *Denkbilder*, which shun theory and argumentation and 'present' or 'stage' various problems and insights. No longer an 'extra', the child here holds a central place, not only in 'Construction Site', but also and especially in the sections titled 'Enlargements', 'Toys', 'Stamp Shop' and other pieces. Here, the idea of the 'penetration' of the book by the reading child is reiterated and motifs merely hinted at in earlier writings made explicit. First, the motif of a 'closeness' between the child and the world of things, which annuls the *principium individuationis* and the separation subject/object. This closeness is 'tactile', a knowledge of the object that does not proceed from detached observation through the sense of vision, but is sensorial and sensual, 'passionate' (*leidenschaftlich*) like the embrace of a lover who penetrates the boudoir of the kitchen (*GS* IV·1: 114; *SW* 1: 464). It becomes interpenetration when the child plays hide-and-seek and an act of redemption of the object (a fundamental motif in the 1930s) in the child's collection (*GS* IV·1: 115–6, 134–7; *SW* 1: 465–66, 478–80).[14] The important

---

sight', unlike the adult whose gaze is laden with tedium, familiarity and habit. In the Berlin *memoires*, Szondi continues, the distance is the one of time, and the defamiliarisation aims at the recovery of the child's receptivity as redemptive. For Gilloch, Szondi's argument fails to conjugate distance with 'proximity': he argues that remembrance enacts an interplay of distance and proximity which subjects the city to a process of 'enlargement'. Recalling the experiences of the child, for whom the city is unfamiliar, the adult does not make the city 'smaller' and thus easier to describe, but rather makes himself small, like a child, and recaptures the child's mimetic 'closeness' to the world of things. Szondi's 'distance' must thus be included into a dialectic with proximity: the aim is the recovering of the child's 'at first sight', a new understanding that is a 'not-knowing' but as such is close to things and a critical tool to disrupt the bourgeois adult's sense of superiority. See Szondi 22ff; Gilloch *Walter Benjamin* 92ff; Gilloch *Myth* 43ff, 60ff. None of these authors relates 'distance' to the question of 'aura', which produces the perception of 'distance, however near it [the object] may be' (*GS* VII·1: 355; *SW* 3: 105). It is nevertheless an important point in the present argument because it is related to the question of perception: unlike in the artwork essay, in 'On Some Motifs in Baudelaire' aura has no negative connotation and is described as the association of memory and perception that cluster around an object. Here aura is the gaze that the inanimate or natural objects return to us, and is related by Benjamin to the *mémoire involontaire*, as in the early writings perception (or 'pure' perception) was related to the Platonic anamnesis. Aura thus corresponds to the positive connotation of *Erfahrung* and can here be related to the gaze of the child. The modern decline of the aura is compared to the loss of the 'ability to look' (*GS* I·2: 644–48; *SW* 4: 337–9), that ability that still characterises the child. For the question of aura see Stoessel; Fürnkäs.

14. The connection between child and collector is fundamental and is emphasized in many writings, from 'One-Way Street' to the Berlin memoires to *The Arcades Project*. In the 1931 piece 'Unpacking My Library', Benjamin dwells on the peculiar relationship with objects that both child and collector present: it 'does not emphasize their functional, utilitarian value [*Funktionswert, Nutzen*]—that is, their usefulness [*Brauchbarkeit*]—but studies and *loves* them as the scene, the stage, of their fate'. This relationship has thus something

theme of the bourgeois apartment is introduced here: a 'gloomy' space, it is
the 'rotten, dismal edifice in whose closets and crannies the most ignomini-
ous instincts are deposited' and where eroticism is neutralized and transformed into commodity fetishism, the fulcrum of the bourgeois *phantasmagoria*.[15] Through play, the child transforms this gloomy environment into an
enchanted space, a place of mystery, exoticism and adventure; thus play is
an enchanting, 'mythic' activity, but one that *disenchants* the adults' myth
through playful enchantment: 'magical experience [*magische Erfahrung*] becomes science [*Wissenschaft*]. As its engineer, the child disenchants [*entzau-
bert*] the gloomy parental apartment' (*GS* IV·1: 116, also 144; *SW* 1: 466, also
484).

Another fundamental motif is that of nature and *Technik*: bourgeois modernity is a 'fallen' condition, in which nature is approached without respect
and exploited 'rapaciously', snatching 'the fruit unripe from the trees in order to sell it most profitably': 'through necessity and greed' bourgeois society has 'denatured [*entartet*] itself' (*GS* IV·1: 101; *SW* 1: 455). The last piece
of the book, 'Zum Planetarium', is fundamental. For the ancients, Benjamin writes, human intercourse with nature and the cosmos was an 'ecstatic trance' (*Rausch*), in which they were able to 'gain a certain knowledge of
what is nearest to us and what is remotest from us, and never of one without
the other' (*GS* IV·1:146; *SW* 1:486). Bourgeois modernity betrayed Mother
Earth in the attempt to dominate the cosmic powers. Technology was understood as 'the mastery of nature', but ultimately rebelled against its masters, turning 'the bridal bed into [the] bloodbath' of World War I. However,
to consider technology the mastery of nature is for Benjamin the same as
to trust a 'cane wielder who proclaimed the mastery of children by adults
to be the purpose of education'. Education, Benjamin argues, is rather 'the
indispensable ordering of the relationship between generations and therefore mastery (if we have to use this term) of that relationship and not of
children'. Likewise, technology is the 'mastery not of nature but of the relation between nature and man'. It is the organisation of human contact with
the cosmos and, as such, is the 'genuine cosmic experience' (*echter kosmischer
Erfahrung*). The will to dominate, the Enlightenment myth of cumulative
progress, the estrangement of man from nature, ended in the rebellion of

'magical' and '*passionate*', so different from the utilitarian one of adults and bourgeois. As
such, this relationship 'saves' the object from the fate of the commodity, that is, both from
usefulness and fetishism: child and collector 'can accomplish the renewal of existence [*die
Erneuerung des Daseins*]' of the object, for them 'collecting is only a process of renewal'. 'To
renew the old world [*die alte Welt erneuern*]', through tactility, renaming, acquisition, '—this
is the task of childhood and collecting (*GS* IV·1: 389–90; *SW* 2: 487, my emphases). See
Köhn, and Gilloch *Walter Benjamin* (100ff).

15. In 'Moscow' Benjamin had already described the "petty [sic]-bourgeois rooms" as
'battlefields over which the attack of commodity capital has advanced victoriously; nothing
human can flourish there again' (*GS* IV·1: 327; *SW* 2: 30).

technology, a 'frenzy of destruction' and annihilation (*GS* IV·1: 146–8; *SW* 1: 486–7). Only the child, in its prelapsarian, non-hierarchical relationship with nature, seeks harmony rather than mastery, and therefore has a 'correct' approach to technology.[16] This question of technology will be especially important in *The Arcades Project*, whilst books, mimesis, play and language will constitute the kernel of the Berlin *mémoires*. All these notions will receive a more exhaustive exposition in the writings of the 1930s, but they are already present and defined in the works of the 1920s.

PLAY AND PEDAGOGY

Between 1928 and 1930 Benjamin published a number of important reviews and essays dealing with play, toys and pedagogy. Usually taken as *marginalia* in his work, they can be considered the core of his theory of the child: at its centre lays the notion of play, which is what differentiates the child's experience from that of the (bourgeois) adult. The analysis of toys provides the starting point. In an article on a toy exhibition at the Märkisches Museum in Berlin ('Old Toys' 1928) and two reviews of Karl Gröber's *Kinderspielzeug aus alter Zeit: Eine Geschichte des Spielzeugs* ('The Cultural History of Toys' and 'Toys and Play' 1928),[17] Benjamin argues that toys are constructed by adults and usually 'tend to show what the adult understands [*sich vorstellt*] by toys rather than what the child demands [*verlangt*] from them' (*GS* IV·1: 514; *SW* 2: 101, translation modified). They are in a certain sense 'imposed on [the child] as cult implements' and are thus a 'site of conflict, less of the child with the adult than of the adult with the child' (*GS* III: 128; *SW* 2: 118). Toys are laden with the culture and the prejudices of their time, most of all with the idea of childhood of their time: adults use the needs of the child as a 'pretext of satisfying childlike ones' (*GS* III: 128; *SW* 2: 117). The image of the child has nevertheless changed enormously since the end of the eighteenth century, since it has finally been recognised that children are not just 'men

---

16. This point is emphasised in the important 1930 'Theories of German Fascism', a review of the collection of essays *War and Warriors* edited by Ernst Jünger. War is here again defined as the 'slave revolt on the part of technology': although technology, as a new configuration of the *physis*, has the 'power to give nature its voice', the 'depraved' use of it made by humans gives 'shape to the apocalyptic face of nature' and reduces it to silence. This depraved use is the 'attempt to redeem, mystically and without mediation, *the secret of nature*, understood idealistically, through technology' and is a sign of the 'incapacity of people to order their relationships to one another in accord with the relationship they possess to nature through their technology'. Children's relationship, instead, 'curious' but 'sober' [*nüchtern*], 'possess in technology not a fetish of doom but *a key to happiness*' [*einen Schlüssel zum Glück*]: only they can listen to the voice of nature, the 'secret password', and thus shape technology mimetically and harmoniously (*GS* III: 240, 247–50; *SW* 2: 313, 319–21, my emphases).

17. See also 'Russische Spielsachen' (1930, *GS* IV·1,2: 623–5), 'Berliner Spielzeugwanderung I' and 'Berliner Spielzeugwanderung II' (1930, *GS* VII·1: 98–105, 105–111).

and women of a reduced scale' and, most of all, that play is not the 'imitation [*Nachahmung*] of adults'. The old notions of child and play determined
a pedagogy in which the adult was 'the ideal in whose image the educator
aspired to mold [*bilden*] the child' (*GS* IV·1: 514, III: 128, 129; *SW* 2: 101, 118,
119). The recognition of the child's peculiarity produces different notions of
toys and play. The former, Benjamin writes, become 'toys' 'only afterwards,
partly through the child's power of imagination' [*Bildkraft*]. They are not
the work of adults, but 'the result of children at play': 'a child wants to pull
something, and so he becomes a horse; he wants to play with sand, and so
he turns into a baker; he wants to hide, and so he turns into a robber or a
policeman'. Thus the artefact is appropriated by the playing child, 'mislaid,
broken, and repaired', and only then does it become a toy. 'Imitation', Benjamin concludes, 'is at home in the playing, not in the plaything' (*GS* III:117
also IV·1: 515, III: 128, 116; *SW* 2: 116, also 101, 115, 118).

Here returns the question of the relationship with the object: the child
enjoys the 'harmonious combinations of the most heterogeneous materials—stone, plasticine, wood and paper' and is 'chaste' (*keusch*) in their use;
its world is a 'microcosm' where 'wood, bones, wickerwork, and clay are
the most important materials, all of which were already used in patriarchal
[that is, pre-bourgeois, and thus prelapsarian] times, when toys were still a
part of the production process that found parents and children together'.
The available technology conditions the construction of the toy, but in its
'chaste' use of the materials the child exemplifies the question of technology, that is, of a non-dominating and more harmonious relationship between
man and nature (*GS* III: 115–6, 129–30; *SW* 2: 115, 119). Another important
point is the anti-individualist nature of play: in 'Old Toys', Benjamin writes
that, in play, 'even the most princely doll becomes a capable proletarian
comrade in the children's play commune' (*GS* IV·1: 515; *SW* 2: 101). In 'Toys
and Play', the 'schematic individualism' and the picture of the child given by
the 'psychology of the individual' are each undermined by the child's play:
the child's worldview demands to be seen as 'collectivist' (*GS* III: 128; *SW*
2: 117–18). The child lives in a world that is not only prior to distance from
the object, but also prior to bourgeois 'possessive individualism'. Here, Benjamin seems to identify the *principium individuationis* with bourgeois possessive
individualism, and the child's absence of individualism with a revolutionary
collectivist and proletarian ideal.

The conclusion to 'Toys and Play' gives a positive definition of children's
play as an experiment with objects and rhythms, based on 'repetition', in
which we 'first gain possession of ourselves'. 'For a child repetition is the
soul of play,' Benjamin writes, 'nothing gives him greater pleasure than to
"Do it again!".' Benjamin finds the explanation in Freud: 'every profound
experience [*tiefste Erfahrung*] longs to be insatiable, longs for return and repetition until the end of time, and for the reinstatement of an original condi-

tion from which it sprang'. Not only the mastery of 'frightening fundamental experiences', but also and most of all the enjoyment of 'one's victories and triumphs over and over again, with total intensity': a child 'creates [*schafft*] the entire event anew and starts again [*fängt an*] right from the beginning'. *Spielen* as repetition is not a 'doing as if' [*So-tun-als-ob*], but a 'doing the same thing over and over again' [*Immer-wieder-tun*], the transformation of 'shattering experience [*erschütterndsten Erfahrung*] into habit [*Gewohnheit*]' (*GS* III: 131–2; *SW* 2: 120). This is a difficult point in Benjamin: repetition will become in the 1930s the core of the phantasmagoria of modernity, the hellish 'eternal return' of the same (*ewige Wiederkehr*), which is the *fundamental* form of the 'mythic consciousness' (*AP* D10,3); and habit, the anaesthetic that numbs the senses and understanding of the bourgeois adult. Burkhardt Lindner stresses that Benjamin lacked a coherent theory of myth and this threatens to undermine his analysis of the child. Here, myth, magic and animism are pitted against civilising rationality (as its 'disenchantment'[18]), but elsewhere rationality itself is denounced as the exacerbation of myth.[19] Despite the force of Lindner's criticism, it can nevertheless be argued that repetition functions differently in play and in modern myth: in the former it is a *wieder-tun*, a 'doing' again, a 'creating' [*schaffen*] the event anew, a starting [*anfangen*] everything from the beginning, therefore an active stance; in the latter, a *Wieder-kehr*, a passively suffered *re-turn* of the same numbing spectres, over and over again. Repetition remains problematic for Benjamin because he cannot make up his mind and oscillates between these two mutually exclusive alternatives.

These concepts coagulate into a specific theory of pedagogy in two important essays, 'Program for a Proletarian Children's Theatre' (1929), written with Asja Lacis, and 'A Communist Pedagogy' (1930). Benjamin's pedagogic writings of these years are strongly Brechtian in content and language: he met Brecht through the Latvian Asja Lacis in 1929, and the influence of both would be very strong thereafter.[20] The tone of these writings is strongly anti-bourgeois and revolutionary, their explicit context proletarian and communist Russia and its advances in the field of education. Although they betray a 'faith' in communist utopia, they are nonetheless a translation into Lacis' theatrical frame of Benjamin's own long-standing ideas on childhood. The referent of 'A Communist Pedagogy' is in fact bourgeois education,

18. Gilloch insists on this point: play is both mythic and demystifying insofar as 'the "magic" of the child's imagination' is disruptive and subversive, and as such it is the 'antithesis of the mythology of the adult' which is fetishistic and reifying. Thus the child as a figure of redemption 'unravel[s] the mythic from within' and disenchants the city through enchantment. See Gilloch *Myth* 84–5.

19. See Lindner. For an overview of the concept of myth in Benjamin see Hartung.

20. While the Brechtian influence is widely acknowledged, that of Lacis is usually downplayed by the critics. For an analysis of the importance of Lacis for Benjamin's theory of pedagogy see for example Ingram.

communist pedagogy itself is defined merely *ex negativo*. The bourgeois system revolves around the two poles of 'psychology' and 'ethics': psychology establishes the 'nature of the child' and ethics sets the 'goal of education', the formation of the good citizen. It thus 'hypostatizes an absolute childhood or adolescence' and 'a no less absolute concept of adulthood and citizenship which it tricks out with the attributes of idealist philosophy'. It is predicated on 'abstract data' and its strategy is 'insinuation and empathy' (*Insinuationen und Einfühlungen*); it thus prolongs the capitalist separation of theory and practice and 'colonizes' childhood with the demands of commodity society.[21] What the new communist ideal proposes is an education firmly anchored in concrete reality, and thus 'nonhumanist and noncontemplative, but *active* and *practical* universally; it is the product of universal readiness [*Bereitsein*]' (*GS* III: 206–9; *SW* 2: 272–5, my emphases).

To the bourgeois 'unsystematic system', Benjamin opposes a revolutionary pedagogy in 'Program', the system of which would be the 'framework' [*Rahmen*] of theatre. It is a 'framework' because it does not propose an abstract 'idea' *towards* which education leads, but an 'objective space' *within* which it is allowed to develop. Theatre itself is feared by bourgeois educators because it 'unleashes' (*aufruft*) in children 'the most powerful energies of the future', when 'reality and play *merge into one* [*sich verschmelzen*]' (*GS* II·2: 764–5; *SW* 2: 202, translation modified). This merging requires, in proletarian theatre, that the attitude of the adult be radically modified: the pedagogue must give up his or her domineering role and become a 'leader' (*Leiter*) whose influence is merely 'indirect' and 'mediated by subject matter, tasks, and performances'. The 'moral personality' of the adult, the 'superior standpoint' that leads to an attempt at direct influence, the 'knowing better and wanting better' of bourgeois education, must be 'neutralized'. Only this neutralisation allows for the release of the 'true genius of education—namely, the power of observation' (*Beobachtung*).[22] Bourgeois pedagogical love is 'sentimental and vain', it aims at imposing a set of values and behavioural patterns on the child; proletarian theatre is not concerned with contents, but with 'tensions' (*Spannungen*), that is, relationships and—one might extrapolate— 'constellations' and in it the adult's love must be 'unsentimental', that is, it must abandon the attempt at influence and courageously embrace 'mere observation' (*GS* II·2: 765–6; *SW* 2: 203).[23]

---

21. See 'Kolonialpädagogik' *GS* III: 272–4.

22. See the meaning of *Beobachtung* in the idea of nature of the early Romantics, *GS* I·1: 58–61; *SW* 1: 147–8.

23. The negative reference of this essay is not merely bourgeois education; in it Benjamin also briefly settles his differences with the *Jugendbewegung*, in which he was active until ten years before. The *Jugendkultur* attempted to achieve a 'hopeless compromise' with bourgeois society: it channelled youthful energies into a self-centered reflection, which 'can never be activated in a political way'. This 'idealistic self-reflection' drains the enthusiasm of youth and gradually and imperceptibly replaces the former ideologies (German idealism) with

It is the adults, therefore, who learn in proletarian theatre, and what they learn are *signals*: 'every childhood action and gesture becomes a signal', not of a psychoanalytic unconscious, but rather 'a signal from another world, in which the child lives and commands', from a world that is prelapsarian and thus potentially redemptive and revolutionary. The task of the leader is to 'release children's signals from the hazardous magical world of sheer fantasy and apply them to materials'.[24] The fulcrum of this pedagogy is the child's *gesture*,[25] based on improvisation, where the 'creative [*schöpferische*] innervation is in an exact correspondence to receptive [*rezeptive*] innervation'. The child's mode of reception is, as in the Romantic theory of Nature, 'pure' and 'unmediated', its improvisation thus 'creative', 'inventive' and tied to action (Buck-Morss *Dialectics* 264). And, unlike in bourgeois education, it is never the single child, but rather the 'collective' that acts.[26] Gesture, improvisation and collectivity mark the scope of education: 'childhood achievement is always aimed not at the "eternity" of the products but at the "moment" of the gesture. The theatre is the art form of the child because it is ephemeral' (*GS* II·2: 766–7; *SW* 2: 204, translation modified).[27] Performance as the 'radical unleashing [*Entbindung*] of play' is aimed not at inculcating in children a system of values or notions, but at the 'fulfilment' [*Erfüllung*] of their childhood. It is thus not a moment of notional learning, but rather a 'great creative pause' in the process of upbringing, where the child's imagination is liberated and, as in the pagan carnival, roles are inverted and it is

---

bourgeois contents. The child's mind is, as in the bourgeois model, merely 'subjugated', it remains apolitical and idealistically self-centered (*GS* II·2: 768; *SW* 2: 205).

24. Hans-Thies Lehmann relates the children's signals to Benjamin's theory of language: the signal is the 'name', the language that speaks *in* the person: 'The presubjective signalling of the child's gesture transfers the expression from the realm of subjectivity into the "objective" collective realm of the body. In between *vouloir-dire*/meaning to say and the body, lies the realm of the gesture, an intermediate realm in which, unhampered by "culture", that which is mute becomes eloquent' (189).

25. Gerhard Fischer relates the gesture to both the 'profane illuminations' of the Surrealism essay and the shock of the writings on Baudelaire and Paris, the *caesura* that interrupts the continuum of time and opens up the messianic (211).

26. The collective, Fischer argues, emphasises the difference from the abstract and hypostatized child of bourgeois education: it is a part of a group, product of specific sociocultural circumstances and with specific needs and priorities. See Fischer (212).

27. This point is dangerously close to the vitalism and irrationalism of the *Lebensphilosophie* of Klages or Jung: the fact that, as Lehmann puts it, 'reflection and moral consideration, delay, planning ahead and thinking, spoil everything in a situation where the main point is child-like, playful, bodily innervation. *Decisive experiences are formed before or beyond intention, in interrupting it*'. Nevertheless, Lehmann argues that Benjamin is concerned with 'localizing non-conscious impulses and structures in the realm of practical expressive behaviour, not with their ideological hypostatization. They have a concrete place, such as the theatre, the text, and the child's gesture. Benjamin attempts to give this de-subjectivization a political name when he describes the child itself, and not merely the community of children, as the "child's collective"' (*GS* II·2: 766), Lehmann (189).

the adults who learn.[28] They learn from the child's gesture 'the *secret signal* [*geheime Signal*] of what is to come', the password that allows them to become 'truly revolutionary' subjects (*GS* II·2: 768–9; *SW* 2: 205–6).[29]

EXPERIENCE AND MEMORY

In Benjamin's 1930s writings the figure of the child appears above all in the Berlin *memoires*. The fragments of 'A Berlin Chronicle' were written in the first half of 1932 in Ibiza, re-worked into a first version of 'Berlin Childhood around 1900' between 1932 and 1934, and then further revised into a second version in 1938. As a project, they cover almost the whole decade and run parallel to the essays and notes flowing from and into *The Arcades Project*. I will attempt in this section to analyse the Berlin *mémoires* in relation to the problem of experience. With Benjamin's interest focussing on the analysis of urban modernity, the question of experience becomes central, but also forks into two antinomian directions: not the ones that lead either to Berlin or to Paris, but rather, the dialectical contradiction between an enthusiastic embrace of modernity as revolutionary and liberating and a melancholic yearning for the world that had been lost. To the first belong 'The Destructive Character' (1931), 'Experience and Poverty' (1933), 'The Author as Producer' (1934) and the Artwork essay (1936); to the second, the Berlin *mémoires*, 'The Storyteller' (1936) and the writings on Kafka, Proust and Baudelaire. When confronted with the experience of modernity and the loss of traditional experience, Benjamin cannot choose, or better, he only ever makes strategic, temporary and reversible choices.

'Experience [*Erfahrung*] has fallen in value', Benjamin writes in 'Experience and Poverty': today no one knows precisely what it is, and even less how to communicate it. 'A completely new poverty has descended on mankind', with the developments in technology that led to the horrors of World War I. But the 'new barbarism' that constitutes the poverty of human experience is, for Benjamin, a 'positive' development: it forces humanity to 'start from scratch; to make a new start; to make a little go a long way; to begin with a little and build up further, looking neither left nor right'. The new barbarian is the 'naked man of the contemporary world who lies screaming like *a newborn babe* [*Neugeborenes*] in the dirty diapers of the present', a 'de-humanized' (*entmenschte*) being who rejects the 'civilization' of old humanism, does not yearn for new experience, nor to free him- or herself from experience, but longs 'for a world in which they can make such pure and decided use of their poverty … that will lead to something respectable'. In this new world, 'na-

---

28. This notion can be fruitfully compared with Bakhtin's concept of 'carnevalesque' (122–37).

29. Buck-Morss in fact argues that the consequence—or the goal—of bourgeois education and socialisation is 'their defeat as revolutionary subjects' (265). See also Zipes.

ture and technology, primitiveness and comfort, have completely merged' and the new barbarian is about to begin 'anew and with few resources', prepared to 'outlive [*überleben*] culture, if need be' (*GS* II·1: 213–9; *SW* 2: 731–5). The same principle informs 'The Destructive Character', who destroys the old world in order to make room for the new (*GS* IV·1: 396–8; *SW* 2: 541–2); or 'The Author as Producer', where the revolutionary writer is urged to forsake his or her aura, adopt the technical and technological innovations and become an 'operating' writer (*GS* II·2: 683–701; *SW* 2: 768–82); and especially the Artwork essay, where the cathartic and revolutionary power of technological reproducibility results in the 'shattering of tradition' and the 'liquidation of the value of tradition in the cultural heritage', which will allow the 'renewal of humanity' (*GS* VII·1: 354–5; *SW* 3: 104–5).[30]

The incipit of 'Experience and Poverty' is almost literally recycled in 'The Storyteller', but thereafter the two essays proceed in opposite directions. In the latter, the loss of experience (*Erfahrung*) means the loss of the 'lore of the past' and its 'wisdom' (*Weisheit*), the loss of memory and the transformation of experience into information (*GS* II·2: 438–65; *SW* 3: 143–66). The problem of modernity is thus the separation of experience and memory: this is the central issue in Benjamin's work throughout the 1930s, explicitly and most thoroughly analysed in 'On Some Motifs in Baudelaire'. To 'vitalistic' experience as *Erlebnis*—'inner lived experience', singular, individualistic, irrational and ultimately mythical (Dilthey, Klages, Jung)—Benjamin there counterposes *Erfahrung* as theorised by Bergson: an experience structurally grounded on memory (*Gedächtnis*), tradition and a collective and relational existence. The problem with Bergson's position, nonetheless, is that it is anti-historical: he excluded the 'blinding' experience of 'large-scale industrialism' from his concept of experience, so that in his theory *Erfahrung* can only be constructed as an 'afterimage' (*Nachbild*) of the modern (*GS* I·2: 608–9; *SW* 4: 314). The Bergsonian insight is developed by Proust (a cousin of Bergson's wife), who would attempt to 'produce *Erfahrung* … in a synthetic way under today's social conditions'. Thus Bergson's *mémoire pure* becomes the *mémoire involontaire*, a form of recollection in which the past arises when put into constellation with an event in the present. The problem with

---

30. The destruction of experience that constitutes this new barbarism entails a renunciation of the original innocence and wholeness that the prelapsarian child represents; the *newborn babe* which is an allegory of this new barbarism is thus not the child of the 1920s writings, nor the one of the Berlin memoires, but rather what today is called the 'posthuman', a *non-innocent* and *non-whole* mixture of 'nature and technology, primitiveness and comfort', a fresh start that does away with all that the prelapsarian child represented. The antinomy that informs Benjamin's writings in the 1930s, his Janus-like looking melancholically backwards and, simultaneously, enthusiastically forward, can be represented by the opposite images of the prelapsarian child and the posthuman. However, whereas the prelapsarian child is the main focus of Benjamin's writing on this figure, the posthuman receives much less attention.

Proust, however, is that this is entirely based on *chance* (*Zufall*), and thus 'part of the inventory of the individual who is isolated in various ways' (*GS* I·2: 610–11; *SW* 4: 315–16). The politics of such experience are endangered by its own structure; it needs to be historicised and, in order to achieve this, Benjamin enlists Freud. In *Beyond the Pleasure Principle*, Freud had written that the threatening and shocking stimuli of modern life leave traces in the unconscious: 'if need be', the consciousness can be 'trained' to cope with stimuli, and dreams and recollection (*Erinnerung*) are part of this training. Incorporated into conscious memory, the *Erlebnis* of modern life can thus be emancipated and transformed into Baudelaire's poetic *Erfahrung* (*GS* I·2: 612–5; *SW* 4: 317–18). Benjamin describes Baudelaire's *correspondances* as an '*Erfahrung* which seeks to establish itself in crisis-proof form' (*krisensicher*). They are the 'data of recollection' (*Eingedenken*),[31] in which the past 'murmurs', and, importantly, they '*do not occur by chance*' (*GS* I·2: 638–40; *SW* 4: 333–4, my emphasis). What Benjamin attempted by rejecting both the vitalistic *Erlebnis* of *Lebensphilosophie* and the overly rational *Erfahrung* of Neo-Kantian tradition was to construct a different type of experience that would be *dialectical*. This is 'a learning process over time', Martin Jay argues, 'combining negations through unpleasant episodes as well as affirmations through positive ones to produce something akin to a wisdom that can be passed down via tradition through the generations' (146).

The argument of 'On Some Motifs in Baudelaire' is complex and cannot be explored in detail here[32]; this long introduction can, however, provide a theoretical grid for the analysis of the Berlin *memoires*. 'A Berlin Chronicle' and *Berlin Childhood Around 1900* are usually read as Proustian texts, even though many elements suggest the presence of a more complex theoretical apparatus. These two texts, especially *Berlin Childhood*, repropose (sometimes with the same words), explore and represent themes and motifs that accompanied the figure of the child in the 1910s and 1920s: the mimetic relationship with things and nature, expressed in the passion for collecting[33];

31. *Gedächtnis*, *Erinnerung* and *Eingedenken* can be translated as memory, recollection and remembrance, where the first presents a connotation of a gathering of unconscious data, the second of an isolated individual memory and the third is the term most recurrent in *The Arcades Project* for the construction of the dialectical image. In 'The Storyteller' we find: 'it is *remembrance* [*Eingedenken*], the muse-derived element of the novel, which is added to recollection [*Gedächtnis*], the muse-derived element of the story, the unity of their origin in memory [*Erinnerung*] having disappeared with the decline of the epic' (*GS* II·2: 454; *SW* 3: 154)

32. For an analysis of this essay and of the concept of experience see for example Andrew Benjamin (122–40); Jay; Abbas (216–39).

33. See the 'tactile' inhabiting of books (*GS* VI: 514–5; VII·1: 396–7; *SW* 2: 631–2; 3: 356); the passion of collection (*GS* VII·1: 408–9; *SW* 3: 367); tactility and the 'sock' (*GS* VII·1: 416–7; *SW* 3: 374); 'Hiding Places': identity and playing hide-and-seek (*GS* VII·1: 418; *SW* 3: 375–6); colour and perception (*GS* VII·1: 424; *SW* 3: 380); tactility and *principium individuationis* (*GS* IV·1: 250; *SW* 3: 389); collection and 'tidying up' (*GS* IV·1: 283–7; *SW* 3:

a prelapsarian relationship with language and name[34]; the bourgeois apartment as prison[35]; play as demystifying and thus redemptive.[36] I will not again explore these themes, which have been analysed above, even though they are presented more systematically and with greater depth in these late writings.[37] What I want to explore here is the relationship of the child to experience and memory, which is the founding point underlying the other issues.

Memory (*Gedächtnis*), Benjamin writes in 'A Berlin Chronicle,' is:

> not an instrument for exploring the past but its theatre [*Schauplatz*]. It is the medium of past experience [*des Erlebten*], just as the earth is the medium in which dead cities lie buried. He who seeks to approach his own buried past must conduct himself like a man digging. This determines the tone and bearing of genuine reminiscences [*echter Erinnungen*]. They must not be afraid to return again and again to the same matter; to scatter it as one scatters earth, to turn it over as one turns over soil. For the matter itself is merely a deposit, a stratum, which yields only to the most meticulous examination what constitutes the real treasure hidden within the earth: the images [*Bilder*], severed from all earlier associations, that stand—like precious fragments or torsos in a collector's gallery—in the sober room of our later insights. True, for successful excavations a plan is needed. Yet no less indispensable is the cautious probing of the spade in the dark loam, and it is to cheat oneself of the richest prize to preserve as a record merely the inventory of one's discoveries, and not this dark joy of the place of the finding, as well. Fruitless searching is as much a part of this as succeeding, and consequently remembrance must not proceed in the manner of a narrative or still less that of a report, but must, in the strictest epic and rhapsodic manner, assay its spade in ever-new places, and in the old ones delve to ever-deeper layers.(*GS* VI: 486–7; *SW* 2: 611)

401–4); 'the lamp': objects and mimesis (*GS* VII·2: 792–4; *SW* 2: 690–3). See Leslie (11ff); Weidmann (95–105; Schweppenhäuser (145–65).

34. See the episodes of Aunt Lehmann (*GS* VI: 472; VII·1: 398–400; *SW* 2: 600–1; 3: 358–9); *Markt-Halle* (*GS* VI: 475; VII·1: 402; *SW* 2: 603; 3: 360–2); Brauhausberg (*GS* VI: 495; *SW* 2: 617); the snowstorm 'speaks' to the child (*GS* VII·1: 396–7; *SW* 3: 356); the Mummerehlen: words and mimesis (*GS* VII·1: 417–8; *SW* 3: 374). See Gilloch *Myth* 6off; Kahn (142 ff).

35. Benjamin describes the child he was as a 'prisoner' enclosed within the well-to-do 'old and new West End', a 'ghetto' and a 'fiefdom' (*GS* VI: 471; IV·1: 287–8; *SW* 2: 599–600; 3: 404); see the humiliating shopping sprees with the mother (*GS* VI: 499; *SW* 2: 620); the interior as the dead reign of the immortal commodity (*GS* VI: 500–2; *SW* 2: 621–2); the courtyards as openings (*GS* VI: 503; *SW* 2: 623); poverty as an unknown, external experience (*GS* VI: 518; *SW* 2: 634); the child as 'threshold dweller', waiting to cross the boundary (*GS* VI: 461–2; VII·1: 395; *SW* 2: 600; 3: 354). See Gilloch *Myth* 76ff; Richter 214ff.

36. See 'hiding places' (*GS* VII·1: 418; *SW* 3: 375–6). See Gilloch *Myth* 85ff.

37. Critics, quite correctly, usually base the analysis of the child in Benjamin on these writings. The most thorough analysis of the Berlin *mémoires* is by Anna Stüssi.

If read through the lens of 'On Some Motifs in Baudelaire', this programmatic passage clarifies some important points: the project of the Berlin *memoires* as an archaeological excavation of the past is not simply a bite into the
Proustian madeleine. The archaeologist proceeds with the determination to
unbury the treasure, is not afraid of hard work or temporary failures, and
most of all proceeds with a *plan*. It is true that chance has its play in the success of the research, that its fruits are torsos, fragments and ruins, not a complete and organic narrative, but a fragmentary rhapsody.[38] Nevertheless, the
voluntaristic tone of this passage is clear. The Berlin *mémoires* cannot be read
as merely a Proustian abandonment to the chances of the *mémoire involontaire*,
as many commentators suggest.[39] They are not a collection of private and
singular *Erlebnisse*, but rather an attempt to transform these into collective
and relational *Erfahrungen*. Unlike Proust's work, this is a project with a precise politics, that of a reconstitution of the relationship, lost in modernity,
between experience and memory, so that the archaeology of the experience
must be seen as its rescue. The interrelations of past and present, child and
adult, memory and setting, thus superimpose Baudelaire's *correspondances* and
their political project over Proust's *mémoire involontaire*.

This is why Benjamin refuses to define his project as autobiography[40]:
the singular and irrational *Erlebnis*, the 'substance that life is made of', cannot be captured by commemoration, and in its singularity has no political
value. By 'spatializing' his reminiscences, Benjamin screens out the individuality of memory and transforms it into the communal *Erfahrung* of places,
moments and situations, of the relational experience of Berlin around 1900.
The short preface to 'Berlin Childhood' states that biographical features
and the continuity of experience will recede in his project so as to give space
to the *images* 'in which the experience of the big city is precipitated in a child
of the middle class'. While the experience of a country childhood could still
present a (premodern) continuity, obedient to nature and its cycles, the metropolitan experience cannot be so 'customized' (*geprägt*). Emancipation from
loss of experience can rather be performed in metropolitan modernity by a

---

38. For the labyrinthine and city-like structure of memory see for example Szondi (22);
Gilloch (66ff); Richter (45ff).

39. See Kahn, also Gilloch *Myth* especially 57ff. Both Kahn and Gilloch recognise a
connection with Baudelaire's *correspondances* and that the Berlin *mémoires* are 'exercises
in critical historiography rather than wistful nostalgia' (Gilloch 60) and the nexus with
The Arcades Project, but they remain anchored to the argument of the Proustian *mémoire
involontaire*.

40. The famous definition of 'A Berlin Chronicle' reads: '[f]or autobiography has to do
with time, with sequence and what makes up the continuous flow of life. Here, I am talking
of a space, of moments and discontinuities. For even if months and years appear here, it
is in the form they have at the moment of commemoration [*des Eingedenkens*]. This strange
form—it may be called fleeting or eternal—is in neither case the substance that life is
made of' (*GS* VI: 488; *SW* 2: 612, translation modified).

political act of remembrance that becomes a true 'historical experience' (*geschichtliche Erfahrung*) (*GS* VII·1: 385; *SW* 3: 344). The Berlin *memoires* are recollections of the city at a specific time, a precise historical (and not merely individual) experience the rescue of which is attempted. This is the connection between this project and the historical analysis of the prehistory of modernity in *The Arcades Project*.

CHILDHOOD AND AWAKENING

In *The Arcades Project* the child occupies a secondary position: the critique of bourgeois modernity focuses on the bourgeois consumer, leaving the child's alternative form of experience only implicit. The figure appears in the critique neither of the bourgeois interior nor of commodity fetishism and is barely mentioned in the analysis of the collector. However, it does appear as central in three thematic areas: the question of technology, the analysis of labour and the motif of awakening. *Technik* was defined in 'Zum Planetarium' and also in the Surrealism essay as the human organization of *physis* (see *GS* II·1: 310; *SW* 2: 217), as mastery not of *physis*, but of the relationship between man and cosmos. Modernity can no longer master this relationship: the attempt to transform technology into the mastery of nature resulted in the horrors of the Great War; the aesthetization of technology, extreme examples of which include Italian Futurism and Jünger, ended in a 'frenzy of annihilation'. Mastery of the man/nature relationship entails the ability to understand it and thus to give it symbolic representation. This is what modernity cannot do and this is where the child is important: in its prelapsarian approach to nature, the child operates like ancient mythologies, producing a symbolic representation of its configuration. Technology as a new configuration of nature needs an ever new symbolic representation: 'by the interest it takes in technological phenomena,' Benjamin writes, 'by the curiosity it displays before any sort of invention or machinery, every childhood binds the accomplishments of technology to the old world of symbol' and thus achieves 'something great and irreplaceable for humanity' (*AP* N2a1). The task of childhood is thus 'to bring the new world into symbolic space,' to do what grownups cannot, that is, 'recognize the new once again' (*das Neue wiedererkennen*) (*AP* K1a,3). There is no antithesis, for Benjamin, between the symbol-space of nature and that of technology, as Klages argued, but rather the latter is simply a new configuration of *physis*: this new configuration needs new 'images' and these are what the child discovers and incorporates 'into the image stock of humanity' (*AP* K1a,3). The child's relationship to technology is thus informed not by the 'aura of novelty,' as in the adult (for which the artefact is 'merely new'), but rather by the 'aura of the habitual,' by the same aura as in nature (*AP* N2a1). The technological artefact returns the gaze of the child not as the commodity returns that of the adult, but in

the sense of the 'pure perception' of the Romantics. It is thus a mimetic relation.[41]

Technology as the mastery of nature also pertains to the 'inauthentic'
(uneigentlich) discourse of labour as the 'exploitation' (Ausbeutung) of nature,
which treats nature merely as the booty (Beute) of human pillage. This discourse reinforces, and is in turn reinforced by, the practice of the exploitation of human labour. Labour, Benjamin argues, is characterized by the exploitation of nature by man and, when the order of production is founded
on the exploitation of labour, then 'raw materials' are given the 'semblance
[Schein] of 'value" (AP J75,2). A relationship to nature not based on exploitation would result in human beings 'authentically' (eigentlich) unexploited,
and vice versa. The child's mimetic relationship to nature becomes here the
model of a new concept of labour: play as respectful and undemanding aims
'not at the propagation of values but at the amelioration of nature' (AP J75,2).
The question of labour and technology thus finds its resolution in play. Benjamin found this model in Fourier, a central reference for The Arcades Project:
'[t]o have instituted play as the canon of a labor no longer rooted in exploitation is one of the great merits of Fourier' (AP J75,2). The travail passionné of the
Harmonians in the falanstery is based on children's play, where 'all places
are worked by human hands, made useful and beautiful thereby' and action
is the sister of dream (AP J75,2). Convolute 'W' is dedicated to Fourier and
many other entries relate to children's role in the phalanstery.[42] It is significant that Fourier's descriptions read like the descriptions 'of color illustrations in children's books' (AP W16a,1): the anti-positivistic children's form of
perception illustrates a relationship to the natural world (and technology) in
which labour, as Benjamin writes in 'On the Concept of History', 'far from
exploiting nature, would help her give birth to the creations that now lie dormant in her womb' (GS I·2: 699; SW 4: 394). This form of labour is not, for
Benjamin, a regression to pre-capitalist and pre-modern models of work, but
'presupposes highly developed forces of production, such as only today stand

---

41. Benjamin does not connect this 'bringing the new world into symbolic space' with
the 'poverty of experience' that characterises this new world, thus an ambiguity is hidden
here: the prelapsarian child produces a symbolic representation of a new world that brings
about the end of the concepts of original innocence and wholeness that the child represents.
Its mimetic relation with technology drags him or her away from the Romantic myth and
towards the 'shattering of tradition', the 'liquidation' of its values and its myths, including
the myth of original innocence and wholeness; thus towards a 'renewal of humanity' (GS
VII·1: 353–4; SW 3: 104) and the 'newborn babe' that represents the 'new barbarian' of
'Experience and Poverty' (see GS II·1: 213–9; SW 2: 731–5).

42. In it children's tastes and passions would be given free reins in order to discover their
'vocation'; by organising them in different hierarchies and 'hordes' (AP W12,4, W12,6,
from W14,1 to W14a3) and giving them tasks they enjoy (like the collection of garbage
and the cleaning of slaughterhouses and latrines; AP W2,1, W12,1), Fourier includes the
pleasure principle into education (and thus work). See Hollington (118).

at the disposal of humanity' (*AP* J75a).

Michael Hollington writes that what appealed to Benjamin in Fourier was the vision of 'human happiness as a kind of game' in which action is the sister of dream (J75,2) (Hollington 124). This statement, and thus the whole discussion of the child, requires qualification: that action and dream intertwine in play does not endorse a 'return to childhood', nor entail that the modern adult take refuge from loss of experience into a childish dream-state, into an *infantilisation* of experience. Benjamin is not proposing a 'politics of infancy'. The polemic against Surrealism revolves precisely around this point: the Surrealists rediscovered myth and dream in the metropolis, but emphasised merely the moment of intoxication, which they strived to inhabit. Surrealism remained therefore politically 'inadequate' and 'undialectical' (*GS* II·1: 307; *SW* 2: 216): 'Aragon persists within the realm of dream' reads an entry in *The Arcades Project*; 'mythology' is his 'impressionistic element'. Benjamin's project, on the contrary, is concerned 'to find the constellation of awakening [*Erwachen*]' and thus to 'dissolve' (*auflösen*, that is, 'find a solution for') 'mythology into the space of history' (*AP* N1,9). A number of entries in Convolute 'K' relate the child to dreaming and awakening: the 'historical configuration' of childhood is a 'dream configuration'; 'every epoch has such a side turned toward dreams, the child's side [*die Kinderseite*]' (*AP* K1,1). But what Benjamin's project seeks is a 'teleological moment in the context of dreams.' This moment is 'waiting' (*das Warten*), which is the figure of childhood: '[t]he dream waits secretly for the awakening; the sleeper surrenders himself to death only provisionally, waits for the second when he will cunningly wrest himself from its clutches. So, too, the dreaming collective, whose children provide the happy occasion for its own awakening' (*AP* K1a,2). The child is a figure of waiting, and thus a figure of awakening, a dream of the future and a figure of hope.

A passage from 'One-Way Street' further elucidates the point: to be 'still half in league with the dream world' is self-betrayal, a *childish* posture, as distinct from a dialectical valorisation and use of childhood; 'only from the far bank, from broad daylight, may dream be addressed from the superior vantage of memory' (*GS* IV·1: 86; *SW* 1: 445). Only retrospectively, from the vantage point of adulthood, can childhood become a revolutionary model of experience: to paraphrase the Surrealist slogan, Benjamin wanted to win the energies of childhood for the revolution, not to dwell within it. For Benjamin, childhood *stands* for an alternative model of experience, which the retrospective gaze of the adult can win for the revolutionary project. The child must grow up, society must awaken from its child-like dreaming state, childhood must end and give way to true *maturity*. The bourgeois boasting pretension of maturity is thus itself a childish illusion: bourgeois modernity is *the* state of dreaming, of myth, of false consciousness, and is therefore a state of infancy. The bourgeois patronising attitude toward childhood dismisses precisely those characteristics of the child's world which could deliver it from such infancy: it is a 'sentimental fantasy' saturated with impotence (*AP* J63a,1).[13] Benjamin proposes rather a 'politics of childhood', a revolution of experience based on the recovery and re-use of those pre-bourgeois potentialities that the bourgeois model of education, socialisation, production and consumption has stolen from the child, and therefore from the adult.

As with the question of myth, to which it is related, the question of dreaming and awakening remains opaque in Benjamin (Lindner 41). The fusion of childhood with collective history, Buck-Morss notes, is but an insight, although a puzzling one, and receives no analytical clarification (Buck-Morss *Flaneur* 133). Recovering the dreams of the personal and collective *Kinderseite* can certainly be read as a salvage of experience through the remembering of a 'truer', pre-bourgeois and prelapsarian experience of childhood. But at the same time these dreams, the wish-images that populate childhood and child-like epochs, present a potential for disruption and discontinuity that does away with experience as such and foreshadows a mechanical, technological scenario in which the innocence and wholeness of the prelapsarian child has no meaning. Benjamin's work is torn between these two possibilities.

---

43. The whole passage reads: 'The dream of having children is merely a beggarly stimulus when it is not imbued with the dream of a new nature of things in which these children might one day live, or for which they can struggle. Even the dream of a "better humanity" in which our children would "have a better life" is only a sentimental fantasy reminiscent of Spitzweg when it is not, at bottom, the dream of a better nature in which they would live. (Herein lies the inextinguishable claim of the Fourierist utopia, a claim which Marx had recognized [and which Russia had begun to act on].) The latter dream is the living source of the biological energy of humanity, whereas the former is only the muddy pond from which the stork draws children. Baudelaire's desperate thesis concerning children as the creatures closest to original sin is not a bad complement to this image.' (*AP* J63a,1)

11

Experimental Set-ups:
Benjamin on History and Film [1]

Tara Forrest

Among the many fragments which constitute Walter Benjamin's *The Arcades Project* is a highly evocative passage from Joseph De Maistre's 1821 book *Les Soirées de Saint-Pétersbourg*. In this passage, which Benjamin describes as 'important' (*AP* J86,2), De Maistre recounts the sense of disarray generated by an earthquake that has shaken the foundations of a natural history museum:

> One can form a perfectly adequate idea of the universe by considering it under the aspect of a vast museum of natural history exposed to the shock of an earthquake. The door to the collection rooms is open and broken; there are no more windows. Whole drawers have fallen out, while others hang by their hinges, ready to drop. Some shells have rolled out into the hall of minerals, and a hummingbird's nest is resting on the head of a crocodile. What madman, though, could have any doubt of the original intention, or believe that the edifice was built to look this way? ... The order is as visible as the disorder; and the eye that ranges over this mighty temple of nature reestablishes without difficulty all that a fatal agency has shattered, warped, soiled, and displaced. (*AP* J86,2)

In Siegfried Kracauer's 1927 essay on photography, a similarly evocative image emerges in his analysis of the scrambling of 'natural reality' performed by the intermingling of the undated, disorganised contents of a massive photographic archive. The images contained in this archive have, Kracauer writes, 'lost [their] relationship to the present' (Kracauer 'Photography' 62). That is to say, the historical 'place' of each image is, from the

---

1. This chapter draws on material contained in my book *The Politics of Imagination: Benjamin, Kracauer, Kluge*.

viewer's perspective, not something that is easily determinable.

In a similar vein to the intermingling of the natural history exhibits described by de Maistre, Kracauer argues that the hodgepodge of images contained in the photographic archive produces a situation in which the viewer's 'habitual' understanding of the 'relationship among the elements of nature' is suspended (Kracauer 'Photography' 62). Unlike de Maistre, however, for Kracauer it is neither straightforward, nor desirable, to reestablish the previously ordered relationship between these elements by seeking—as if they were parts of a jigsaw puzzle—to reinstate them to their so-called 'natural' positions. On the contrary, Kracauer claims that the freeing up of the order of nature performed by the jumbling of the photographic images encourages the viewer to reconceive the possibilities of the past and the present outside of the evolutionary conception of history espoused by those who 'subject [...] the historical process to the very kind of necessity which we are accustomed to attribute to the workings of nature' (Kracauer History 36).

In Benjamin's writings on history, and in Kracauer's final book, *History: The Last Things Before the Last*, the relationship between the natural sciences and historicist accounts of history are discussed in some detail. For both Benjamin and Kracauer, what is problematic about the practice of 'assimilating historiography to natural science' (*SW* 4: 401) is the degree to which it naturalises the idea that history is constituted out of a series of causally related events that are bound together (under the banner of abstract concepts such as 'culture', 'enlightenment', and 'objective spirit'(*SW* 4: 403)) by a form of evolutionary progress. 'Historicism', Benjamin writes,

> contents itself with establishing a causal nexus among various moments in history. But no state of affairs having causal significance is for that very reason historical. It became historical posthumously, as it were, through events that may be separated from it by thousands of years. (*SW* 4: 397)

For Benjamin, what is problematic about the evolutionary bent of historicism is the extent to which it naturalises the choices and decisions made by those in positions of power. 'The rulers at any time', he writes, 'are the heirs of all those who have been victorious throughout history' (*SW* 4: 406). Historicism, in this sense, can thus be seen as a form of 'empathy with the victor' (*SW* 4: 406). Its delineation of political decisions and events as stepping stones in history's so-called march of progress toward the future creates a climate within which it is difficult to conceive of the possibilities of the past and the present outside of the parameters established and maintained by the ruling status quo.

In his reading of Benjamin's 'On the Concept of History', Kracauer argues that in order to critique this model of historical development, one must also critique the concept of chronology upon which it is based—a model within which the passing of time is heralded as 'the matrix of a meaningful process' (Kracauer *History* 150). Within this schema, de Maistre's description of the shake-up of the natural history exhibits could be seen to exemplify what Benjamin describes as the 'blasting of historical continuity' (*AP* N10a,1) performed by a political historiographical practice that has liberated itself from the 'vulgar historical naturalism' (*AP* N2,6) characteristic of historicist accounts of history. In a similar vein to Kracauer's analysis of the disordered state of the photographic archive, the jumbling of the natural history exhibits (so whimsically embodied in the image of the hummingbird's nest that has landed on the head of a crocodile) could be said to open up a space within which the historical 'place' of the exhibits (and, by extension, the relationship between the past and the present) can be re-imagined and re-explored.

In Benjamin's 1936 essay 'The Work of Art in the Age of its Technological Reproducibility', film's capacity to shake up the so-called natural order of things is described as one of its key virtues. Indeed, what binds Benjamin's writings on history to his analysis of the radical possibilities of film is the extent to which the mode of perception facilitated by the film practice outlined in the 'Work of Art' essay is associated with the opening up of an 'image space' within which the natural order of things is momentarily suspended. In a passage that resonates strongly with the effects of the earthquake described by de Maistre, Benjamin argues that the significance of film lies in its capacity (through devices such as framing, close-up, slow motion, and editing) to 'explode [...] the prevailing world into rubble' (Koch 210) and, in doing so, to open up a space within which the possibilities and limitations of both the past and the present can be re-imagined and re-explored. In this regard, Benjamin writes,

> film manages to assure us of a vast and unsuspected space of play [*Spielraum*]. Our bars and our city streets, our offices and furnished rooms, our railroad stations and our factories seemed to close relentlessly around us. Then came film and exploded the prison-world with the dynamite of a tenth of a second, so that now we can set off calmly on journeys of adventure among its far-flung ruins [*Trümmern*]. (*SW* 4: 265; *GS* I.2: 499-500)[2]

Thus, in a similar vein to Kracauer's analysis of the active, creative mode of engagement facilitated by the scrambling of the photographic archive, Benjamin argues that film (contra sculpture or painting) shakes up our perceptual habits and, in doing so, encourages us to view the world around us, as if for the first time, from a rejuvenated perspective.

In 'This Space for Rent' (a short fragment in 'One-Way Street' which anticipates a number of the concerns outlined some ten years later in the 'Work of Art' essay), Benjamin draws a distinction between the distant, con-

---

2. I have slightly modified the translation.

templative gaze characteristic of the art critic, and the visceral, distracted mode of perception cultivated by advertising and film. In a critique of the contemplative gaze that sustains the art critic's mode of analysis or interpretation, Benjamin states that only

> [f]ools lament the decay of criticism. For its day is long past. Criticism is a matter of correct distancing. It was home in a world where perspectives and prospects counted and where it was still possible to adopt a standpoint. Now things press too urgently on human society. The 'unclouded', 'innocent' eye has become a lie, perhaps the whole naïve mode of expression sheer incompetence. (*SW* 1: 476)

For Benjamin, the attentive, concentrated gaze of the art critic stands in stark contrast to the distracted, imaginative mode of perception cultivated by film. In contrast to the contemplative manner in which one gazes at a sculpture or a painting, Benjamin argues that the shock-like organisation and sensation of film cultivates a spectatorial relationship more akin to the mode of perception cultivated by life in the modern city—the 'distracting element' of which is 'primarily tactile, being based on successive changes of scene and focus which have a percussive effect on the spectator' (*SW* 4: 267).

For Benjamin, what is significant about the manner in which film 'hurls' (*SW* 1: 476) itself at the spectator is the extent to which it shatters the distance which sustains the sovereign, contemplative gaze (with all its pre-formed ideas, values, and prejudices)—opening up a space within which the film could animate thoughts and associations in the viewer which might challenge 'the optical illusions' generated by one's own 'isolated standpoint' (*SW* 1: 453).[3] Moreover, although the shock-like organisation of film does, to a certain extent, cultivate a mode of perception analogous to the distracted mode of perception associated with urbanisation, Benjamin argues that the camera's capacity to extend the spectator's vision beyond the realm of subjective intention means that film is ideally placed to counter the diminution in the capacity for perception, experience and imagination that he associates with modernity.

In a response to an article by Oscar A. H. Schmitz which anticipates Benjamin's analysis, in the 'Work of Art' essay, of the radical potential of the medium, film's capacity to open up 'a *new realm of consciousness*' is described in no uncertain terms:

> To put it in a nutshell film is the prism in which the spaces of the immediate environment—the spaces in which people live, pursue their avocations, and enjoy their leisure—are laid open before their eyes in a com-

---

3. In support of this claim, Benjamin quotes Georges Duhamel, who states of the mode of perception cultivated by film: 'I can no longer think what I want to think. My thoughts have been replaced by moving images'. (*SW* 4: 267)

prehensible, meaningful, and passionate way. In themselves these offic-
es, furnished rooms, saloons, big-city streets, stations, and factories are
ugly, incomprehensible, and hopelessly sad. Or rather, they were and
seemed to be, until the advent of film. The cinema then exploded this
entire prison-world with the dynamite of its fractions of a second, so that
we can take extended journeys of adventure between their widely scattered ruins. (*SW* 2: 17)

Film, in this context, thus performs a similar function to Benjamin's
analysis of the rejuvenation in the capacity for perception and imagination
facilitated by hashish.[1] By placing a 'prism' between the spectator and his or
her environment, the spectator is able to gaze anew at that which 'had previously floated unnoticed on the broad stream of perception' (*SW* 4: 265).

In his 1960 book *Theory of Film: The Redemption of Physical Reality*, Kracauer— following Benjamin—argues that what is significant about film is
the extent to which the camera's capacity to extend our vision beyond the
realm of subjective intention facilitates a mode of perception that challenges
our previously held conceptions about the material world. Film, Kracauer
argues, 'renders visible what we did not, or perhaps even could not, see before its advent'. It enables us to 'redeem this world from its dormant state'
by allowing us to 'experience it through the camera' (Kracauer *Theory* 300).

In contrast to Kracauer, however, (who is explicit in his critique of films
that are organised around the creation of a whole with a purpose) what is, to
a certain extent, elided in Benjamin's emphasis on the differences between
the total image presented by painting and the fragmented organization of
film, is a detailed discussion of the perceptual effects generated by a film
practice that is organised around the creation of a sense of autonomy and
unity—effects which complicate the distinction between contemplation and
distraction outlined in the 'Work of Art' essay.

In fact, the closest that Benjamin does come, in the 'Work of Art' essay,
to discussing the spectatorial ramifications of such a film practice is in the
relationship he draws between the captions which accompany images in illustrated magazines, and the manner in which filmic images (or shots) are
pieced together in the editing process. 'The directives', he writes, 'given by
captions to those looking at images in illustrated magazines soon become
even more precise and commanding in films, where the way each single image is understood appears prescribed by the sequence of all the preceding
images' (*SW* 4: 258). Elaborating on this idea in an evocative comparison between the image of continuity striven for by certain filmmakers and historians, Benjamin states that, in film, the 'continuous musical accompaniment'

4. Benjamin's experiments with hashish, which began in 1927 and continued sporadical-
ly over the next seven years, are discussed in the writings collected in (Benjamin, *On Hashish*). I have discussed these experiments in some detail in Chapter 2 'The Politics of Aura
and Imagination in Benjamin's Writings on Hashish' in my book: (Forrest, pp.43-63.).

undermines the 'downright jerky rhythm of the image sequence'—the latter
of which 'satisfies the deep-seated need of this generation to see the 'flow' of
'development' disavowed' (*AP* H°,16).[5]

What is significant about these comments is not only the degree to which
they furnish a link between Benjamin's writings on film and history, but the
extent to which they establish his concern with the degree to which the
shock-like organisation and sensation of film can be undermined when the
autonomy of each fragment is subordinated to a piece of a larger picture, or
a cog driving a larger narrative—a process which could be said to culminate
with classical editing practices via which images are cut together to draw the
spectator in, and lead him or her through, the world of the narrative.

The roots of Benjamin's aversion to such a film practice can, in part, be
traced to his friendship with, and writings on, Bertolt Brecht—whom Benjamin first met via Asja Lacis in 1929, and whose delineation of the mode
of engagement fostered by epic theatre provided Benjamin with a model for
the active, 'testing' spectator outlined in the 'Work of Art' essay.[6] In the second version of 'What is Epic Theatre?' (in which he expands on ideas elaborated in an essay of the same title written some eight years earlier in 1931)
Benjamin evokes an image of epic theatre that is in keeping with his analysis
of the fragmentary, shock-like organisation of film:

> Epic theatre proceeds by fits and starts, in a manner comparable to the
> images on a film strip. Its basic form is that of the forceful impact on one
> another of separate, sharply distinct situations in the play. The songs, the
> captions, the gestural conventions differentiate the scenes. As a result, in-
> tervals occur which tend to destroy illusion. These intervals paralyse the
> audience's readiness for empathy. (Benjamin *Understanding Brecht* 21)

Anticipating Benjamin's criticism of autonomous works of art, Brecht
argues that the 'fusing' together of the artwork's various elements produces a
'*Gesamtkunstwerk*' ('total work of art') within which each of the elements serves
as 'a mere "feed" to the rest'—a process that does not exclude the spectator, who is drawn into the work of art as a 'passive' participant (Brecht, 'The
Modern Theatre' 37-38).

In stark contrast to this passive mode of engagement, Brecht argues that
the 'radical *separation of the elements*' (Brecht 'The Modern Theatre' 37) characteristic of epic theatre cultivates a spectator who is actively encouraged to
participate in the meaning-making process which is generated, but not cir-
cumscribed directly by, the various situations that are presented by the play.
Within this schema, the audience retains a critical distance from the action

---

5. 'To root out any trace of "development" from the image of history', Benjamin writes
in this passage, 'is no less the tendency of this project'. (*AP* H°, 16).

6. For a more detailed discussion of Benjamin's relation to Brecht, see (Witte 122-26)
and (Tiedemann 190-98).

on stage. The spectator is not drawn passively (via processes of character identification) into a fictional world, but is situated outside as an observer who brings his or her critical faculties to bear on the scenarios presented by the play. 'The essential point', Brecht claims, is that epic theatre 'appeals less to the feelings than to the spectator's reason. Instead of sharing an experience the spectator must come to grips with things' (Brecht 'The Epic Theatre' 23).

In Benjamin's writings on Brecht, this coming 'to grips with things' is framed very much within the terms employed in Benjamin's writings on history—terms which, transposed to a discussion of film, provide us with a clearer sense of the stakes of his analysis of the radical possibilities of the medium. In language remarkably reminiscent of that employed in both 'Convolute N' of *The Arcades Project* and 'On the Concept of History', Benjamin claims that the significance of epic theatre lies in its capacity to 'expose the present' (Benjamin *Understanding Brecht* 100). 'Epic theatre', he states, 'makes life spurt up high from the bed of time and, for an instant, hover iridescent in empty space' (Benjamin *Understanding Brecht* 13). The situation it reveals (as if 'by lightening') is 'the dialectic at a standstill' (Benjamin *Understanding Brecht* 12-13); a phrase which Benjamin employs in his writings on history to refer to those moments of '*Jetztzeit*' ('now time') which—in their disruption of the false sense of continuity propagated by historicism—open up a space within which one is able to reconceive the possibilities of the past and the present.[7]

In Benjamin's writings on Brecht, it is the 'interruption of the action' characteristic of epic theatre which encourages the audience to 'treat elements of reality as if they were an experimental set-up' (Benjamin *Understanding Brecht* 99)—an idea he explores via an analysis of the image of history presented by epic theatre. The epic dramatist, Benjamin writes,

> will tend to emphasize not the great decisions which lie along the main line of history but the incommensurable and the singular. 'It can happen this way, but it can also happen quite a different way'—that is the fundamental attitude of one who writes for epic theatre. His relation to his story is like that of a ballet teacher to his pupil. His first aim is to loosen her joints to the very limits of the possible. (Benjamin *Understanding Brecht* 7-8)

Transposing these ideas to film, one could say that it is the loose, fragmentary structure of a film practice which is not organised around a sense of unity that prompts the viewer to draw upon his or her own experience and imagination in an attempt to engage with the materials on screen.[8] In contrast, however, to the image of the distant, reasoning spectator out-

---

7. See, for example, (*AP* N2a,3).

8. In 'What is Epic Theatre?' (Second Version), Benjamin notes that 'the events shown on stage ... must be of such a kind that they may, at certain decisive points, be checked by the audience against its own experience'. (Benjamin *Understanding Brecht* 15-16)

lined by Brecht (the contours of which resemble, in part, Benjamin's negative delineation of the art critic), the mode of spectatorship cultivated by the
film practice for which Benjamin argues is more akin to the active, imaginative mode of perception which—in Benjamin's writings on hashish[9] and
mimesis[10]—is associated with a rejuvenation in the capacity for perception
and experience. Indeed, in a similar vein to his analysis of the extent to
which the intoxicated gaze of the hashish eater animates face-like qualities
inherent within objects and spaces, Benjamin argues that the image spaces
opened up by the camera reveal to the spectator 'physiognomic aspects, image worlds, which dwell in the smallest things' (*SW* 2: 512)—the presence of
which 'assure us of a vast and unsuspected space of play [*Spielraum*]' (*SW* 4:
265; *GS* I.2: 499)[11].

As Miriam Hansen has argued, it is this emphasis on film's capacity to
open up a 'vast and unsuspected *Spielraum*' which ties Benjamin's analysis of
the possibilities of the medium to 'the radical unleashing of play' cultivated by proletarian children's theatre and, more specifically, to his analysis of
the connection between 'receptive innervation' and creativity exhibited in
the activities of children (Hansen 'Room-for-Play' 142-43). Indeed, expand-
ing on this idea, one could say (within the terms of the framework set out by
Benjamin in the 'Work of Art' essay) that, in a similar vein to his analysis of
the guiding function of the leader in Proletarian Children's Theatre (*SW* 2:
203)[12], the task of the filmmaker is not to dictate, nor circumscribe the audience's behaviour, but rather to encourage them to engage imaginatively
with the images on screen.

As Kracauer states in an important passage in his essay on photography
which anticipates Benjamin's analysis of the significance of the fragmented,
'piecemeal' organisation of film, the basis for this active, creative mode of
engagement can only be realised 'whenever film combines parts and segments to create strange constructs'. In a passage reminiscent of De Maistre's
description of the intermingling of the natural history exhibits, Kracauer
argues that 'the game film plays with the pieces of disjointed nature is reminiscent of *dreams* in which the fragments of daily life become jumbled'. 'This
game', Kracauer states, 'shows that the valid organization of things remains
unknown' (Kracauer 'Photography' 62-63).

For Benjamin (and, indeed, for Kracauer), the task of film is not to provide the audience with an image of an alternate reality. As Benjamin states
in his analysis of proletarian children's theatre, 'what is truly revolutionary

9. See (Benjamin, *On Hashish*).

10. See 'Doctrine of the Similar' (*SW* 2: 694-98) and 'On the Mimetic Faculty' (*SW* 2:
720-22).

11. Translation modified.

12. For a discussion of the origins of Benjamin's interest in proletarian children's theatre, see (Lacis).

is not the propaganda of ideas, which leads here and there to impracticable actions and which vanishes in a puff of smoke upon the first sober reflection at the theatre exit' (*SW* 2: 206). Rather, what is revolutionary is the extent to which the 'unsevered connection between perception and [creative] action' (Buck-Morss *Walter Benjamin* 263) exhibited, for example, in children's play can be rejuvenated by a film practice which—in 'stir[ring] up the elements of nature' (Kracauer 'Photography' 62)—encourages the audience to reconceive the possibilities of the past and the present.

bibliography

Bibliography

Abbreviations throughout the text refer to the following sources from Walter Benjamin:

AP   Benjamin, Walter. *The Arcades Project*. Trans. Howard S. Eiland and Kevin McLaughlin. Cambridge, Mass.: Harvard UP, 1999.

GS   Benjamin, Walter. *Gesammelte Schriften*. Ed. Rolf Tiedemann, Hermann Schweppenhäuser, Hella Tiedemann-Bartels and Tillman Rexroth. Frankfurt: Suhrkamp Verlag, 1972–89. 7 vols.

SW   Benjamin, Walter. *Selected Writings*. Ed. Marcus Bullock, Michael W. Jennings, Howard Eiland and Gary Smith. Cambridge: Harvard UP, 1996–2003. 4 vols.

The following Benjamin works are also referred to throughout the book:

Benjamin, Walter. *Illuminations*. Ed. Hannah Arendt. New York: Schocken Books, 1969.

Benjamin, Walter. *Gesammelte Schriften*. Ed. Rolf Tiedemann, Hermann Schweppenhäuser, Hella Tiedemann-Bartels and Tillman Rexroth. Frankfurt: Suhrkamp Verlag, 1972–89. 7 vols.

Benjamin, Walter. *The Origin of German Tragic Drama*. Trans. John Osborne. London: New Left Books, 1977.

Benjamin, Walter. *Moskauer Tagebuch*. Frankfurt am Main: Suhrkamp, 1980.

Benjamin, Walter. *Moscow Diary*. Ed. Gary Smith, Trans. Richard Sieburth. Cambridge, Mass., London, England: Harvard UP, 1986.

Benjamin, Walter. *Gesammelte Briefe*. Band 1. 1910–18. Eds. Christoph Gödde and Henri Lonitz. Frankfurt am Main, Suhrkamp, 1995.

Benjamin, Walter. *Selected Writings*. Ed. Marcus Bullock, Michael W. Jennings, Howard Eiland and Gary Smith. Cambridge: Harvard UP, 1996–2003. 4 vols

Benjamin, Walter. *The Arcades Project*. Trans. Howard S. Eiland and Kevin McLaughlin. Cambridge, Mass.: Harvard UP, 1999.Benjamin, Walter. *Berlin Childhood around 1900.* Cambridge: Harvard UP, 2006.

OTHER SOURCES

Abbas, Ackbar. 'Walter Benjamin's Collector: The Fate of Modern Experience.' *Modernity and the Text: Revisions of German Modernism.* Ed. Andreas Huyssen and David Bathrick. New York: Columbia UP, 1989.

Abbas, Ackbar. *Hong Kong: The Culture and Politics of Disappearance.* Hong Kong: Hong Kong UP, 1997.

Agamben, Giorgio. *Homo Sacer: Sovereign Power and Bare Life.* Trans. Daniel Heller-Roazen. Stanford: Stanford UP, 1998.

Agamben, Giorgio. *Potentialities: Collected Essays in Philosophy.* Trans. Daniel Heller-Roazen. Stanford: Stanford UP, 1999.

Agamben, Giorgio. 'The State of Exception' Norris 284–97.

Aragon, Louis. *Le libertinage.* Paris: Gallimard/L'Imaginaire, 1977.

Arendt, Hannah. *The Origins of Totalitarianism.* San Diego: Harcourt Brace and Company, 1979.

Augé, Marc. *Non-places: Introduction to an Anthropology of Supermodernity.* London and New York: Verso, 1995.

Bakhtin, Mikhail. *Problems of Dostoevsky's Poetics.* Trans. Caryl Emerson. Minneapolis: U of Minnesota P, 1984.

Bauman, Zygmunt. *Globalization: The human consequences.* Cambridge: Polity Press, 1998.

Benjamin, Andrew. 'Tradition and Experience: Walter Benjamin's *Some Motifs in Baudelaire.*' *The Problems of Modernity: Adorno and Benjamin.* Ed. Andrew Benjamin. London and New York: Routledge, 1989.

Benjamin, Andrew. *Philosophy's Literature.* Manchester: Clinamen Press, 2001.

Benjamin, Andrew. 'Benjamin's modernity' *The Cambridge Companion to Walter Benjamin.* Ed. David S. Ferris. Cambridge: Cambridge UP, 2004. 97–113.

Benjamin, Andrew, ed. *Walter Benjamin and History.* London: Continuum International Publishing Group, 2005.

Benjamin, Andrew. 'Literary Potential: The Release of Criticism.' *Literature and Philosophy: A Guide to Contempory Debates.* Ed. David Rudrum. Basingstoke: Palgrave Macmillan, 2006.

Benjamin, Andrew. *Style and Time: Essays on the Politics of Appearance.* Evanston, Illinois: Northwestern UP, 2006.

Betsky, Aaron. *Queer space architecture and same sex desire.* New York: Morrow, 1997.

Borges, Jorge Luis. 'Tlön, Uqbar, Orbis Tertius.' *Collected Fictions.* Trans. Andrew Hurley. New York: Viking, 1998.

Bröcker, Michael. 'Sprache.' Opitz and Wizisla 740–73.

Brodersen, Momme. *Walter Benjamin: A Biography* Trans. Malcolm R. Green and Ingrida Ligers. London & New York: Verso, 1996.

Buck-Morss, Susan. 'The *Flâneur*, the Sandwichman and the Whore: The Politics of Loitering.' *New German Critique* 39 (Fall 1986): 133.

Buck-Morss, Susan. *The Dialectics of Seeing: Walter Benjamin and the Arcades Project*. Cambridge, Mass., London: MIT Press, 1989.

Bullock, Marcus Paul. *Romanticism and Marxism: The Philosophical Development of Literary Theory and Literary History in Walter Benjamin and Friedrich Schlegel*. New York: Peter Lang, 1987.

Burke, Edmund. *A Philosophical Enquiry into the Origin of our Ideas of the Sublime and the Beautiful*. Ed. James T. Boulton. Notre Dame, Ind. and London: U of Notre Dame P, 1968.

Capra, Fritjof. *The Web of Life*. New York: Anchor Books, 1996.

Caygill, Howard. 'Non-messianic Political Theology in Benjamin's "On the Concept of History".' A. Benjamin 215–26.

Caygill, Horward. *Walter Benjamin: The Colour of Experience*. London and New York: Routledge, 1998.

Chauncey, George. *Gay New York: Gender, urban culture and the making of the gay male world 1890–1940*. New York: Basic Books, 1994.

Cohen, Margaret. *Profane Illumination: Walter Benjamin and the Paris of Surrealist Revolution*. Berkeley: U of California P, 1993.

Cohen, Tom. *Hitchcock's Cryptonymies*. Minneapolis: U of Minnesota P, 2005.

Cohen, Tom. *Ideology and Inscription* Cambridge, UK: Cambridge UP, 1998.

Cornell, Drucilla, Michel Rosenfeld and David Gray Carlson, eds. *Deconstruction and the Possibility of Justice*. London: Routledge, 1992.

Delany, Samuel. *Times Square Red, Times Square Blue*. New York, London: New York UP, 1999.

Deleuze, Gilles and Félix Guattari. *A Thousand Plateaus*. Trans. Brian Massumi. Minneapolis: U of Minnesota P, 1987.

Derrida, Jacques. 'Force of Law: The "Mystical Foundations of Authority".' Trans. M. Quaintance. Cornell et al. 3–67.

Derrida, Jacques. *Of Grammatology*. Trans. Guyatri Chakravorty Spivak. Baltimore: Johns Hopkins UP, 1976.

Derrida, Jacques. *Writing and Difference*. Trans. Alan Bass. Chicago: U of Chicago P, 1978.

Derrida, Jacques. *The Other Heading: Reflections on Today's Europe*. Trans. Pascale-Anne Brault and Michael Naas. Bloomington: Indiana UP, 1992.

Derrida, Jacques. *Acts of Literature*. Ed. Derek Attridge. New York: Routledge, 1993.

Derrida, Jacques. *Force de Loi: Le 'Fondement mystique de l'autorité'*. Paris: Galilée, 1994a.

Derrida, Jacques. *Specters of Marx: The State of the Debt, the Work of Mourning, & the New International*. Trans. Peggy Kamuf. London: Routledge, 1994b.

Derrida, Jacques. *Politics of Friendship*. Trans. George Collins. London: Verso, 1997.

Derrida, Jacques. *Monolingualism of the Other or the Prothesis of Origin*. Trans. Patrick Mensah. Stanford: Stanford UP, 1998.

Derrida, Jacques and Dufourmantelle, Ann. *Of Hospitality: Ann Dufourmantelle invites Jacques Derrida to Respond*. Trans. Rachel Bowlby. Stanford: Stanford UP, 2000.

Derrida, Jacques. *Paper Machine*. Trans. Rachel Bowlby. Stanford: Stanford UP, 2005.

Derrida, Jacques. *Sovereignties in Question*. Trans. Thomas Dutoit and Outi Pasanen. New York: Fordham UP, 2005.

Doderer, Klaus. 'Walter Benjamin and Children's Literature.' Trans. Anne O'Connor. Fischer 169–76.

Doyle, Christopher. *Don't Try for me Argentina: Photographic Journal*. City Entertainment: Hong Kong, 1997. N. pag.

Fischer, Gerhard. 'Benjamin's Utopia of Education as *Theatrum Mundi Et Vitae*: On the *Programme of a Proletarian Children's Theatre*.' Fischer 201–218.

Freud, Sigmund. 'Die Traumdeutung.' *Studienausgabe*. Eds. Alexander Mitscherlich, Angela Richards and James Strachey. 10 vols. Frankfurt am Main: Fischer, 1969–1979. Vol. 1.

Friedrich, Hans-Edwin. 'Hausgreuel—Massenschund—radikal Böses: Die Karriere des Kitschbegriffs in der ersten Hälfte des 20. Jahrhunderts.' *Kitsch. Faszination und Herausforderung des Banalen und Trivialen*. Ed. Wolfgang Braungart. Tübingen: Niemeyer, 2002. 35–58.

Fürnkäs, Josef. 'Aura.' Opitz and Wizisla 95–146.

Giedion, Sigfried. *Bauen in Frankreich: Bauen in Eisen, Bauen in Eisenbeton*. Leipzig and Berlin: Klinkhardt & Biermann, 1928.

Giesz, Ludwig. *Phänomenologie des Kitsches: Ein Beitrag zur anthropologischen Ästhetik*. Heidelberg: Rothe, 1960.

The Gleaners and I. Dir. Agnés Varda. Ciné Tamaris, 2000.

The Gleaners and I: Two Years Later. Dir. Agnés Varda. Ciné Tamaris, 2002.

Gilloch, Graeme. *Myth and Metropolis: Walter Benjamin and the City*. Cambridge: Polity Press, 1996.

Gilloch, Graeme. *Walter Benjamin: Critical Constellations*. Cambridge: Polity Press, 2002.

Goffman, Erving. 'Performances.' *The presentation of self in everyday life*. Harmondsworth, England: Penguin, 1990. 17ff.

Goldstein, Rebecca. *Betraying Spinoza: The Renegade Jew Who Gave Us Modernity*. New York: Schocken, 2006.

Gramsci, Antonio. *Prison Notebooks*. 3 vols. New York: Columbia UP, 1991–2007.

Greenberg, Clement. 'Avant-garde and kitsch.' *Art and Culture: Critical Essays*

Boston: Beacon, 1961.

Gubser, Michael. *Time's Visible Surface: Alois Riegl and the Discourse on History and Temporality in Fin-de-Siècle Vienna*. Detroit: Wayne State UP, 2006.

Hamacher, Werner. '"Now": Walter Benjamin on Historical Time.' Trans. N. Rosenthal. A. Benjamin 38–68.

Hamacher, Werner. 'Afformative, Strike: Benjamin's "Critique of Violence".' *Walter Benjamin's Philosophy*. Eds. Andrew Benjamin and Peter Osborne. London: Routledge, 1994. 110–38.

Hanssen, Beatrice and Andrew Benjamin, eds. *Walter Benjamin and Romanticism*. New York and London: Continuum, 2002.

Hartung, Günter. 'Mythos.' Opitz and Wizisla 552–72.

Haverkamp, Anselm. 'Anagrammatics of Violence: The Benjaminian Ground of *Homo Sacer*' Norris 135–44.

Haxthausen, Charles W. 'Reproduction/Repetition: Walter Benjamin/Carl Einstein.' *October* 107 (Winter 2004): 47–74.

Hegel, Georg Wilhelm Friedrich. *Phenomenology of Spirit*. Trans. A. V. Miller. New York: Oxford UP, 1977.

Hollington, Michael. 'Benjamin, Fourier, Barthes.' Fischer 113–128.

Imai, Yasuo. 'Benjamin und Wyneken: Zur Entstehung des Pädagogischen Denkens bei Walter Benjamin.' *Neue Sammlung: Vierteljahres-Zeitschrift für Erziehung und Gesellschaft* 36.1 (January–March 1996): 35–47.

Ingram, Susan. 'The Writings of Asja Lacis.' *New German Critique* 86 (Spring–Summer 2002): 159–77.

Jay, Martin. 'Experience without a Subject: Walter Benjamin and the Novel.' *new formations: a journal of culture/theory/politics* Issue dedicated to The Actuality of Walter Benjamin. 20 Summer (1993): 145–55.

Jacobs, Carol. *In the language of Walter Benjamin*. Baltimore: Johns Hopkins UP, 1999.

Jennings, Michael. *Dialectical Images: Walter Benjamin's Theory of Literary Criticism*. Ithaca and London: Cornell UP, 1987.

Joyce, James. *Ulysses: The Corrected Text*. Ed. Hans Walter Gabler. New York: Viking, 1986.

Kafka, Franz. 'Poseidon.' *The Complete Stories*. Ed. Nahum N. Glatzer. New York: Schocken, 1971.

Kahn, Robert. *Images, Passages: Marcel Proust et Walter Benjamin*. Paris: Éditions Kimé, 1998.

Karpfen, Fritz. *Der Kitsch: Eine Studie über die Entartung der Kunst*. Hamburg: Weltbund-Verlag, 1925.

Kittler, Friedrich A. *Gramophone, Film, Typewriter*. Trans. G. Winthrop-Young and M. Wutz. Stanford: Stanford UP, 1999.

Köhn, Eckhardt. 'Sammler.' Opitz and Wizisla 695–724.

Lehmann, Hans-Thies. 'An Interrupted Performance: On Walter Benjamin's Idea of Children's Theatre.' Trans. Olaf Reinhardt. Fischer 179–

200.

Leslie, Esther. 'Future Murmurs: Walter Benjamin's *Berlin Childhood.*' *Aura Rosenberg, Berliner Kindheit.* Göttingen: Steidl Verlag, 2002.

Leslie, Esther. 'Ruin and Rubble in the Arcades.' *Walter Benjamin and the Arcades Project.* Ed. Beatrice Hanssen. London: Continuum International Publishing Group, 2006. 87–112.

Levin, Thomas. 'Walter Benjamin and the Theory of Art History.' *October* 47 (Winter 1988): 77–83.

Lindner, Burkhardt. 'The *Passagen-Werk,* the *Berliner Kindheit,* and the Archaeology of the "Recent Past".' *New German Critique* 39 Fall (1986): 38–40.

Löwy, Michael. *Fire Alarm: Reading Walter Benjamin's 'On the Concept of History'.* Trans. Chris Turner. London: Verso, 2005.

Lukács, Georg. *History and Class Consciousness.* Cambridge: MIT Press, 1972.

Mack, Michael. *Anthropology as Memory: Elias Canetti and Franz Baermann Steiner's Responses to the Shoah.* Tübingen: Niemeyr, 2001.

Mack, Michael. *German Idealism and the Jew: The Inner Anti-Semitism of Philosophy and German Jewish Responses.* Chicago: U of Chicago P, 2003.

Mack, Michael. 'Transzendentaler Messianismus und die Katastrophe der Entscheidung: Anmerkungen zu Carl Schmitts und Walter Benjamins Eschatologie.' *Leben, Tod und Entscheidung: Studien zur Geistesgeschichte der Weimarer Republik.* Eds. Stephan Loos and Holger Zaborowski. Berlin: Duncker & Humbolt, 2003. 155–166.

Martin, Stewart. 'W.G. Sebald and the modern art of memory.' *Radical Philosophy* 132 (July/August 2005): 18–30.

Marx, Karl. *Capital.* Trans. Ben Fowkes. Vol. 1. London: Penguin Books, 1990.

Mehlman, Jeffrey. *Walter Benjamin for Children: An Essay on His Radio Years.* Chicago and London: U of Chicago P, 1993.

Menninghaus, Winfried. *Walter Benjamins Theorie der Sprachmagie.* Frankfurt am Main: Suhrkamp, 1980.

Miller, J. Hillis and Manuel Asensi. *Black Holes: or, Boustrophedonic Reading.* Stanford: Stanford UP, 1999.

Ngai, Jimmy. *Sichu Wang Jiawei, Luo Sahji [Four Films by Wong Kar-wai, Los Angeles].* Hong Kong: Chen Mi-ji, 1994.

Norris, Andrew. 'The Exemplary Exception: Philosophical and Political Decisions in Giorgio Agamben's *Homo Sacer.*' Norris 262–283.

Norris, Andrew, ed. *Politics, Metaphysics, Death: Essays on Giorgio Agamben's Homo Sacer.* Durham: Duke UP, 2005.

Olin, Margaret. *Forms of Representation in Alois Riegl's Theory of Art.* University Park: Pennsylvania State UP, 1992.

Opitz, Michael. 'Ähnlichkeit.' Opitz and Wizisla 15–49.

Opitz, Michael and Erdmut Wizisla, eds. *Benjamins Begriffe.* Frankfurt am

Main: Suhrkamp, 2000.

Osborne, Peter. 'Non-places and the spaces of art.' *The Journal of Architecture* 6 (Summer 2001): 183–94.

Podro, Michael. *The Critical Historians of Art.* New Haven and London: Yale UP, 1982.

Polheim, Karl Konrad. *Die Arabeske. Ansichten und Ideen aus Friedrich Schlegels Poetik.* Munich, Paderborn andVienna: Schöningh, 1966.

Proust, Marcel. *Finding Time Again.* Trans. Ian Patterson. Ed. Christopher Prendergast. London: Penguin Books, 2002.

Reimann, Hans. *Das Buch vom Kitsch.* Munich: Piper, 1936.

Richter, Gerhard. *Walter Benjamin and the Corpus of Autobiography.* Detroit: Wayne State UP, 2000.

Richter, Jean Paul. 'Vorschule der Ästhetik', 'Levana oder Erziehlehre', 'Politische Schriften' *Sämtliche Werke.* Ed. Norbert Miller. Vol. 5. Munich: Carl Hanser Verlag, 1987.

Rickels, Laurence A. 'Suicitation: Benjamin and Freud.' *Benjamin's Ghosts.* Ed. Gerhard Richter. Stanford: Stanford UP, 2002.

Riegl, Alois. *Die Entstehung der Barockkunst in Rom: akademische Vorlesungen aus seinen hinterlassenen Papieren.* Ed. Arthur Burda und Max Dvořák. Munich: Maander, 1987.

Ronell, Avital. *The Telephone Book* Lincoln: U of Nebraska P, 1989.

Santner, Eric L. *On Creaturely Life: Rilke, Benjamin, Sebald.* Chicago: U of Chicago P, 2006.

Schlegel, Friedrich. *Kritische Friedrich-Schlegel-Ausgabe.* Vol. 2 (*Charakteristiken und Kritiken I*). Ed. Hans Eichner. Paderborn, Munich, Vienna, Zürich: Schöningh, 1967.

Schmitt, Carl. *Political Romanticism.* Trans. Guy Oakes. Cambridge Mass.: MIT Press, 1986.

Scholem, Gershom. *Walter Benjamin: The History of a Friendship.* London: Faber & Faber, 1982.

Scholem, Gershom. *The Messianic Idea in Judaism* New York: Schocken, 1995.

Scholem, Gershom. *Zohar: The Book of Splendor.* New York: Schocken, 1949.

Schweppenhäuser, Hermann. 'Physiognomie eines Physiognomikers.' *Zur Aktualität Walter Benjamins.* Ed. Siegfried Unseld. Frankfurt am Main: Suhrkamp, 1972.

Shakespeare, William. 'The Tragedy of Hamlet, Prince of Denmark.' *The Riverside Shakespeare.* Ed. G. Blakemore Evans. Princeton: Houghton Mifflin, 1974. 1135–97.

Simmel, Georg. *Goethe.* 3rd ed. Leipzig: Klickhardt & Biermann, 1918.

Simay, Phillipe. 'Tradition as Injunction: Benjamin and the Critique of Historicisms.' A. Benjamin 137–155.

Sorel, Georges. *Reflections on Violence.* Ed. Jeremy Jennings. Cambridge:

Cambridge UP, 1999.

Spinoza, Benedictus de. *Opera*. Ed. Carl Gebhardt. 4 vols. Heidelberg: Carl Winters Universitätsbuchhandlung, 1925.

Stoessel, Marleen. *Aura, Das vergessene Menschliche: Zu Sprache und Erfahrung bei Walter Benjamin*. Munich: Carl Hanser, 1983.

Stüssi, Anna. *Erinnerung an die Zukunft: Walter Benjamins 'Berliner Kindheit um Neunzehnhundert'*. Göttingen: Vandenhoeck & Ruprecht, 1977.

Sussman, Henry. *Actualities of Aura: Textual Studies of Walter Benjamin*. Ed. Dag Petersson and Eric Steinskog. Svanesund, Sweden: Northern Summer UP, 2005.

Sussman, Henry. 'The Afterlife of Judaism.' *Provocations to Reading*. Ed. Barbara Cohen and Dragan Kujundžić. New York: Fordham UP, 2005.

Sussman, Henry. *boundary 2*, 30 (2003): 169–97.

Sussman, Henry 'Hegel, Glas, and the Broader Modernity.' *Hegel after Derrida*. Ed. Stuart Barnett. London and New York: Routledge, 1998.

Sussman, Henry. 'Between the Registers: *The Arcades Project*, The Talmud, *Glas*.' *The Task of the Critic*. New York: Fordham University Press, 2005.

Szondi, Peter. 'Walter Benjamin's City Portraits.' Trans. Harvey Mendelsohn. *On Walter Benjamin: Critical Essays and Recollections*. Ed. Gary Smith. Cambridge, Massachussetts and London, England: MIT Press, 1988.

Turner, Mark. *Backward Glances: Cruising the queer streets of New York and London*. London: Reaktion Books, 2003.

Virilio, Paul. *The Lost Dimension*. New York: Semiotext(e), 1994.

Warner, Michael. *The trouble with normal*. Cambridge Mass., Harvard UP, 2000.

Weber, Samuel. 'Storming the Work: Allegory and Theatricality in Benjamin's *Origin of the German Mourning Play*.' *Theatricality as Medium*. New York: Fordham UP, 2004. 160–80.

Weber, Thomas. 'Erfahrung.' Opitz and Wizisla 230–59.

Weidmann, Heiner. *Flanerie, Sammlung, Spiel: Die Erinnerung des 19. Jahrhunderts bei Walter Benjamin*. München: Wilhelm Fink Verlag, 1992.

Wellbery, David E. *The Specular Moment: Goethe's Early Lyric and the Beginnings of Romanticism*. Paolo Alto: Stanford UP, 1996.

Wohlfarth, Irving. 'The Politics of Youth: Walter Benjamin's Reading of *The Idiot*.' *Diacritics* 22.3/4 Fall–Winter (1992): 160–172.

Wohlfarth, Irving. 'Et Cetera? The Historian as Chiffonnier.' *Walter Benjamin and The Arcades Project*. Ed. Beatrice Hanssen. London: Continuum, 2006. 12–31.

Wong Kar-wai, dir. *2046*. Jet Tone Production, 2004.

Wong Kar-wai, dir. *Ashes of Time*. Jet Tone Production and Scholar Films, 1994.

Wong Kar-wai, dir. *Chungking Express.* Jet Tone Production, 1994.

Wong Kar-wai, dir. *Days of Being Wild.* Jet Tone Production, 1990.

Wong Kar-wai, dir. *Fallen Angels,* Jet Tone Production, 1995.

Wong Kar-wai, dir. *Happy Together.* Jet Tone Production, 1997.

Wong Kar-wai, dir. *In the Mood for Love.* Jet Tone Production, 2000.

Zipes, Jack. 'Political Children's Theater in the Age of Globalization.' *Theater* 33.2 (2003): 2–25.

Zell, Michael. *Reframing Rembrandt: Jews and the Christian Image in Seventeenth-Century Amsterdam.* Berkeley: U of California P, 2002.

Contributors

Andrew Benjamin is Professor of Critical theory and Philosophical Aesthetics at Monash University, Australia. His most recent book is *Style and Time, Essays on the Politics of Appearance* (2006).

Tara Forrest is Senior Lecturer in Cultural Studies at the University of Technology, Sydney. She is the author of *The Politics of Imagination: Benjamin, Kracauer, Kluge* (2007) and the editor of a special issue of *Cultural Studies Review* on the topic of 'History Experiments' (2008).

Jo Law is an artist and film maker. She currently teaches visual art and media art at the University of Wollongong, Australia.

Michael Mack is a Research Fellow in the Department of German at the University of Reading. His most recent book is *German Idealism and Anti-Semitism* (2004).

George Markus is Emeritus Professor of Philosophy at the University of Sydney. He has published widely on Philosophy of Culture, History of Aesthetics, Modernity, European Philosophy, and Dialectics.

Winfried Menninghaus is Professor of German and Comparative Literature at the Free University Berlin. He has published extensively on German literature and particularly on Walter Benjamin. His most recent book is *Hälfte des Lebens. Versuch über Hölderlins Poetik.* (2007)

Joel Morris is completing a PhD in German at Northwestern University

Charles Rice is Associate Professor of Architecture in the Faculty of Design, Architecture and Building at the University of Technology Sydney. He is the author of *The Emergence of the Interior: Architecture, Modernity, Domesticity* (Routledge, 2007). His writings on Walter Benjamin and architecture have appeared in anthologies including *Intimate Metropolis* (Routledge, 2009), *Critical Architecture* (Routledge, 2007) and *Walter Benjamin and History* (Continuum, 2005), as well as in journals including *Home Cultures* and *The Journal of Architecture*.

Carlos Salzani is a Research Assistant in the Centre for Comparative Literature and Cultural Studies, Monash University Australia.

Peter Schmiedgen teaches philosophy and cultural studies at Macquarie University. He has published on Levinas and Benjamin.

Robert Sinnerbrink is a Senior Lecturer in Philosophy at Macquarie University. His most recent publications include *Understanding Hegelianism* (2007) and *Critique Today* (edited with Jean-Philippe Deranty, Nicholas Smith, and Peter Schmiedgen) (2006)

Henry Sussman is Julian Park Professor of Comparative Literature in the Department of Comparative Literature at the University of Buffalo. His publications include, *The Aesthetic Contract: Statutes of Art and Intellectual Work in Modernity* (1997) and *Psyche and Text: The Sublime and the Grandiose in Literature, Psychopathology, and Culture* (1993).

Lightning Source UK Ltd.
Milton Keynes UK
UKOW02f2331010416

271370UK00001B/105/P